INVESTOR BEWARE!

How to Protect Your Money from Wall Street's Dirty Tricks

John Lawrence Allen

John Wiley & Sons, Inc.
New York • Brisbane • Chichester • Singapore • Toronto

This text is printed on acid-free paper.

Copyright © 1993 by John Lawrence Allen.
Published by John Wiley & Sons, Inc.

This publication is designed to provide accurate and authoritative information in regard to the subject matter covered. It is sold with the understanding that the publisher is not engaged in rendering legal, accounting, or other professional services. If legal advice or other expert assistance is required, the services of a competent professional person should be sought. *From a Declaration of Principles jointly adopted by a Committee of the American Bar Association and a Committee of Publishers.*

Library of Congress Cataloging-in-Publication Data:
Allen, John Lawrence.
  Investors beware! : fighting back against stockbroker abuses while protecting your money / John Lawrence Allen.
    p.   c.m.
  Includes bibliographical references and index.
  ISBN 0-471-58970-5 : $19.95
  1. Stockbrokers—United States. 2. Stockbrokers—United States—Corrupt practices. 3. Investments—United States. I. Title.
  HG4928.5.A43 1993
  332.6'2—dc20   92-41657

Printed in the United States of America

10 9 8 7 6 5 4 3 2 1

To my mother, Marian,
who has graced my life with interminable love
and boundless support;
and to my father, Albert,
who exemplifies integrity and compassion
for his fellow man

Acknowledgments

After the notion of this book began to germinate it was only through the guidance, writing and organizational skills of Lynda Stephenson that I was able to see my ideas grow from a manuscript into a book. My deepest appreciation to Lynda whose humor and creative input endowed my original material with a sense of style and wit.

I am profoundly grateful to Richard Teweles, Ph.D., my much-loved mentor, who graciously reviewed the manuscript and provided innumerable suggestions for changes (all of which were made).

I have been greatly aided by Lori, Dennis, Jeff, and Cathy who helped pick apart the manuscript, put it back together, and endured my endless corrections.

Mere words of adoration can not express my indebtedness to my wife, Cheryl, for providing me the freedom to write this book. Realizing my familial responsibilities, Cheryl thoughtfully adjusted home and family life while munificently providing constructive criticism and advice.

Contents

INTRODUCTION
What's Going On?! *xiii*

SECTION I
What You Need to Know
A Person Armed with Knowledge is Much Harder to Cheat 1

1 Know Your Used Stock Salesperson
Today's New Reality 3

2 Know What Goes On at Your Brokerage Firm
A Peek Behind the Scenes 23

3 Know Your Built-In Investment Roadblocks
What Lies Between You and Your Stock Market Profit? 46

4 How to Spot Others Making a Living Off You
A Proper Introduction 65

SECTION II
Taking Control
*A Person Armed with Knowledge Can Take Action
81*

5 How to Tell If You're Being Cheated
The Warning Signs 83

6 How to Pick a Stockbroker or Money Advisor
Three Checklists 107

7 How to Invest Alone
An Investor's Commonsense Rules 127

8 How to Trade Alone
A Trader's Dozen Rules for Survival 150

9 When to Say No
Investment Products Most Misused 170

SECTION III
Making Wall Street Pay You Back
*A Person Armed with Knowledge Can Beat the
System and Recover Lost Money 191*

10 When You Can Recover Your Losses and Why
Negligent or Fraudulent Acts Explained 193

11 When All Else Fails: How to Get Your Money
   Back
   The Arbitration System 218

12 The Arbitration Hearing
   A Peek Inside 245

   Glossary *261*

   Index *271*

Introduction
What's Going On?!

You, or someone you know, has lost money with the "help" of a stockbroker or money manager. Newspapers and the evening news are filled with stories about people from all walks of life who have lost money through the negligence or outright fraud of "investment experts."

Even the famous aren't immune. Singer/songwriter Billy Joel is on the road again. Why? Because he was led down the road to financial ruin by his business manager—his own brother-in-law. Actor James Caan thought he was set for life. That is, until the money he'd entrusted to business associates disappeared. Basketball legend Kareem Abdul-Jabbar became the oldest man in the NBA when he was forced to play several extra seasons after losing most of his money through bad investment advice.

The powerful aren't immune either. The man seated beside me on an recent L.A.-bound flight, a partner in a prestigious Washington law firm, admitted that he'd been swindled out of $2 million by the son of his best friend.

Then there are the heartbreakers—like the 80-year-old woman, her husband dying of cancer, who entrusted their life savings to a stockbroker's guidance. He lost it all.

What is going on?

Be they stockbrokers, financial planners, or whatever they call themselves, these so-called experts are losing millions of our dollars.

The investors, some of whom you are about to meet, have all lost money in a variety of ways, but there is one common truth that links them all: Their stockbrokers have a hidden agenda of which few investors are aware.

As a former prosecutor in the Los Angeles district attorney's office, I thought I'd seen it all. How wrong I was.

After 30 years investing in the stock market—including five years as a stockbroker and three years as a vice president of investments with two different national brokerage companies—I grew disgusted with the misrepresentation and dishonesty around me, with the outright greed and hucksterism, but most of all, with the surprisingly simple ways that today's industry can and does cheat people.

So I quit.

Today, instead of advising people about investing, I am teaching investors how not to be cheated.

That's the reason for this book. You want to invest for your financial future; yet after researching the theories, checking the mounds of technical data, or just listening to your stockbroker espouse unintelligible jargon, your head is spinning. All you want is to invest without becoming a casualty. Why does that seem so hard in today's investment world?

Because the rules have changed. Today, the investment landscape is drastically, radically different. The personal investor has not been prepared for these incredible changes nor have the agencies we thought would protect us. That is why so many of us are finding our pockets picked clean.

Well, to whom do we turn?

Ourselves. Investment self-defense is the solution. It is time you learned what really happens to your investment dollars, how to tell if your stockbroker is working for you or his own pocketbook, and what you can do to protect yourself. You must, if you are to keep from becoming one of the people cheated in this new arena of investing.

What really goes on in a brokerage firm?

What actually happens to your money once the brokerage firm gets its hands on it?

What are the telltale warning signs that indicate trouble with your stockbroker?

How can you choose a stockbroker or financial advisor wisely?

If a stockbroker commits negligent acts or fraud, can you recover your money?

What products should you avoid? Which ones can cause you financial ruin and what should you do immediately if you own any of these dangerous investments?

You will find the answers to these and many more questions in the pages ahead.

Read on.

What You Need to Know

A Person Armed with Knowledge Is Much Harder to Cheat

Know Your Used Stock Salesperson

Today's New Reality

Joyce and Jack Cash (not their real names) invested their money—$100,000—in Certificates of Deposit (CDs). It was probably all the money they would ever have. Both were near retirement age. Joyce and her husband had spent 35 years of their lives working together installing rain gutters, and now Jack, unemployed, was suffering from Alzheimer's disease. Understanding their situation, a friendly teller at their bank one day suggested to Joyce, "Why not put your money into tax-exempt mutual funds so you won't have to pay income tax on it?"

So Joyce walked into a nearby brokerage firm and met the "broker of the day," the broker assigned to help anyone who walks in without an appointment.

Joyce explained her situation to the stockbroker and her interest in tax-exempt mutual funds. The broker smiled and immediately began telling Joyce of a fabulous investment in a high-yield bond fund that would pay her higher interest rates than she would receive from the bank but "would be just about as safe." Tax-exempt mutual funds were never mentioned again.

"Well, that's fine," answered Joyce, listening to this polished, seemingly trustworthy young man. "As long as my principal isn't at risk and as long as my income will stay constant."

"The principal may fluctuate a little bit," the broker admitted, "but there's very little risk, Mrs. Cash." "After all," he pointed out, "these are high-yield corporate bonds."

Two years passed. Joyce, now widowed and living on the income from the bond fund selected by the broker, received a call from the young man. Her high-yield bond fund was not doing so well; he needed to put her into a safer investment. Again, Joyce trusted him, and within a month, her income was cut in half. The broker had not mentioned that she would lose $27,000 by moving out of the fund.

"What happened?" she demanded to know. "I told you I couldn't afford to lose any principal!"

"Well, the junk bonds in the fund caused the fund to drop dramatically, and . . ."

"Junk bonds? What junk bonds?" Joyce had just been told that her high-yield bond fund contained junk bonds. Her stockbroker was guilty of a little omission of fact so widespread in the sale of junk bond funds that it inspired an article in *The Wall Street Journal*. Joyce stormed in to see the branch manager, but to no avail. Since nothing had been put in writing, it was her word against the broker's.

At about the same time, 70-year-old Ed Monk, Sr., (another pseudonym) withdrew $52,000 from his CDs to invest in a Dean Witter government bond fund. When the fund went down in price, a broker talked him into switching into another of the firm's funds, a high-yield bond fund, with assurances that it was safe. Ed Monk, Sr., agreed to the switch but made it clear that he didn't want "to get into risky stuff." When the junk bonds fell apart, Ed Monk, Sr., lost $21,000. Quickly, he made the broker sell out. His son, Ed Monk, Jr., incensed by his father's loss, took his father to confront the broker. The broker swore he had given Ed Sr. a prospectus explaining the fund. Ed Sr. swore he never saw it, and even if he had, the elder Monk admitted he wouldn't have known what he was reading.

But the best line came from the broker. He turned to the distraught Ed Sr. and comforted the older man with the statement that a lot of people had made the same investment and were hurting worse than he was. To which Ed Jr., aghast, said: "You're telling me you've done the same thing to other senior citizens?"

As such stories pile up and, ultimately, show up in the arbitration system, the average investor is grudgingly beginning to understand the true nature of today's investment scene. Several California junk bond victims compared notes and found themselves laughing darkly at how their brokers all used the same lines. Each of the different stockbrokers had said that he was so confident in the fund that he had put his own elderly parents in it. One of the victims commented, "That's an old dodge. I'm an old salesman; I should have known better."

It's like the line attributed to a Wall Street bond trader in one of today's best-selling exposés: "C'mon, people, we're not selling truth!"

And that, sadly enough, seems to be the new fact of investing life.

The October 1987 stock market crash has made most investors think harder and worry more about their money's fate—even in the hands of the most reputable firms. These firms know it, so they hustle to add new, more professional-sounding job titles, such as financial consultants, investment advisors, and money managers, to their normal herd of stockbrokers.

Eighth Wonder of the World

Despite their fears and worries, investors continue to patronize brokerage firms. "It's the Eighth Wonder of the World that clients keep coming back ..." one former Prudential Securities Incorporated stockbroker said in a recent *Business Week* article.

So why do investors go to a brokerage firm today?

Because we need help. The problem is, the help is often picking our investment pockets and we seem helpless to control it. We want to trust. We expect the professional to be professional, to work in our best interests just like our accountants, doctors, or dentists, the true professionals in our lives. It is hard to comprehend that this expectation of stockbrokers is a thing of the past. For some people, the betrayal of trust by a stockbroker is just too much.

An article in the *Los Angeles Times* told about an elderly man who, after losing his life savings in bonds during the collapse of Lincoln Savings and Loan, took his own life. He left a note in his typewriter dated Thanksgiving Day: "There is nothing left for me of things that used to be. My government is supposed to serve and protect . . ." But it hadn't. He was one of over 17,000 investors who lost a total of more than $200 million when Lincoln and its parent company went bankrupt. Most of the bondholders were over 60 years old. Who would have thought that savings and loan bonds would be so risky?

The truth is, even a CD has a small amount of risk. Every investment does. No one wants to hear that. For our own investment self-defense, though, it is the first thing we must remember. The more potential gain on an investment, the more risk there will be.

If a CD has an element of risk, what about a stock or a bond? A limited partnership or a mutual fund? You know the answer, no matter what your stockbroker or financial planner may tell you: There is always some degree of risk. Unfortunately, in today's investment world, the brokerage companies and the brokers who work for them commonly overstate the opportunity for profit and grossly understate the possibility of loss.

Burying Your Money in the Garden

No doubt, all of this is enough to make you want to grab a shovel and just hide your money under the tomato plants. But that's not the answer either, because inflation will eat away at the money faster than gophers will. You and I both know that we must do something with our money.

As the elderly man in the *Los Angeles Times* article sadly discovered, we cannot rely on the government or other agencies to protect us either, not in today's financial reality. In California alone, the U.S. Attorney's office gets over 6,000 complaints a year about financial fraud, a 50% increase from five years ago. Yet the staff in its enforcement department hasn't kept up with the enormous growth in claims.

So, what is the answer? Knowledge—knowledge, caution, and foresight.

We must learn to protect ourselves. That begins with the First Three Questions of Investment Self-Defense:

1. Why am I seeking financial help?
2. Who *are* these people I'm entrusting with my hard-earned money?
3. For whom is the stockbroker really working?

Why Am I Seeking Financial Help?

In the pages ahead, I shine a white-hot spotlight down the dark hole into which most investors feel they are throwing their money. You'll learn the answers to lots of questions. But first, let's focus on the question, "Why am I seeking financial help?" Before you leave home to visit a brokerage firm, ask and answer it. Do you need income without endangering your nest egg? Do you want greater return than you can get in a bank? Is your goal long-term growth to protect yourself from inflation? Or do you want to speculate, aware of the risks, hoping to make a great amount of money?

Once you have that answer, tie up a bundle of questions to take to your stockbroker. (See Chapter 6 for a detailed list.) And when you're sitting across from your broker hearing explanations, listen closely. If you aren't getting clear and precise answers, keep asking or leave. Contrary to what you may believe, a stockbroker is not a financial wizard with a bag of investment magic the common mortal cannot understand.

Who *Are* These People I'm Entrusting with My Hard-Earned Money?

Stockbrokers were once considered professionals, on the same prestigious level as an accountant or a lawyer. Even today, it seems reasonable to expect that your stockbroker has some sort of financial background, or at least college training in finance, economics, accounting, or business planning.

Don't count on it.

Who is the average stockbroker today? Today's brokers are very much like three "professionals"—Tom, Dick, and Harry—pseudonyms for the most "successful" stockbrokers I worked with during my eight years as a broker. They're all summa cum laude graduates of the top-rated economics departments of prestigious universities, right?

Wrong.

Prior to becoming a stockbroker, Tom was a disc jockey. Dick was a "surf reporter." So, what qualifies them to work with people's money? They could sell. Oh, could they sell. I have seen these two at their most persuasive best. The breadth of humanity was putty in their smooth, dexterous hands.

Harry was even better than Tom and Dick. His experience? Fifteen years selling used cars. This is the man who would write up a sales ticket, hand it to the cashier and loudly proclaim, "Bagged another one, honey. Just made a four figure commission on that one. This is a helluva lot better than selling used cars!" He was no longer a used car salesperson; he was a "used stock salesperson" and he never had it so good. More than a few of his customers, no doubt, were the ones that had been "had."

Lest you think these three stockbrokers—these "used stock salespeople" —were working in polyester suits in some seedy backstreet brokerage house, think again. Their office was just around the corner from Rodeo Drive in Beverly Hills. Thousands and thousands of people just like Tom, Dick, and Harry have flooded the brokerage industry, bringing their sales techniques to the profession of stockbroking. These modern sales techniques have changed the stockbrokerage business into what it is now: A sales business. Unfortunately, it's a far cry from the profession that I found so fascinating when I first started investing in the early sixties.

Today, brokerage houses train their brokers not in the fundamental evaluations of securities or asset allocation, but in how to place cold calls or how to "close the deal"—sales techniques. To put it bluntly, today's stockbroker is little more than a used stock salesperson with the training of a used car salesperson.

The junk bond victim who was himself an old salesperson was right. He heard the old sales lines, but even he didn't want to believe sales pitches were coming from a man he thought to be a professional. Today, the term "stockbroker" has come to be the definition for a financial salesperson, someone who sells products in the securities industry. Stockbrokers sell a wide range of products: insurance, annuities, limited partnerships, closed-end bond funds, unit trusts, commodities, options—much more than just stocks.

The key word is sales. That one-syllable word alone has turned the brokerage industry upside down.

Even the Wall Street firms themselves are beginning to hear the danger in that word. Sales techniques and hucksterism have become so prevalent that some of the largest firms in the world now realize what a monster has been created—and what a financial disaster horrified clients can cause. Merrill Lynch, Inc. recently announced it would begin keeping all its new brokers in training and on salary for two years to curb what has become an epidemic of the hard sell, to encourage "the highest degree of integrity" instead of the reckless quest for higher and higher commissions. Shearson Lehman Brothers, Inc. plans to put one-fourth of its brokers through a new training program that emphasizes service. The National Association of Securities Dealers, Inc. (NASD) has created a special "ethics brochure" stressing "the need for professionalism and fair dealing with investors," and it is sending the brochure to the home of every new stockbroker.

As Peter Lynch, the respected manager of the Magellan Fund, stepped down, he went on record as being disenchanted with the sales techniques and the lack of professional training that most stockbrokers now display.

Best-selling books chronicling Wall Street antics in the eighties and the "Decade of Greed" are all about this influx of unqualified salespeople and the impact they are still having on the industry. The financial professionals of yesterday are retiring or being edged out by the supersalespeople of today. The profession will never be the same.

What, then, should investors do?

You know the old joke about trustworthiness that goes, "Would you buy a used car from this person?" You should be just as wary when dealing with today's stockbrokers, today's used stock sales-people—be they honest yet incompetent or be they thoroughly dishonest—because most are out to pick your pocket for every commission-producing penny they can filch.

It is said that knowledge is power. So let me introduce you to the different personality types you might encounter in today's brokerage house. "Caveat emptor"—investor, beware. And keep your hands over your pockets as you read.

Good News Gus

Anita was never able to save much money. She knew nothing about investing and knew she knew nothing. One day, she received $240,000 from her mother's estate, the bulk of it in stocks, bonds, and CDs. This was not a sum to tuck into her checking account or even in a bank savings account. So she asked her friends and acquaintances for recommendations—the same way she had found her dentist and her doctor. Someone told her about Gus, who was happy to advise Anita how to reinvest her quarter of a million dollars.

Gus's advice came fast and furious. He suggested that she liquidate the CDs and with her permission he wanted to sell off the rest of her mother's portfolio, which consisted of high-grade municipal bonds, triple-A corporate bonds, and blue-chip stocks—all fine investments.

"The yield isn't good enough to provide for your retirement," he assured her. "I want to place the rest of the funds in high-yield bonds." Anita began to feel nervous, but Gus assuaged her concern with a smile.

"Everything I'm doing is in your best interest, let me assure you. This will preserve your capital, 100%. Don't worry."

Nine months later, Anita noticed that she'd lost 10% of her invested capital. Hurriedly, she dialed Gus. But Gus was his usual cheerful self.

"Don't worry about reading your monthly statements and all those silly things," he said. "That's my job, not yours. The value of your portfolio is going to fluctuate up and down with interest rates, but there is nothing to worry about. It's really good news. You're getting such a high return, it doesn't really matter what happens to the portfolio value. So quit worrying now. I'm the professional."

Anita hung up the phone relieved. Two months later, the portfolio had sunk even lower. Anita once again called Gus.

"I told you, Anita, don't worry about what's happening to your portfolio," he responded. "The yield you're receiving is going to more than make up for what the portfolio seems to be losing. It's always going to come back up. Let me take care of your money; you just take care of making it."

Over the next few months, the same scenario continued to happen. Her portfolio kept falling, Anita kept calling, and every time, Gus had an excuse for why she shouldn't be worrying. Finally, two years later, Anita attended a financial seminar, met the speaker, and asked him if he wouldn't mind looking at her portfolio. When he did, the expression on his face made her stomach leap into her throat.

"Why, 80% of your portfolio is invested in junk bonds!" he all but gasped.

"Is that good or bad?" she whispered.

"Lady, you've got a $150,000 loss in your portfolio. What do you think the answer is?"

When Anita got home, she called Gus, and, of course, he was full of bright cheery advice. Even when she met with him, Gus was seemingly nonplussed. All would be well with the world if she'd just leave the worrying to him. At least until she had nothing left in her portfolio.

That's when Anita began calling him Good News Gus.

Where did Anita err? She allowed Gus to have a position of authority and trust that enabled him free rein to do as he pleased with her money. This is violating the first rule of investment self-defense: Don't give control of your money to anyone.

There are Good News Guses in every brokerage firm who will smile and talk the sky blue when the sky is actually falling—falling on your portfolio due to their mishandling of your funds. An honest Good News Gus may not be able to face the idea that he has made a mistake with your money, and he will keep up the smiles while you continue to lose money. A dishonest Good News Gus smiles his way in and out of your pocketbook, knowing that pleasantness covers a multitude of sins. Both have advanced cases of hoof-and-mouth disease, and you should take your money and run at the first sign of their happy talk.

Cold-Calling Clara

"Is this Mrs. Bart Sampson? Good morning, Mrs. Sampson. This here is Clara Wood and I want to tell you about a product that is so revolutionary and will so enhance your personal well-being that no sophisticated investor, like yourself, should turn it down."

Sound familiar? There probably isn't a home in the country that hasn't received some sort of "cold call"; that is, a call from a complete stranger trying to talk all who will listen into placing their money in whatever product the caller happens to be peddling.

It defies the imagination that Mrs. Bart Sampson in Sioux City, Iowa, could pick up the phone, listen to Clara's spiel, and actually sit right down and send Clara $100,000.

But it works. Oh, does it work. The most prodigious Cold-Calling Clara I ever knew was from the South. She'd purr with a sweet Southern drawl and just sit back to wait for the mail to bring her the money. Clara would buy lists from professional services that provided names, addresses, and phone numbers of people in a certain area based upon research data. From those lists, Clara knew all about the financial potential of her telephone prey. Oh yes, she'd know all about you. She'd know you had assets in excess of $200,000, and that you had two cars, children already educated, and a mortgage almost paid. So she would pull out a nifty bond fund suited to your needs and, abracadabra, she was in business. A million dollar business. The Claras of this world, more often than you could stomach, are millionaires. There is even a "cold-calling college" offered by most large brokerage firms from which Clara proudly graduated with honors. In "college," Clara was trained how to meet any objections with persuasive sales techniques. Clara's teachers used high-tech audio equipment to monitor Clara's voice inflection, attitude, and technique in speaking to strangers over the phone, toward one effect: instant rapport.

Now she keeps up her continuing education by purchasing every audiocassette and workbook on sales written and designed by "Super Brokers," teaching her the latest techniques in her chosen specialty. She will probably be on the phone all day because she knows that cold calling is a numbers game—The more you call, the more success you'll have.

One of Cold-Calling Clara's favorite ploys is the use of a reverse telephone directory. She will call your neighbor and sell him a product. Then she will dial your number, begin her pitch, and casually drop your neighbor's name for instant credibility: "Do you know the Sampsons down the block? Well, they just bought quite a large amount of this stock. I'm not at liberty to say how large, but it's that good. The Sampsons certainly believe in its potential." Then she'll probably close with one of the most common lines used by stock salespeople everywhere: "I had so much confidence in this product that I bought some myself."

What do you do? The most effective defense against the Cold-Calling Claras of the world is found in two little words: Hang up.

Trader Dick

"Yes, Mr. Thrump, I'm telling you I'm watching the market all the time. All the time. Nothing gets past me. So I know what's happening out there. It's just a question of getting a jump on it, you know, and I love it. You won't find another broker here as on top of things as I am. I can assure you of that."

Every office has a Trader Dick. He's got one eye on the tape, the other on his computer, and he believes in his trader heart that if he watches the market just right, he can make trades that are profitable for his client and occasionally, when daring enough, for himself. He might have a touch of "trade-itis," which means he is addicted to the chase more than the money. Every bit of news, every fluctuation of the market, every world event keeps him connected to that monitor.

He is probably the guy you see walking down the street with a mobile phone stuck to his ear. Trader Dick always has a theory for why the market goes up or down, and he lives and dies by it—and so, unfortunately, do his clients.

It is not a question of if, as much as when, he will lose his client's money, and then lose the client. He cannot help himself; he has to trade. Usually he has very good intentions. He's not dishonest, really, just inept and addicted to the thrill of the hunt. One correct call will keep him going for months.

Yet, this is the paradox. Although he may be losing your money and maybe even his own with all of his trades, he is generating heaps of money through commissions for the brokerage house and for himself. He actually is making money as you lose it, because each of his trades generates a commission that comes out of your pocket one way or another. Trading is his business . . . his only business.

But what if he's right more than he's wrong with your portfolio? You'll still probably be losing money. You'll have a difficult time overcoming the "commission cost" of doing that business. Commission fees paid on trades throughout the year could send your profits into oblivion. No, not oblivion—rather, into Trader Dick's pocket and the firm's cash flow.

No Brain Bill

Bill is a whole new breed, the stockbroker equivalent of a windup toy. There has never been a job that requires fewer brains to make more money in less time than his, and he's just happy to be here. What does No Brain Bill need to be successful? To be told what to sell and how to sell it. Then watch out, here he comes.

If that sounds strange, it isn't. No Brain Bill is the corporate officers' favorite kind of broker—a salesperson through and through. He is told what to do; he gladly, energetically does it; and his clients are the recipients of all of this no-thought exuberance.

Here is how Bill's day begins. He greets the pile of photocopied papers on his desk with relief. These papers explain what the brokerage firm wants to push that day—what products were left over or unsold from yesterday. Stapled to many of them are printed scripts for Bill's sales pitches. He glances at all of them, then pulls out and savors one specific piece of paper, the one showing he is currently number one in the sales contest for a free trip to Bermuda. Then he turns up a little radio-like speaker box on his cluttered desk, called an "SR4" or "squawk box," which broadcasts from the firm's headquarters in New York. It's always chock-full of recommendations, ideas, and helpful information with which he can fill his selling day without an ounce of contemplation or evaluation on his part. His bosses here and on Wall Street know what they're doing, he tells himself. Look at all this information. It has to be right.

He checks his watch. It's time for the morning sales meeting hosted today by an outside distributor of a limited partnership, to be sold through the brokerage firm. Yesterday's sales meeting offered him another sales-promoted contest to Las Vegas, his favorite city, but today's distributor is offering a high commission payout instead. He can't ignore that.

This morning's spokesperson is happy to announce to Bill and his colleagues that in addition to the large commission normally offered with every sale of their product, the firm will also be offering a "trailing quarter commission." That means any stockbroker selling the product could have a few bucks trickling in as long as his clients own the product. This impresses Bill. He decides to find out exactly what this product is, information the distributor is only now offering.

Back at his desk (the day is still young) he quickly looks over a few of the scripts offered in the packages he's received from his firm and pulls out a couple. He is ready to sell. He picks up the phone and calls you.

And he is hoping that you're not using your brain, either.

Seminar Sam

YOU ARE INVITED TO A SEMINAR ON
FINANCIAL PLANNING
COME LEARN HOW TO MAKE YOURSELF
FINANCIALLY INDEPENDENT
IN THE DIFFICULT YEARS AHEAD
FREE LUNCH PROVIDED

Sponsored by Big Time Investments, Inc.
Cordially, Sam E. Newman
Your friendly neighborhood stockbroker

"Mrs. Cleaver? Did you receive my invitation to the seminar on Sunday? I hope you can make it. I'd love to help you and Mr. Cleaver plan for your family's financial security. Yes, it's absolutely free, no obligation. That I can assure you. I'm in charge, and I am proud to be able to bring this financial expert to our get-together. She can provide you with life-changing advice during these all-important years. I hope you can be my guest. You can? Superb."

Seminar Sam is a used stock salesperson on the cutting edge. His chosen specialty is the latest fashion in gaining customers for brokerage firms: the "Free Information Seminar." Sam loves these seminars and is the one in charge of finding the outside "expert," usually a product spokesperson or some other well-trained sales-person with perhaps a background in law or accounting.

Sam will mail a large batch of invitations, often engraved ones, to either a specific geographic area, to his own clients, or even a blanket mailing to an entire city. The seminars could be on topics such as "Retirement Planning," "Providing for Your Children's Education," or "New Ideas for the Nineties Market." They always meet a particular need or desire of your financial goals. When Seminar Sam has a bit of style, he offers a continental breakfast. Sometimes, if he's trying to pull in a richer clientele, he'll offer a free lunch, especially if the guest speaker will foot the bill.

At the seminar, Sam probably won't even speak. He will politely introduce the "expert" and then listen attentively as the speaker talks generally about finances for a few minutes and then spends the rest of the time speaking quite specifically about how her special investment strategy can meet the financial goals of each and every member of the audience.

Then, at the end of the show, Sam positions himself and his helpers near the doors to enable you and yours to make appointments to come into his office to discuss these illuminating ideas and/or investment opportunities. If nothing else, Sam makes certain you have his card in your hands before you leave.

As we will discuss later in the book, though, the old saying is still very true, especially in dealing with Seminar Sam: There is no free lunch.

The Professor

Probably the single most dangerous personality type in the entire brokerage firm is The Professor. Here is a man who is an expert in his own mind and will gladly guide you through the troubled waters of financial chaos if you will bow to his sage advice.

Why is he so dangerous? Because his sales pitch isn't a sales pitch; it's a lecture. The Professor honestly believes every word he utters and will back up each and every thing he says with several documents and charts. The customer takes one look at The Professor in his bow tie, with his authoritarian air, condescending attitude, and highfalutin language, and he thinks he is in the presence of someone who actually knows what he's doing. The Professor certainly agrees. He attacks his job as if he were writing a thesis—research, research, and more research. That's his secret, along with his higher intellect, of course. He's continually poring over reams and reams of balance sheets, income statements, prospectuses, research reports, and every bit of information he can find on whatever he wants his clients to buy. He reads *The Wall Street Journal, Forbes,* and *Fortune;* watches "Wall Street Week" and "The Nightly Business Report"; subscribes to three charting services and a market timing service—a service that purports to predict the fluctuations of the stock, futures, and interest rate markets. The Professor even makes use of its telephone hotline update service for which he must pay by the minute.

In other words, this man does his homework. And when he does it for you, he expects you to consider his advice golden. There is no questioning his wisdom; he has been known to be offended if you seek confirmation of his ideas elsewhere, especially with any of the other brokers in his office who are decidedly his intellectual inferiors. After all, he has just spent his weekend traveling across the country to inspect the real estate limited partnership deal he is suggesting you invest in. He's seen it with his own eyes. He has worked through the material with his own hands. He has evaluated it with his own highly developed intellect. What more do you want?

Plenty. Because for all The Professor's research and stuffy confidence, you may notice that he still has his day job. In other words, if he's so smart, why is he working here? Once again, all his research puts him no farther ahead in the impossible game of predicting the stock market than anyone else this side of insider trading.

What then is the survival tactic with The Professor?

Do to the Professor what you couldn't do in school: Get up and leave the classroom before you sink any more money into "tuition," before he is the one who fails with your dollars. He cannot teach you any more than any other broker, and his air of authority is a psychological ploy that plays poorly this side of graduation.

An Endangered Species: Jerry and James

When I worked at Shearson Lehman Brothers, Inc., my partner, Jerry, had already been in the stockbrokerage business for over 30 years. He was considered a dinosaur—a relic of a bygone era. Jerry's forte was stocks and bonds; that's what stockbrokers did when he began. He never sold a limited partnership. He never sold an insurance product or an annuity. Mutual funds didn't interest him. He was, plain and simple, a stockbroker. Jerry was not only an excellent stock picker but a superb portfolio manager. He could put together a crackerjack portfolio comprised of bonds with differing maturities and varying levels of yield, so that a portfolio would be able to handle the ebb and flow of inflation and deflation. He was also a whiz at picking stocks. He would ignore all of the research recommendations handed down by the firm and pick his own stocks (rarely done today), and he knew just how to juggle to diversify a client's portfolio. To top that off, he did something few stockbrokers are able to do. He had such a large amount of loyal clients, he never had to worry about making extra money through contests, brownie points, and double commissions. With the confidence derived from a stable clientele and a solid, steady income, he was free to give his clients advice based on what was best for the client, even when it seemed contrary to what the client might deem logical. You always got the unvarnished, expert truth, minus any hidden agenda, with this stockbroker.

Does Jerry sound too good to be true? He is. Jerry's about to retire, disillusioned with the state of the profession today. A talented, honest stockbroker lost.

I'm not saying there aren't some moral, competent, professional stockbrokers working today. I have even defended some stockbrokers when I was convinced they were the ones in the right, being unjustly accused of wrongdoing by "sour-grapes" clients.

James is one of those talented, decent young brokers, working hard to ignore the fluff blowing all around him, trying to stay up with the used stock salespeople without relying on their sales techniques. There are a few like James and Jerry in the brokerage world who are working under high ethical standards, doing the best they can for the client. The key word, though, is few.

It is our responsibility, and ours alone, to see that our stock salesperson is forced to be honest when dealing with us.

How?

The more knowledge we possess, the less opportunity our stockbroker has to deceive us or deviously influence our decisions about investing.

That brings us to The Third Question of Investment Self-Defense.

For Whom is the Stockbroker Really Working?

The moment you walk into a brokerage house and open an account with a broker, you have entered into a mutually exclusive relationship that almost always turns out to be better for the stockbroker than for you.

Why? Commissions.

Because of the wildly varying temptations that lie within the wildly varying commission rates, stockbrokers are caught in the lucrative middle. Always remember that unless a stockbroker buys or sells something for a client, he does not make one red cent. He cannot earn a living by telling clients to keep their money in the bank. In order to survive, he has to advise you to take some action with that money, buying or selling some product of his. In any industry operating on a "commission payout" basis, a basic conflict will always exist between the customer's desire for objective, responsible advice, and the salesperson's need to pay his mortgage, feed his family, and vacation on the right tropical beach.

To be fair, who among us would not find a product offering a large commission just a little more attractive than the rest of the investments in the pile? The difference between $3,000 and $6,000 is enough to taint anyone's objectivity. The mutual fund managers, as well as all those vying for the stockbroker's help to sell their product, know that money doesn't just talk—it croons. Like the siren's song, it is hard, very hard, to ignore. And the result may be professional advice that is legal yet ethically questionable.

The ethical problems arising from the conflict of interest have always been controversial, but now they pose such a real danger to the entire investment landscape that understanding this conflict is absolutely essential for investment survival in this last decade of the twentieth century. You must be deadly honest with yourself about this person who is helping you make some of the most important decisions of your life, always keeping in mind the pressures your broker faces while handling your money.

Let's assume the best of all worlds—that your broker is professionally trained and has the background and operating experience necessary to provide you with the finest advice available. Consider yourself lucky.

But lucky or not, the next thing you must ponder is pivotal to understanding the realities of the profession and your financial well-being. Every time you work with your broker, ask yourself: "What is his ultimate motivation? Is it to make me money, or is it to make him money?"

Does that sound cold-blooded? Put yourself in his shoes. You are at your desk. In walks an elderly couple who want advice about what to do with their maturing CDs. They want to get a better return on their money. What they don't know is that you have bills piling up at home—the mortgage payment, life insurance, a car payment, school tuition, gas, electricity, food bills—because you have not written one ticket (sold any product) all month. In your advice to them, could you ignore the closed-end bond fund offering a double-digit commission? What would you say to a client when he calls to get a quote on AT&T stock that he bought from you at $25 and is now at $30? Would you tell him to hold on to get a higher price? Or would you tell him to sell knowing that if you don't switch him out of that stock and put him into another one, you won't make any money—money you desperately need?

That's a working definition of a conflict of interest if there ever was one. Like a person on a diet who works in an ice cream shop, temptation for a bit of indulgence is ever-present in the modern stock salesperson's world. The honest stockbroker is constantly being pulled between his "dieting" ethical self and the chocolate fudge ripple there for the taking, absolutely free. More often than not, though, it's free at your expense.

Chain of Conflict

The conflict gets worse the farther you go into your local brokerage office. Deciding whether you have a stockbroker like Cold-Calling Clara or a basically honest but misguided person like The Professor is your first concern. But between the transaction you make with the broker and the transaction at the clearing corporation is a maze of departments and employees that finger your money. Above your Good New Gus or No Brain Bill are an astounding number of people looking to make a buck off your buck.

You don't see these people, but they are part of this winding chain of conflict that stretches from the used stock salesperson, past the branch manager and the back office personnel, around the traders, through all of the division vice presidents, and right on up to the president. Most of the departments in a firm are expected to make a profit, just like the stock salespeople. The commission generated from your investments pays for these people's jobs and affects their wheelings and dealings. Your commission is what they use to make their department successful. How, then, can these people be solely concerned with making wise choices to safeguard your financial well-being when your money is helping them meet their own goals and needs? There it is again—the conflict of interest rearing its two-faced head.

Time for a Peek

So, now you have answered the first three questions of smart investing, you have met the types of stock salespeople best avoided, and you know the conflict most stock salespeople face. Your investment consciousness has now been raised a bit, and you are beginning to be aware of what it will take to protect yourself in your relationship with the brokerage industry. Armed with this new information, you're ready to leave the comfort of your own home and trek to a nearby brokerage firm in hopes of making an informed, reasonably smart investment with your money.

Now is the time for a peek behind the scenes of your brokerage firm. What really happens when you visit today's stockbroker? Chapter 2 introduces the rest of the people in the chain of conflict and reveals how much of what they do works against you as an investor.

Know What Goes On at Your Brokerage Firm

A Peek Behind the Scenes

Mr. and Mrs. Cleaver smile tentatively at each other as they look at the tall building they are entering. Sleek, new, it reeks of stability and success.

They have decided that it's time to plan their financial future with the nest egg they've been able to save. Recently they had met Sam Newman at a free financial seminar. Sam invited the Cleavers to visit him today at his brokerage office to talk about investments. So they press the button on the wood-paneled elevator, and they ride up to the 18th floor and the offices of Big Time Investments, Inc.

Walking through the glass doors, they are greeted by the smiling receptionist who is so very cordial as she lets Mr. Newman know they are here. Before they have sunk comfortably into the plush couch and begun one of the articles in *Forbes, Business Week* or *The Wall Street Journal* so amply supplied, Mr. Newman is greeting them with a firm, enthusiastic handshake. He leads them through the heavy oak doors to the beautiful offices beyond.

The Cleavers both notice how everything looks so well-kept and professional. From memories of old movies and TV, they had expected ticker tapes, hustle-bustle, and cubicles full of men in shirt-sleeves on the phone to Wall Street. But this atmosphere is so calm, and, well, calming. The only hustle-bustle they see is at the glass cashier windows across the way where expensively-dressed men are coming and going, handing tickets to serious-looking clerks.

The Cleavers smile at each other again, as Mr. Newman invites them into his quiet, well-appointed office and offers them a seat in his sleek, chrome chairs. Mrs. Cleaver notices the silk plant beside Mr. Newman's desk—a fake ficus, but still very nice—while Mr. Cleaver notices all the gadgets on the desk. There are several computers attached to strange-looking keyboards, with screens that flash in multiple colors. On the other side of the desk there's a little speaker box, a radio squawking about transportation averages, bonds going up ten "ticks," upside volume at 72 million with down-side volume at 47 million, the wholesale price index, and just how good a deal is being offered on 3,000 shares of some company that makes synthetic fertilizer—all followed by a lot of nonsense words neither Mr. nor Mrs. Cleaver comprehend.

Mr. Newman turns the volume all the way down on the box and then smiles at Mr. and Mrs. Cleaver as he hears a few code words from the little speaker, telling him that the synthetic fertilizer company stock is selling for a little under market value, and that every sale of that stock comes with a whopping double commission, together with a pile of bonus points towards this month's sales contest. He makes a mental note as he assesses the couple in front of him.

"Now, Mr. and Mrs. Cleaver," he begins, a serious look on his face. "I need to ask you some questions about your finances that will help me choose the best products for you." For the next few minutes, they go over a financial questionnaire to satisfy the brokerage company's "suitability" requirements. The brokerage company is required to ascertain essential information about a prospective client so that the salesperson can make recommendations that are suitable for that particular client. As Mr. and Mrs. Cleaver go over their finances, their estimated net worth, and their annual income, all of the apprehension they were feeling slowly melts away.

"What is your stated investment objective?" Mr. Newman asks them.

Mr. Cleaver clears his throat. "Well, we don't want to lose any of our money. We'd like it to help our future. I suppose we need some advice."

Mr. Newman nods and quickly fills in the boxes on the suitability forms. Impatiently, he finishes the form, sets it aside, and begins to thumb eagerly through the in-tray stacked full of brochures and prospectuses. Some brokers take a lot more time, asking to see such personal data on clients as their recent income tax statements or making them guess what their next five years' income will be or whether they have any plans to move in the near future. Some even request personal information about mortgages or medical problems. But Sam has another appointment in less than an hour, another couple from the same seminar. Besides, he has something already in mind for the Cleavers. Yes, he does.

"Now," he begins, with a confident smile. "Didn't you say you were interested in tax-exempt income? Then you may want to consider the Really Good Municipal Bond Fund, Inc. The objective of this newly formed, closed-end fund is to generate tax exempt income with investment grade bonds consistent with the preservation of your capital . . ." Mr. Newman notices this couple is listening intently to every word coming out of his mouth. They should be easy to work with.

He hands them a flashy, oversized brochure and continues: "The advantages are numerous: current tax-exempt income from investment-grade quality, tax-exempt municipal bonds; active professional management, too; a proven leader in tax-exempt investing, managing over $15 billion in 38 tax-exempt portfolios; monthly tax-exempt income; a dividend reinvestment option; ready liquidity; and affordability."

"And best of all," he smiles, leaning back in his chair, "you don't have to pay any commission!"

The Cleavers, a bit wide-eyed, are impressed. Mr. Newman's smile widens as he thinks about the fat commission he'll be receiving directly from the fund. It will put him in the next commission bracket and in line for a whopping pay increase. Window office and free prizes, here he comes.

What else is Mr. Newman not telling the Cleavers? Things they don't really need to hear, he tells himself. The word "risk," for instance. After all, how much safer can you get than tax-exempt municipal bonds?

"So," Mr. Newman continues, grabbing his new Mont Blanc fountain pen from his pocket, unscrewing the cap and making a few thick numerical flourishes on a nearby pad, "here's my plan for you. I think we should buy $50,000 worth of this fund. Then let's take $40,000 and put it into a mutual fund that will give you the opportunity to grow with the stock market and overcome the ravages of inflation. This one here," he says as he flips another brochure across the table, "it invests in a broad spectrum of stocks designed to outperform the market averages." These are the exact words Mrs. Cleaver notices on the second page of the brochure. "Once again," Mr. Newman points out, "there's no commission on this one either. Of course, there can be a commission if you decide to sell the fund, but if you hold the fund long enough, there won't be any commission. What do you think?"

The Cleavers stare at the figures and the brochure. What is long enough? Mrs. Cleaver wonders. But she doesn't ask.

"As for the $10,000 remaining, well, Mr. and Mrs. Cleaver, I think we can afford to speculate a little bit. I've just gotten fine reports on a new company, a synthetic fertilizer company, that we just happen to have a special offering on today. You can buy it below what it's selling for in the market. That gives you a profit on the very first day you buy it. It's a fine little company that should do nothing but make you money. Here's another brochure. I guarantee it will be a winner." Mrs. Cleaver takes the third brochure, juggling them all in her lap, as Mr. Cleaver leans over for a look at the numbers Mr. Newman has scribbled down concerning this synthetic fertilizer company. Mr. Cleaver frowns. He stares at Mr. Newman as he begins the same kind of gobbledygook talk that he heard earlier from the little box on the desk, all concerning getting in on the ground floor of this high-tech fertilizer producer, the wave of the future. He'd like to ask a few questions but isn't sure what to ask. And he certainly doesn't want to look dumb. Finally, Mr. Newman pauses. "Well? Do we try these? You'll appreciate the returns. I guarantee."

Mrs. Cleaver smiles at her husband, placing her hand reassuringly on his arm, and Mr. Cleaver's frown turns into a sigh and a smile as they both nod their heads at their new stockbroker. Mr. Newman quickly writes up three tickets, puts them in the pneumatic tube near his desk, and—whoosh—their nest egg is fried. "That's all there is to it," he smiles, getting to his feet. "Welcome aboard," he says, extending his hand. As they shake it, both Mr. and Mrs. Cleaver feel a wonderful sense of relief. They've found someone whom they trust and can turn their financial responsibilities over to. What a load off their minds.

With a few cordial good-byes, the Cleavers leave Mr. Newman's office. As they thread their way through the corridor back toward the heavy oak doors, they hear another broker talking to someone on the phone. "Good morning," they hear, "I'm a financial consultant at Big Time Investments, Inc. Are you interested in tax-exempt income? Then you may want to consider the Really Good Municipal Bond Fund, Inc. The objective of this newly formed closed-end fund is to generate tax-exempt income consistent with the preservation of your capital. The advantages are numerous: current tax-exempt income from investment-grade quality, tax-exempt municipal bonds; active professional management, too; a proven leader in tax-exempt investing, managing over $15 billion in 38 tax-exempt portfolios; tax-exempt income every month; a dividend reinvestment option; ready liquidity; and affordability."

"And best of all, you don't have to pay any commission!"

Mr. Cleaver frowns for a moment, then shakes it off and pushes the door open for Mrs. Cleaver to walk through.

What will happen to the Cleavers? Maybe nothing. But maybe too much. There were too many variables that they needed to consider, and their new stockbroker didn't bring up any of them. The Cleavers didn't ask enough questions and Mr. Newman, their used stock salesperson, didn't offer enough information or time. So here is their reality: The Cleavers have invested in a tax-exempt closed-end bond fund that could go down in value. Because of their low tax bracket, they may lose more money from its lower yield than they will save in taxes. With the mutual fund, if they happen to sell it within a six-year period, they're going to lose a hefty bit in commission. As for the synthetic fertilizer company, nobody knows what kind of a stink it's going to raise when it begins to compete with the organic fertilizer companies—in other words, when the synthetic fertilizer hits the fan. And, most importantly, nobody mentioned the "R"-word—RISK.

The Cleavers will now go home, receive monthly statements which they will give only the most casual of glances, and will not talk to Mr. Newman again for months.

The Cleavers are not unusual. Whatever your age or need— parents planning for your children's education, middle-aged couple concentrating on making the best of your peak earning years, or retirees planning to make your senior years financially secure—most investors wish they could hand the reins of their money management to another person and relax.

Most of us would rather trust others than worry about finances ourselves.

Worry Now or Worry Later

How can people trust their life savings to a virtual stranger and never call back to check on it? Yet it happens all the time. We want someone else to do the worrying for us. Too often, though, we pay the penalty of greater worries down the line because the financial advisors—the used stock salesperson, Seminar Sam, The Professor, Trader Dick, and the rest of the well-dressed gang—don't worry enough. After all, it's not their money.

Relinquishing control over your own funds is the absolute worst thing you can do for your investment self-defense, however nice it sounds.

Besides, these big-time Wall Street firm professionals don't have such a good batting average lately. If the Cleavers had done a little homework, even as little as reading the newspaper headlines, they would have found out that many of the major brokerage companies have trouble turning a profit.

Am I making this up? No. These are facts that have graced most of the country's newspapers the last few years. Shearson Lehman Brothers, Inc. lost $998 million in 1990. Prudential Securities Incorporated has done so poorly that Prudential Insurance, the parent company, has been forced to come to its rescue to the tune of $1 billion since 1981 when it paid $385 million to buy the brokerage company. Those are just two of the professional "success" stories of the major firms on Wall Street, the ones spending fortunes on commercials and advertising to make sure we, like the Cleavers, still believe in their financial know-how. And we think they know something we don't know about making money?

So, what is the answer?

The answer is to be an educated, self-reliant client—if you are going to be a client at all. Let's take a peek at the goings-on behind those heavy oak doors. There is nothing the Cleavers saw or heard that they couldn't have understood. There was quite a bit they would have found very helpful as they shopped for the best financial advice available.

Broker's Jargon

"Listen, Mr. Robinson, your SMA doesn't give you sufficient buying power to increase your long position. On the other hand, the short interest is not very high right now, broker call rates are going up, the put-call ratios are neutral, the sentiment indicators slightly bearish, the M1 figures are expected to increase tomorrow, and the PPI looks like it's accelerating; add to this a retest of a Fibonacci resistance level, the breaking of a trend line, the penetration of the 39-day moving average, and the slightly overbought configuration in the momentum index, and we better err on the side of caution right now.

"But we could still get a quick pop, and you'll participate in the move, because of your bull spread position."

Talk about bull spread.

It's too easy to feel overwhelmed with the "brokerese" you hear from your stock salesperson. Frankly, the idea may be to overwhelm or impress you. Or it may be that the stock salesperson is so "into" the Wall Street lingo that it's crept into his normal English and he just can't help himself. It really doesn't matter. What matters is that you don't let the gobbledygook stand in the way of understanding anything and everything the stock salesperson is telling you. If what he is saying has anything to do with your money, you have every right to ask him to repeat his words in plain English—and if needed, to explain. If that takes awhile, so what? Think how long it took you to save that money. Now, what is that compared to a little time spent understanding what could happen to your life if your money is lost?

So don't let your "financial consultant" charm or confuse you with jargon. There is not one thing he can say that you cannot understand. If he is sensitive enough to your needs, he should either define his terms or not use them in the first place. Remember this: He will know from your first demand for plain English that you are one client that wants to be an informed, hands-on investor. If that seems to bother him, then you have learned a lot about him, too. Maybe he's not the right broker for you.

SR4: The Hoot 'n Holler Box

"Beverly Hills, can you hear me? Let's hear it for Beverly Hills. Boca Raton, how's the sun out there? Okay, let's get the show on the road. Currently the market is up 17 on moderately active trading. The tick is a plus 320, advances are two to one on the upside, upside volume is 31 million shares, downside volume is 27 million shares . . . The autos are under pressure because of a sell recommendation issued by Merrill Lynch this morning. . . . Bonds are down ten ticks. . . . Good morning from the syndicate department. Today we've got an unusual offer—300 thousand shares of Willy Dilly Company . . ."

All this happy chatter is coming from the little brown speaker box on Mr. Newman's desk. The speaker box is the "hoot 'n holler box," the SR4, or squawk box. It's an in-house radio station that most large firms use to talk to their stock salespeople in the trenches, giving market updates, commentary, and ideas for products to sell at special deals to their clients, ideas like the Cleavers' synthetic fertilizer stock.

At both brokerage firms where I worked, the squawk box had a daily schedule of events, not unlike programs for a radio or television station, in which brokers could plan to tune in to get the latest scoop on the hottest new product that the brokerage firm was trying to sell. Intermixed between all of the product sales and promotional announcements were little bits of technical and fundamental analysis always geared to the sale of something. I disagreed so often with the technical analysts, I came to realize that their interests were biased, just like the rest of the firm's recommendations. The analysts slanted their coverage positively to "going long" (buying) so often that it became obvious it was what they were supposed to do. In fact, if I ever agreed with the technical analyst about a product, it made me very uncomfortable. I wasn't the only one. The "research advice" I heard may have been good for the firm in general, an unloading of a stock here, a pushing of another there, but the advice was usually just downright bad and left more than a few No Brain Bills in the lurch facing irate clients.

But good or not, when it came to recommendations, the SR4 broadcasters knew how to get the broker's attention and how to do it discreetly. The nonsense words the Cleavers did not understand are an example of the coded words meant for that very situation—the broker can be talking to a customer and understand the commissions and perks the stock offers without the customer understanding a thing.

That bit of information alone might have made the Cleavers think a little longer before sinking their money into synthetic fertilizer.

Air of Professionalism

Mr. Cleaver had been caught off-guard by the calm, professional atmosphere of Big Time Investments, Inc. Not too long ago the firm's name was Big Time Brokerage Company, and its offices were a storefront full of frenetic activity, with excitement in the air, ticker tapes, and rolled-up shirtsleeves.

When I began dabbling in the market over 30 years ago, such a storefront business was much closer to the truth. The idea was to create excitement, a bull-pen frenzy that would be contagious for investors, some of whom were walk-ins. The individual offices were huddled together, and on Thursdays, when the money figures were released, there was standing room only. You could literally feel the excitement. It was not far from the thrill of gambling, in theory or practice.

I think of a man named Mike when I remember that contagious excitement and the impact it had on the investors in the offices. One day, I was working in my bull-pen desk area, talking on the phone with Damon, my trading link who was on the floor of the Chicago Mercantile Exchange, one of the oldest futures exchanges in the United States. Our offices were so crunched together I could hear everything going on in the cubicles around me. In the one next door, a guy was yelling and cursing at the top of his voice.

"Hey," I said, taking my headset off and leaning over the partition, "keep it down. I'm trying to trade over here."

That's when I got my first eyeful of Mike. His face was pock-marked, his mustache was thick, he was biting on a filterless cigarette, and he wore a beautiful blue designer jacket that cost more than most people spend on a wardrobe. A smaller, younger version of him stood nearby, obviously an offspring. The two of them smelled like a cigarette factory. Mike took a short, nervous drag off his cigarette and offered me an apology, smoke rolling out with each word. He was sorry, but the "damn market is limit down and I'm long 25 contracts of silver (worth about $3 million)."

I went back to my own worries. In my earphone I could hear Damon yelling something about the Federal Reserve and interest rates. But I could still hear Mike, and he had just said, "To hell with it. Buy ten more contracts."

I was trying to ignore him when I noticed that his son, a true facsimile of dear old Dad down to the expensive jacket and half-chewed cigarettes, was standing in my booth. He tapped me on the shoulder.

"What do you think the market's going to do?"

"What market?" I said.

"That market you trade. The S and P? That's what you called it?" He was referring to the Standard & Poor stock index futures.

"I'm just about to get out and make a fair profit, but I think it's going to go a lot higher."

With that, Mike Jr. took out a coin and said, "Tails, I go long (buy), heads I go short (sell). Whichever way it lands, you trade 25 contracts for me."

Heads it was. I leaned over to the booth where Mike Sr. was standing and asked his broker, "Is this guy for real? Do you want me to take his order?"

The broker nodded, so I looked at Mike Jr., giving him a chance to back out. With a few earthy responses and a wave of his hand, he said, "It's all a gamble anyway. Go ahead and put the order in."

Forty minutes later, Mike Sr. was down another $75,000. He told me to get out of the S and P's, and he and Mike Jr. got out—out of the office and into their Rolls Royce waiting outside. I found out later Mike's total losses were in excess of $1 million, and because he had gone way past his available cash playing the market, he had to be sued for payment. That's the way the atmosphere could infect you. That's the way it was meant to infect you.

Now the whole appearance has changed. Instead of a storefront shop filled with the flurry of excitement, brokerage firms wish to convey the image of a professional atmosphere. So a few years ago, Big Time Brokerage Company and other big-time companies leased fancy offices in new buildings alongside lawyers, accountants, and other professionals. A few brokerage firms, like Big Time Brokerage Company—now Big Time Investments, Inc.—also changed their names to fit the image. The brokers now have individual offices and are called financial consultants, registered representatives, or account executives. To feed the image, some firms also employ "money managers," and "financial planners." (Such new "careers" are part of a new species of financial jobs discussed in Chapter 4.) Most of the modern stock salespeople's work is done over the phone and any thought of gambling has been removed from the customer's mind.

Yet, the risk hasn't changed. Only the wrapping it comes in.

Hidden Commissions

"And best of all, you don't have to pay any commission!"

Remember when Mr. Newman, in pushing the Really Good Municipal Bond Fund, saved that statement until last? He knew exactly what effect those words would have on the Cleavers. No commission, he said. Yet Mr. Newman made a hefty commission on it from the other end, a perfect example of one of the many ways the stock salesperson makes commissions off your money without you knowing it. Stockbrokers are under a moral obligation not to charge excessive commissions, but moral obligations only stretch as far as the morals of the stockbroker. So many ways to make hidden commissions exist, and so many new ones are created with each new product, that a complete list would be impossible. It goes on every day behind the scenes in a multitude of ways. Here are just a few examples that will remind you that the broker, once again, has a real conflict of interest in serving you.

Switch Idea

When I was working in the brokerage industry, rarely a month would pass when someone didn't hand me a "switch idea."

Switch ideas are one of the many creations cooked up by the brokerage community for the purpose of generating commissions that otherwise wouldn't be generated. The concept is to call up your client and present the client the idea of switching from a bond he presently owns to another bond, allegedly for a higher interest rate return. The broker using a switch idea isn't concerned about the interest rate. He's interested in the double commission he and the firm will get from the bond switch. And guess what? You as the customer will never know how much that commission was.

To Lump or Not to Lump

Another method of charging excessive commissions is for the stock salesperson to purchase a limited number of shares below the "break point." Say you authorize him to purchase 1,000 shares of a $10 stock. The average commission would be about $275. But instead of one purchase of 1,000 shares, let's say the salesperson makes ten purchases of 100 shares. Instead of the normal $275, he can actually make up to $700 in commissions—right out of your pocket. This is a common practice.

But he's not supposed to do that. In fact, he's not supposed to do that even if you ask for the ten separate purchases yourself. The stockbroker is supposed to lump them together for you, allowing for the smaller commission. You should be charged for one 1,000-share commission, not ten smaller commissions totaling a nice little extra sum for him. Whether he lumps or doesn't lump, though, is entirely up to him, if the firm doesn't catch him.

Bonds: A Net That Catches Your Money

Bonds are a classic hidden-commission product. Brokerage firms have a nice practice of buying bonds on a net basis. That means that the commission you pay is already in the price of the bond when it's quoted to you—it won't even show up on the confirmation slip you receive in the mail. You never know if the broker made $10, $100, $1,000, or any other amount on any bonds that you bought. Mr. Newman can quote a 20-year bond to the Cleavers that yields 9%. But since his company bought a pile of them cheaply, the yield can be in reality nine-and-a-quarter percent. And guess who pockets that 1/4%? A broker can essentially do whatever he wants when it comes to the commissions he puts into the bonds you buy. All he needs is approval from the brokerage firm. So, think about it. Who really needs your bonds switched? You or the broker?

The watchdogs of each big firm, the compliance departments, try to set maximum allowable commissions. Only a few short years ago, the abuses were so bad that even the firms themselves had to fire off memos to their stock salespeople, threatening to automatically reverse such overcharged commissions—if caught, of course.

Payouts: To Gross or Not to Gross

Probably the single highest-paying commission available to a securities salesperson is that derived from the sale of limited partnerships and other direct investment products. Remember No Brain Bill's product meeting? In order to promote products that salespeople will sell, the dealers and wholesalers not only offer higher commissions but award contest points toward free trips to Bermuda or Europe to any broker reaching a specific point total. The dealers desperately need the broker to sell the dealers' own products.

So do the brokerage companies. Here is what the brokerage company offers the salesperson: The more commissions you generate, the more income you make. Sounds simple, doesn't it? This is only the beginning, however, because a broker keeps a percentage of his *total* production generated for the brokerage company. A new salesperson, for example, might generate $100,000 in gross commissions during his first year in the business. At most firms he would probably be given a payout of about 25%, or $25,000. However, a more seasoned salesperson might generate $500,000 gross commission in a calendar year. His payout might be 40% or $200,000. Superbrokers, those producing gross revenues of over $1,000,000 to the brokerage firm, could earn a payout of 50% or more. The higher the gross commission the salesperson generates, the higher the payout he receives and, of course, the more money he makes for himself. Get the picture? The brokerage firms build in an incentive for the salesperson to sell, sell, sell, so he can make, make, make.

Now, of course, we're back into conflict of interest problems. Why should a salesperson purchase a certificate of deposit or a treasury bill when he can place a client in a mutual fund or limited partnership with two, three, or four times the commission involved? Especially when he knows that the larger his commission is, the larger his ultimate payout for the year will be?

Telemarketing: Cold Calling

Cold-Calling Clara's sales technique of choice is the most used sales technique in the industry. I have seen branch managers hand out stacks of three-by-five-inch cards to their brokers, listing not only names, addresses, and financial data, but personal information, including occupation, number of kids, and whether the family owns a dog. The brokers' assignment, should they choose to accept it— and the branch manager chooses that they do—is to pick up the phone, call these people, and try to sell one of the firm's products. They are supplied with scripts and are given the basic operating knowledge of how to overcome investors' objections. If they only sell to 1% of their targets, they're considered successful.

When you met Cold-Calling Clara, you learned that many large firms actually offer a "cold-calling college" for their brokers. Cold calling offers so much potential income that many brokers are constantly trying to find new methods to increase their telemarketing production. Brokerage offices around the country are constantly bombarded with seminars, books, and courses with the latest and greatest cold-calling secrets to success.

Why would anyone turn over thousands of dollars to a disembodied voice from the other side of the country? It seems hard to believe, but it's done every day. The cold callers with the reverse telephone directory system can even make you think they come with a recommendation. After all, they know your neighbors and may even be "handling some assets for them." I had one call me just the other day using that ruse, and no doubt, so did you.

Using these ploys, some of the No Brain Bills I know make $300,000 a year. It takes so little expertise that I've seen stockbrokers hire college students, hand them a script, and pay them to dial for dollars by reading the script to anyone who answers the phone. The optimum telemarketing hours, as anyone who's been interrupted at home by such a call knows, are from 4 to 9 P.M. While this is a violation of security laws, it never seems to be an issue.

The worst of the lot are the boiler room operators who are set up just to defraud you. The number of these are mushrooming right along with the "legitimate" (I use the term loosely) telemarketers. Recently, a Southern California telemarketing scam made the national papers. Three men were convicted of a $5 million "boiler room" scam in which they sold phony precious metals to hundreds of customers. The money went to "sales commissions, overhead, personal expenses, and paying back earlier investors." The victims' individual losses ranged from $1,000 to $150,000. The entire scheme was perpetrated over the phone.

The Rest of the Gang

At the end of Chapter 1, you met the rest of the people in your brokerage firm and learned about the chain of conflict that snakes its way through every brokerage house, from the branch office manager past the back office personnel, around the trading department, and right up to the president and the rest of upper management.

Next, learn how these four groups of Wall Street employees can mishandle your money—without even a proper introduction.

Branch Office Manager

In the movie *Wall Street,* director Oliver Stone did an excellent job of portraying the typical branch manager in action. Upon noticing the phenomenal production of a relatively new broker, the branch office manager moved the fledgling into a beautiful corner office complete with outside window and executive secretary. The manager announced to the entire branch office that this particular broker had done an outstanding job and not only should be admired for his hard work and production but should be looked upon as someone to idolize. This bright young man had rocketed to super-broker status through insider trading—a crime for which he was later exposed and which caused the branch manager to say that he had been suspicious of the young man all along.

This, sadly, is the way it is. The branch manager's success rides on his salespeople's success. The manager's income is based upon the bottom line of the office—the more commissions the office generates, the more money the branch manager makes. Few questions are asked; lots of "Attaboys," though, are freely offered.

If you were a branch manager and Stockbroker Schwartz, whose total production was under $100,000 last year, has suddenly produced $600,000 in commissions in six months, would you call him in and say: "Okay, Schwartz, stop whatever you're doing until I can check to see if it's all right."

Or are you going to call Schwartz into your office and say: "Keep up the good work! You're doing great."

Bluntly, even though branch managers should be watchdogs over their stockbrokers, making sure their work is professional, few managers are concerned with how well the brokers perform for their clients; they are far more concerned with the amount of money the broker is making for the company. The branch managers have little choice if they want to stay employed. Even the sincere, competent branch manager will feel the same conflict of interest pressure the stockbroker feels.

In my eight years in the industry, I never once sat down with a branch manager and discussed the overall performance of any of my clients. We never had meetings to discuss the rates of return, the interest income, or an overall evaluation of my clients' portfolios. But I can assure you that I had plenty of meetings in which we discussed my production level and how it could be increased.

Back Office Personnel

"Well, thank you for the transaction," your stockbroker says to you with a big smile and a shake of your hand. "That's all there is to it! Let me just take the ticket over to the cashier, and we're all set. Claudine will stamp it, and then we'll sign some forms. Your money is in good hands."

You follow your stockbroker to the window and there behind the glass is a paper-shuffling clerk, a middle-aged woman with a little weight problem and a big attitude problem.

"Here, Claudine!" the stockbroker chirps.

"Hmmmph," Claudine grunts, stopping her paper-shuffling just long enough to grab the ticket from the window opening, stamp it, and plop it on top of the rest of her papers.

"Thank you, Claudine," the oblivious stockbroker croons.

"Hmmmph," comes Claudine's churlish response.

Claudine and the rest of the back office personnel spend their days shuffling papers, stamping tickets, and handling reams and reams of paper, all designed to keep the stockbroker and the company both healthy and untouched by litigation problems. Their chief function is to protect the brokerage company from liability and claims due to any false moves by errant stockbrokers.

People like Claudine in the understaffed back office are over-worked and among the lowest paid workers in any industry, yet they are vital to the company's well-being and must always put the company first. One slip and they could be out of a job.

They also help the firm make money on your money. A perfect example is how your money market account might be handled. You may not know it, but whenever you deposit money into a money market account, you lose between one and two days of interest. If it's a Friday or a holiday, make that three or four days of lost interest. This might seem like a trivial matter, but if you're depos-iting a hefty amount of funds, the interest you lose can be dramatic. Who's getting the use of the money during that time? The brokerage firm, through the work of the back office personnel. Next time you make a deposit into your money market account, take a look at your month-end statement. You may find this to be true.

These back office people don't feel a conflict of interest as much as they feel just plain overworked for little reward. If they hurt you, it's not out of malice but through screwups, due to the amount of work dumped on them and the pressure, all out of proportion to their status. Claudine has every right to be surly, so don't be surprised if she is.

Trading Department

"OMIGOSH! Who the hell bought so much stock of this stupid synthetic fertilizer company?! We've got to move it and move it fast. Make it the special offering today, or we're going to lose a pile and somebody's going to have to pay and pay big!"

The brokerage firm's trading department just bought too much of a stinky stock. The brokerage firm, you see, also trades its own accounts, and its actions have an effect on you. The trading de-partments are trying to make money independent of the stock-brokers. So if one of these traders goofs and uses the firm's capital to buy too much stock of some less-than-great company, the trader must get rid of that pile. How does he do it? Sometimes he gets on the in-house radio station, the squawk box, and announces a terrific deal on a stock now available to the salespeople working with the public. They can sell it at a special price and his siren's song tells them of amazingly high commissions and payout.

Then stockbrokers like Mr. Newman help unload it onto clients like the Cleavers. The stockbroker has made money, and the trader has gotten rid of his pile of unwanted stock and also made money for his department. Of course, the downside is that Mr. Newman may not really know it's a stinker of a stock, at least not until his clients start making a stink themselves.

Upper Management

Let me state the obvious: Securities companies exist to make money. The fact that to make money someone has to lose money is not the point. Survival is.

Such must be the credo of those in upper management, the high-priced, high-positioned executives in the large Wall Street firms, because they are constantly under pressure to invent new products for your broker to sell, ones which will generate more commissions for their companies.

A great example of this credo in action is the invention of closed-end bond funds, much like the one the Cleavers sunk $50,000 into with a trusting smile. Following the 1987 stock market crash, the small investor left the stock market in such dramatic numbers that the industry had to find a way of generating commissions. So this idea was born—the now-infamous closed-end bond fund, a little trick to take a portfolio of bonds, tie them together with a little ribbon, and sell them as a new offering. Everybody seemed to have a closed-end bond fund right after the '87 crash. And everybody seemed to be selling them to any and all clients showing the slightest interest.

Why? When a brokerage company brings out a new offering, and the company acts as its own underwriter, the sums of money made during the initial public offering phase are in the huge range. As we've already seen in the case of Mr. Newman's commission windfall, the stock salesperson, at the end of this vast "distribution network" also stands to make commissions in the huge range, a small fact usually not mentioned to the clients.

Several of the funds, like the Cleavers' Really Good Municipal Bond Fund, had the gall to promote and advertise in the prospectuses that their bond fund was good for "preservation of capital and high current income." These are the two things the majority of investors want to hear. So the public believed and bought. Those sterling words of comfort were on the inside of the brochures—in print. Mrs. Cleaver even noticed them. The fine print buried in the prospectus, where the unpleasant information was placed, stated that this was a risky investment but Mrs. Cleaver never noticed it. Most clients can't read this part of the prospectus without the aid of a magnifying glass, and even if they could, they would need an interpreter to explain it.

Yet I have no doubt that when many of the funds lost more than 20% in value, many brokers were pointing to this specific part of the prospectus in their hurried explanations to their angry clients. In the words of a current song, large print giveth and small print taketh away.

Still, even today these closed-end bond funds are being sold to those who are absolutely unaware of their risks. I suppose the truth is that this kind of product isn't really meant to make money for its investors; it's meant to generate quick returns for the firms and high commissions for the salespeople under the thin guise of possible high returns for the supposedly educated consumer. The funds, invented by upper management, can lose investors' money like crazy and still make big bucks for the funds' management teams.

Obviously, the chain of conflict goes all the way to the top. And you, the client, are at the very bottom of the chain (a situation we'll discuss more in Chapter 3). That is a fact the knowledgeable investor must never forget when working with any brokerage firm.

Dishonest Stock Salespeople

So far, most of our discussion has been about the relatively honest stock salespeople who skate along the edge of the rules, however fast or furious. Mr. Newman wasn't necessarily dishonest. He was just self-serving and not above capitalizing on the Cleavers' financial needs.

How about the dishonest ones? There are hundreds of ways a dishonest stockbroker can cheat you. In Chapters 9 and 10, I'll explore the most obvious products and practices abused, the negligent acts committed, and what can be done about it, but for now, here's a quick look at some of these acts. I have already mentioned gouging for exorbitant commissions. Here is a short list of some of the other things a dishonest or incompetent stockbroker might do as he dips into your investment pocket:

- Overtrading accounts
- Unauthorized trading
- "Churning" accounts over and over for the commissions
- Misrepresenting the possible risks or true nature of products
- Fraudulently inducing a customer to buy a product
- Providing advice unfounded in fact
- Making unsuitable recommendations not in keeping with a client's financial condition, sophistication, or risk tolerance

Acts, with such names as Failure To Obey, Suitability, Churning, and Offloading a Loser, violate various rules of the Securities and Exchange Commission (SEC), NASD, and New York Stock Exchange Constitution.

That's the bad news.

The good news is that you can recover monies lost because of such negligent, intentional, or illegal acts. That topic is discussed in Chapter 10.

But Somebody's Making Money on Wall Street

Perhaps an obvious thought has occurred to you by now. Do any of these used stock salespeople make money off investments themselves, or do they just make money off our money? Wouldn't you think that if a financial advisor's advice is so good, he would follow it himself? And if he is truly a professional, why does he need your business? Can't he make enough money investing and trading his own account?

The answer is simple. Few millionaires made their financial fortune in the stock market. They may have enhanced their wealth by proper long-term investing, but they probably didn't make it in the stock market. Most people who make really big money in the stock market are inside stock manipulators or traders—people who have information not accessible to the average investor. They use that inside information to make vast sums of money, often hazarding a few years of jail time before they can spend it.

As for investing their own money, the number of brokers that invest their own funds in the stock market is limited and that means that they are aware of the grave risks in buying stocks and prefer to place their money in the bank. Or even worse, they tried investing their money in the stock market and lost it all.

My favorite broker excuse for not investing a broker's money is: "I can't invest my own money in the stock market. Why, I'd have a conflict of interest between taking care of my money and watching out for my client's money!"

Think about it. If a broker does not have the faith to put his own money in his recommended investments, then why should you have the faith to put your money in them?

The Attitude

There's one last lesson to be learned from your peek into the brokerage firm. Except for the exceptional few who are driven by their own decent ethical standards, it is the stock salesperson's attitude, an attitude no doubt shared by his firm, that fuels almost all the practices you've read about.

Some years ago, I was at one of those Hollywood parties you read about, listening to the latest Hollywood gossip, watching for the occasional celebrity to float by, when I overheard a stockbroker—a member of his firm's elite Director's Circle (said membership requiring the production of over $1 million in commissions during the calendar year)—bragging to a group of party-goers. His comments went something like this:

> *Can you believe how smart the brokerage company is? It comes out with a secondary offering of its own stock at around $30 per share because, like we all know, it doesn't know a thing about making money. Of course, management puts a lot of pressure on us brokers to sell the damn thing. And believe you me, I sold a ton of that crap. The smart money on the street, of*

course, was shorting the stock. They all knew how much trouble the company was in and none of the real professionals would buy a single share. Right after the offering, the company starts to report quarterly losses and laying people off left and right.

So—what happens? The stock begins to drop. All the way down below $10 a share. And what does the company do? Make a tender offer to buy back all those shares at $11 a share. Pretty slick, right? It sells to the stupid public at $30 a share, buys it back at $11 a share, and pockets over $19 a share!

I couldn't stand it. I actually butted into the circle and bluntly asked the man, "Don't you find anything morally reprehensible about that? You have the whole thing backwards. The customer is the one who was taken. You can't be that cold."

The man looked at me as if I were crazy. Finally, he shrugged and, with a casual glance around the circle of listeners, he said: "You place your bet and you take your chances."

What kind of an industry rewards this kind of thinking?

Maybe it's always been this way. Maybe the brokers are now more willing to admit that they are salespeople first and foremost, and the sale is the most important thing. Yet I still believe that most stockbrokers once had a modicum of concern about properly serving their clients, no matter what the cold reality is today.

The major Wall Street firms are perhaps the biggest reasons the investment industry has taken this decidedly dangerous turn against the individual investor. They are not assisting you in your quest toward stock market profits; they are themselves an impediment to success.

In fact, Wall Street today places so many invisible roadblocks in the way of the individual investor that making money with your investments is more like gambling than you would like to believe. The commissions you must overcome create potential investment problems before your money has even left the cashier's hands. After you have invested, there is another world of obstacles between you and the money you'd like to make. It's a world full of roadblocks most investors aren't even aware of. What's between you and that legendary "market killing"? That's next, in Chapter 3.

Know Your Built-In Investment Roadblocks

What Lies Between You and Your Stock Market Profit?

You've bought that stock. Now you watch the papers every day, expecting it to go up, up, up and make your pockets jingle, jangle, jingle.

Instead, your stock goes up a little, then down a little. And then down, down, down.

What happened?

The next morning you notice a story in the paper. The company whose stock you've bought held a press conference the night before to announce some manufacturing problems. How did the stock go down before the story broke about the company?

Information.

It's the ultimate commodity on Wall Street. News makes the market go up and down. And the person with the information edge is the one who will profit from it. When you capitalize on it illegally, it's called insider trading and carries potential jail time. When exploited legally, it's a game of minutes, even seconds sometimes. And the people trying to buy stocks to get a hefty return are always in search of it. Wall Street knew about your company's problems before they ever hit the newsprint. That's why the stock went down before you picked up the paper or turned on your computer.

This is the way it happens: A major event occurs in the boardroom of a corporation, or a new discovery is made in the laboratory at a pharmaceutical company. The pending announcement or discovery descends down the information pipeline at mind-boggling speed. Its usefulness and effectiveness diminishes as the number of people who have it increases. Unfortunately, the customer—the individual investor—is usually at the end of the line; he acquires the information as it's trickling out the end of the pipeline.

Therein lies the problem. Whether it's a news release from Apple about a new computer line or a financial officer at a bank explaining why the bank had to write off $100,000,000 in bad loans, or a research report from a major brokerage house, investors are at the end of the information pipeline, always the last to know.

This dynamic is one of the biggest roadblocks you'll encounter as you try to make money in the market. It's one of the obstacles discussed in this chapter that you, the investor, must overcome to be successful in the investment world.

Surprisingly enough, it's also one of the biggest roadblocks professional investors on Wall Street must overcome. They don't do as well as you might think. Professionals are fishing for information all the time. The desperate need for information creates a propaganda, tip, and rumor mill beyond imagination, and all of this can affect you.

So in this chapter, we'll peek into the world of Wall Street to see how it operates and what it means for the personal investor who scans the morning business section searching for news about his or her stock.

New News/Old News

Once you read about a news event in a paper, or hear a story discussed on the evening news, it's usually too late to profit from the "old" news. Unfortunately, most investors don't seem to grasp the basic axiom that the stock market discounts news events. In fact, many experts believe that the market discounts future events by as much as six months. What does that mean for you, the investor?

Let's take a closer look at a classic example. I'll use XYZ Corporation by way of illustration; however, the story has been repeated since the earliest days of the stock market and no doubt will occur again and again as long as there are two or more people who hold an opinion about the value of a stock.

It's early Tuesday morning, and George and Helen have just finished making breakfast together. As George sits down to a fresh cup of coffee and Helen takes a big bite of her scrambled eggs, he opens the morning paper to the business section. There George discovers a news story about XYZ Corporation. "Helen," George says, frowning, "it says here that XYZ is going to cut its dividend because it's had an earnings slowdown and won't have sufficient income to maintain the dividend at its present level." Helen puts down her fork, suddenly losing her appetite. "It's even talking about laying off as many as 1,000 employees," George reads on, "and shutting down a couple of factories. And if that's not enough, it's going to cut the dividend entirely, not just reduce it. We better call our broker before the stock market opens and figure out what we should do about the situation."

But Helen has a more immediate question: "George, when's the last time you looked up the price of that stock? We haven't talked to our broker in well over three months."

"I checked on the stock about a month-and-a-half ago, and it was selling at $42 a share," George answers, rifling through the newspaper to the stock tables while Helen waits over her cold eggs.

When George finds the stock tables from the previous day, he exclaims, "I can't believe this! XYZ closed at $30 a share yesterday—why that's close to its low for the past year. I don't understand how the stock could have gone down before the news came out. Why didn't we hear from our broker?"

For the next few strained minutes, George and Helen sit around the breakfast table discussing what their next move should be. Should they buy more stock now that it's this low? Or better yet, should they sell the stock before the company is really in trouble?

Not waiting for the stock market to open, George calls up Tom, his broker, to find out what he might know.

Tom is quick to point out that he is right on top of things. "I've got a news story about XYZ on my computer, George, and it looks as though it's not doing too well," Tom tells him. "I think we should consider selling it because it's very possible, according to the article, that it might cut its dividend altogether."

Covering up the mouthpiece of the receiver, George turns to Helen and tells her what Tom thinks. "At least we haven't lost any money on the stock," he says, "but I sure am sorry to see our profits go down the drain and the stock go down so quickly without any warning. Should we sell?"

Helen nods, but not convincingly. "If we do, what will we put our money into?"

George hesitates, then says into the phone, "I guess you'd better go ahead and sell it."

Right or Wrong?

Did they do the right thing? Unfortunately, George and Helen just might be selling the stock at the wrong time. Why? Because George and Helen, like most investors—even the professional ones—do not appreciate this fact: The individuals who are intimately familiar with the internal affairs of XYZ expected the dividend cut and have been selling XYZ stock for the past two months. The slow, steady decline in the price of the stock had already discounted the dividend cut. George didn't know that those who sold their stock two months ago, in anticipation of a dividend cut, had already made a profit while the other uninformed investors, like George, are now selling because the bad news just hit the street.

Once news becomes public property, it has entirely lost its value. The only exception might be in the unusual situation of a news item leaked to help push the price of a stock up or down. The smart investors on Wall Street make money by purchasing or selling securities in *anticipation* of developments, by discounting conditions *before* the public has knowledge of them. To state it more simply: The majority of investors are constantly trying to invest based upon past events. They make the erroneous assumption that present conditions will continue. In fact, our whole scheme of life is, to some degree, based upon this assumption. Any trader who is truly a professional will be the first to point out that news events are most bullish at a market top and most bearish at a market bottom.

Casting Shadows

Unfortunately, professionals as well as individual investors throughout the world get caught up in the perception that things will continue as they are. If the market is going ever higher, we better get in right now before it's too late. I have heard it said that a coming event casts its shadow before the event arrives; this shadow is what the professional trader is looking for, not the event itself.

This "discounting mechanism" is powerful enough to be worthy of great consideration, but that's the topic of another book. I just want you, the reader–investor, to be aware of its vast importance.

Bear in mind, however, that some events cannot be discounted. No one could have anticipated the San Francisco earthquake, or the Florida orange freeze, or the assassination of John F. Kennedy. They cast no shadows at all. And no one can deny the direct implications each of these events had on the population at large as well as individual investors.

Who's at the Controls?

It doesn't take one very long to understand that information is the ultimate commodity on Wall Street. The information revolution, which to a great extent was made possible by the advent of the personal computer, is placing vast amounts of information at the individual investor's fingertips. By connecting to any one of a dozen data bases or information services, you can study just about anything your heart desires. In fact, information is so valuable that major corporations and companies such as Dow Jones & Company Inc., CompuServe, and other information data banks are making fortunes by charging for the use of their information.

But it is the person who *controls* the information, not the one who *receives* it, that profits the most. The closer you get to the information source, the more you are able to make use of it. Imagine that you are hiking through the back country of the Sierra Nevada mountains in search of the purest and cleanest drinking water anywhere on earth. Where are you going to find that water? The obvious answer is the closer you get to the source, the cleaner and purer the water will be. If you're lucky enough to be one of the privileged few who make it to the top of those mountains and find a clean, unspoiled pool of water made up of freshly melted snow, only then would you appreciate the taste of one of nature's finest gifts. The farther you get from the source of the water, the more contaminated, processed, and chlorinated the water will be.

Information is no different. Information is so rapidly transmitted in this shrinking global environment that to make use of it requires lightning-fast decision-making as well as execution. The farther you get from the information source, the more the news event or story may have been edited, altered, or exaggerated. Remember the game we played as youngsters in which we sat around a room and told a story to the person seated to our left, and by the time the story came back from the person to our right it had very little resemblance to what we initially said? That's what happens to the information most of us receive at the end of the pipeline. Unfortunately, the people in a position to make the most use of the information, those closest to the source, must do so at the peril of violating securities laws and possibly spending a little time behind bars. This is the infamous insider trading you've heard so much about: "Insiders" profiting from information that is not generally known to the public and only available to a few "inside individuals," such as directors, officers, or employees of a corporation about to disseminate an important announcement. Of course, that's not to say that it still isn't done frequently, because it is. The overwhelming, seducing power of pure, clear information can blind many even to the threat of imprisonment.

Don't, Don't, Don't

What does this mean to you and me? Obviously we can't trade on inside information because either we don't have access to it, or even if we did, it's illegal. How, then, should we treat the information that does trickle down to us?

First you must realize that there are a couple of basic "don'ts" that can save you a lot of money if you can just adhere to them.

Don't buy a stock based upon a tip. The "tippor" (the person from whom you are getting the tip) might tell you he has information that nobody else has. But if this is the case, why then would he be parting with this information? Out of the goodness of his golden heart? Hardly. If it's so valuable, wouldn't he keep it to himself?

The same is true of rumors: Don't buy a stock based upon one. It's amazing how fast a rumor can spread. And since information is passed so readily from one location to another, rumors are not limited to geographic areas. A rumor on the floor of the New York Stock Exchange will be heard in Switzerland at the same time that it's spoken in London. Everyone is a member of the same electronic global village.

A Principle for All Seasons: Efficient Markets Hypothesis

There is a basic operating principle upon which all markets are constituted. In order for you to fully appreciate the inability to invest based upon information in the form of news events, rumors, and tips, I feel compelled to explain it. The principle has been developed over many decades and, quite to the frustration of all the major brokerage companies, letter writers, chart services, research analysts, and economists, is as relevant and correct today as it was when first postulated. It's not limited to U.S. markets, either; this comprises all markets throughout the world. It's called the efficient markets hypothesis.

More than a few books have been written on the subject, and I would do it a disservice to believe that I could reduce the collective thoughts, research, and analysis of professors from the likes of Cambridge and Harvard in a paragraph or two. For those who are not inclined to delve into econometric research—even though it has direct implications on their investment dollars—I offer this simple summary statement of the principle: "Brokers cannot predict markets, but they act as if they can." That, basically, is what the efficient market hypothesis is all about. It is not limited to brokers, however; it applies to market letter writers, timing services, technical analysts, and economists—all purveyors of information.

In the interest of clarity and succinct reasoning as well as brevity, I quote here from my mentor and much-loved colleague, Dr. Richard Teweles, author of *The Complete Guide to Preventing and Resolving Brokerage Disputes*. He has reduced to a few pages what otherwise might take a reader several hundred pages to comprehend:

> Whether markets are efficient, and to what degree, has been argued for many years and the argument seems destined to rage on for many more years to come. This subject may seem academic to some, but it is important and should be carefully noted by all who are interested in financial markets. It is particularly important to realize that there are those who reject the concept, but ignore evidence that does not support their position or simply make up their minds with no evidence at all.

> **What Is It?**
> A detailed analysis of the efficient markets hypothesis is left to specialized investment books, but the concept deserves careful consideration here.
>
> Basically, it is assumed that the marketplace is made up of large numbers of well-informed seekers of profits who have the financial means and incentives to act quickly to take advantage of opportunities. There are a limited number of financial vehicles relative to the large numbers of researchers, salespeople, advisors, and customers who wish to take advantage of them. Only a few thousand security issues, futures, and options trade actively, whereas the number of people actively interested in trading is in the millions. There is great incentive to acquire information and act upon it quickly while it still has value.
>
> Given the speed with which information gets disseminated, its influence on prices is quite likely to exert itself quickly and accurately. A market which adapts quickly and accurately to

events or anticipated events is said to be efficient. If opportunity is already reflected accurately in price, there is small comfort for those who seek opportunity in financial vehicles regarded as overpriced or underpriced.

Various degrees of efficiency have been described, but the most popular description is that which considers efficiency in three versions: weak, semistrong, and strong.

The weak form indicates that all information that can be yielded by price alone is immediately reflected in price and therefore cannot have forecasting value. This does not set well with those who like to draw trendlines on charts, follow one or more moving averages, or rely upon simplistic, inadequately researched computer programs.

The semistrong version maintains that all publicly available information is immediately reflected in price. This means that reading financial newspapers, magazines, and market letters, or listening to brokerage house gossip, financial reports on the radio, or developments on the television might be interesting and explain why prices have already moved, or what events might cause them to move in the future. These sources, however, would have no value for forecasting prices. Events which have occurred and the anticipation of events which might occur are both already reflected in price. This version of the hypothesis is hardly popular with purveyors or users of such information. It reduces fundamentalists to explainers of the past rather than predictors of the future. Although this may be of intellectual interest to some, it is certainly much less exciting than successful forecasting.

The strong version of the theory is even more discouraging. It maintains that all legitimate information, published or not, regardless of the effort needed to obtain it and no matter how quickly it is acted upon, is already reflected accurately in price. Even illegitimate forces such as trading based upon inside information or the activities of manipulators are reflected quickly in prices and therefore exemplify rather than defeat the concept of efficiency.

Implications of the Theory
The efficient markets hypothesis does not maintain that prices will not change, or that price levels cannot change rapidly and

materially, or that large amounts of money cannot be made by some investors. Neither does it maintain that some investors will not make money consistently. Naturally, if the price level of any market, whether American Telephone & Telegraph preferred stock or options on hogs, moves significantly higher, those who are long will make money and those who are short will lose. The point is that if the change in price levels is random, such changes cannot be consistently and accurately predicted by most people and, possibly, not by anyone. It is further likely that those who are long, for whatever reason, will credit their financial acumen and those who are not long or who are short will blame their bad luck or their brokers.

The undisputable fact is that there is no credible body of evidence in the financial literature that indicates that the weak and semistrong forms of the hypothesis are not true. There are some who maintain, probably correctly, that there are apparent exceptions to the strong form, but this makes no difference to most investors who do not have the resources, skill, judgment, and personal discipline to achieve good results in markets which are so close to pure efficiency.

What this means is that those who make unusually high returns in the markets over time are those who have good resources and extraordinary judgment. Consistently high returns cannot be made by those who rely exclusively upon naive charts, simple programs designed for their personal computers, or suggestions made by advisors who in turn rely upon equally simplistic devices. Most people who invest are usually long and most markets, particularly in stocks, usually go up, so it becomes rather easy to give credit where credit is due.

Actually the best that can usually be done is to be long in a diversified portfolio of financial instruments in a rising market, and short in a falling market. Of course, it would be most attractive to find a device which would outperform such investing, and it is still necessary to forecast the direction of the market, but there is simply nothing in the financial literature to indicate that there is anything better for most investors than the basic strategy of buying and holding a portfolio incorporating a satisfactory level of risk.

For those who live on the sale of information and commissions on trading, the efficient markets hypothesis is, of course, anathema. The investor who rejects the theory should do so based upon acceptable evidence of its deficiency rather than because of a brush of the hand from those who may have considerable personal interest in its rejection. One should be particularly careful not to be misled by those who claim an outstanding record in the market, but who are unwilling to provide specific significant evidence of satisfactory performance.

The implications and dangers of this concept from the point of view of those who have the duty to make reasonable recommendations should be evident. Making recommendations without reasonable (valid) support may well be taken as fraudulent. If brokers wish to take positions in the market in their own accounts based upon a formation on their dogeared charts, the only risk is to their own pocketbooks. When they suggest that their customers trade on such a basis, however, either the trades had better be profitable or the brokers should be prepared to support the predictive ability of their "chart signals." This is not to imply that brokers insure their recommendations or that charts may not help sharpen and focus personal judgments. If brokers, however, assert that chart formations lead to consistently adequate investment returns, the evidence had better support the assertions. The same is true of recommendations based upon shallow fundamental analysis.

Purveyors of Information: Up Close and Personal

The efficient markets hypothesis, as I've said, casts a shadow over all the purveyors of information. What lies between you and your stock market profits? These purveyors of information—a group of people that you will probably never meet. But you are going to get up close and personal with them, now and in Chapter 4, and the closer you come to understanding how they work, the less likely they will be able to pick your pocket.

Research Reports: Sales Scripts in Disguise

Now that you know that information for the most part cannot help you make money unless you have acquired the information illegally or have relied upon information that makes you an insider and subject to a nasty prosecution, you must ask yourself: "Why, then, do brokerage companies spend so much time and so much money writing 'research' reports?" An entire industry is employed strictly for the purpose of writing research reports. Most major brokerage companies boast a staff of research analysts that, like busy little bees, are daily shuffling reams of paper, walking endless corridors, and holding numerous conversations with corporate officers, all in the interest of providing facts, figures, and conclusions about how well a stock might perform in the future.

You already know that no one can predict how well a stock is going to perform in the future. Then why do these analysts get paid so much money to write so much gossip? The answer lies in the simple fact that research reports are sales tools in disguise. The fact that brokerage companies have staffs of analysts making prognostications based upon the evaluation of management, or the potential for profits in the future, or the pros and cons of a company's balance sheet, should not keep you from your appointed reality check. Think about it. Without research reports, how is the broker going to sell you anything?

A Broker's First Line of Defense

Walk into any brokerage company and in the front reception area you will usually find a display of the latest research reports fresh off the press. This is one sales tool that the broker can rely upon without any threat to his pocketbook, or from the compliance department. Why? Because if a broker is merely following the recommendation of the brokerage company for which he works, it will be difficult if not impossible to hold the broker or the brokerage company responsible merely because the predictions by the research analysts do not come true. Want to check this out for yourself? All you have to do is pick up ten research reports from any brokerage company for the previous year and find out just how well the analysts' predictions performed. Some of the worst picks on Wall Street will be found piled amongst the research rubbish that was yesterday's news even before it was ever printed.

Many an analyst will take exception to these statements, I'm sure, but their jobs depend upon their belief that their work has some meaning—other than that of writing stock sales literature for a salesperson. Their company needs them. Without research, a brokerage company could be held liable for making a stock recommendation without a reasonable basis. In fact, one might go a step further and say that in addition to being a great sales tool, research reports are the first and foremost line of defense against a lawsuit filed by an outraged customer. I could devote an entire chapter to research reports and the lawsuits that were never filed. Because if a broker relies upon a research report, unless it is so grossly incompetent, fraudulent, or downright deceptive that it per se is actionable, that broker usually will not be held accountable for suggesting a stock that the research department has indicated is a proper recommendation.

Don't confuse research and suitability, however. Even if a stock is suggested to be a good recommendation from the brokerage company, that particular stock may be suitable to only certain types of individuals. So suitability and research may be mutually exclusive.

What I am saying is that a broker can rely upon the research department of his brokerage firm to form the reasonable basis for his recommendation to his customer. To that end, a research report is more than a sales tool. It is a formidable line of defense against the assertion that a broker did not have a reasonable basis for making a recommendation.

The Other Guys: The Paper Pushers

So, the research department is made up of salespeople—even if they don't acknowledge they are salespeople. But the research department is not alone in pumping out reams of paperwork destined to fall into the hands of the individual investor. Almost all of the major brokerage companies have at least four other departments that are busily typing away on their word processors through all hours of the day and night in order to come up with suggestions. You know the term: Recommendations. And each of these departments makes them in spades, waiting to "offer" them to anyone willing to listen.

Tea Leaves and Broken Clocks:
The Technical Analysis Group

Technical analysis doesn't work either, as we'll see in the next chapter. But that doesn't stop Wall Street firms from paying six-figure salaries for technical gurus who divine, through tea-leaf reading and other mystical means, to predict not only where the stock market is going, but how soon it will get there and how much you can make along the way. Technical analysts, or "technicians" as they are called in the trade, believe that by observing previous patterns, price movements, or other indicators, they can predict what the future holds for a particular market and even a particular issue. The danger, however, is that every technician, like a broken clock, is right at least once in awhile.

All one need do is take a good look at the technical analyst's recommendations from any brokerage company made over the past few years to see this. Peek ahead, if you'd like, to learn more about technical analysis, but for now keep in mind one overriding thought: Technical analysis reports are just another sales tool in disguise. They are a wolf in sheep's clothing and should be regarded, in many ways, as dangerous as that wolf.

Why? Because if an investor follows the technician's predictions, then the investor must act upon the predictions whether they are right or wrong. This obviously creates the need to buy or to sell, which of course creates more commissions for the broker. The shorter the view of the technician, the more trading he can foster, thus creating greater commissions for the salesperson. It's no accident that many times the technician and the research writer are in unison about a particular stock. It certainly wouldn't speak well for the brokerage company if the research department made a buy recommendation on a stock while the technical department recommended selling it.

So the next time you stop by your neighborhood brokerage office and your friendly stock salesperson hands you the latest technical analysis report, be sure you take it with three grains—no, make that three pounds—of salt, so that you know who's peppering who.

Fundamental Beliefs: Fundamental Analysis

Although fundamental analysis is rooted in the concrete, not the abstract, it too falls short of its alleged predictive powers. "Fundamentalists," as they are called, believe that by studying the performance of a company—that is, its balance sheet, income statement, and cash flow—they can get a better picture of how the stock might perform in the future. Fundamental analysts also keep a careful eye on the dividend yield and the price earnings' multiple as it relates to other stocks in the same or similar fields.

However, be aware of this basic caveat: "Past performance is no guarantee of future performance." Just because a company has paid a dividend for the past 15 years doesn't mean it will continue to pay a dividend for the next 15 years. Western Union was once a powerful corporation but it didn't grow with the information age. American Motors couldn't compete with the Japanese. In fact, it couldn't even compete with other American companies.

If I had to choose between fundamental analysis and technical analysis, I would certainly give more credence to the fundamental approach. However, if the stock market were merely a numbers game, then any engineer could program the balance sheet and income statement of any corporation into his computer and predict precisely what the future held in store—a feat that to this day has never been accomplished. Quite the contrary, give a balance sheet to an engineer and then turn him loose with a computer and his dollars, and he will soon be separated from his money. Why? During the last 40 years, many programs have been written trying to predict the stock market based on the past performance of a corporation; however, they do not take into consideration the ultimate equation—the unpredictable psychology of the human element, something unfathomable to balance sheets and computers.

Also, remember that the next time you purchase a stock mentioned in a research report, the commissions you paid are also helping to pay for the writer's salary. It's nice to think that by counting smokestacks, reams of accounting material, and meeting with management, you could get the upper hand on which is the right stock to buy or sell. If that were really the case, the fundamental analyst wouldn't be telling you about what he has learned, and he wouldn't need the salary garnered through your commissions. He'd be off in the Bahamas on his yacht profiting from the information that he and only he was able to obtain.

Besides, did you ever stop to wonder why 15 different brokerage firms employ 15 different analysts to write 15 different reports on the same company? Can one analyst garner information superior in quality or quantity to the 14 other analysts? The herd psychology on Wall Street is no different from any other walk of life. Usually when one analyst likes a stock, they all like the stock. And conversely, when one analyst puts out a sell recommendation on a stock, all the others flock to it.

Don't Accept the Call: Call Writing

An option is a contract that gives the right, not the obligation, to the buyer of the option to buy (in the case of a call) or to sell (in the case of a put) 100 shares of stock at a specific price, at a specified time in the future. Call writing, in plain English, is selling a call. You are granting to the buyer of that call the right to exercise his option to purchase the stock on which the option is based (the underlying stock) on or before the date the call expires, after which it can no longer be exercised.

It's similar to an owner of real estate granting a 90-day option to purchase his real estate to a prospective buyer. The buyer pays the owner (seller) of the land a sum of money for the buyer's right to exercise the option to purchase the land. If the buyer doesn't exercise his option before the 90 days expire, he has lost his right to exercise the option, and he has lost the premium (price) he paid for the option. As a call writer (seller), you obligate yourself to sell the underlying stock at an agreed upon price if the buyer exercises the option.

Although options are usually suited to only the most sophisticated investor capable of bearing the great economic risk that one undertakes in buying an option, many brokerage companies send out sales literature to stock salespeople encouraging them to solicit options transactions from their customers. They publish papers called "options reports," suggesting which particular stocks have above-average profit potential for "call writing."

But the ultimate purpose of the call-writing strategy is to create double and sometimes triple commission for those foolish enough to not know better. I will happily debate the matter with any stock salesperson who doesn't agree with that statement, under one condition: The salesperson must bring with him a printout of his production run showing the commissions generated from his option program and any stock transactions generated as a result of partaking of the option program.

Call-writing programs can generate excessive commission for the salesperson with little or no reward for the investor. What starts out as a conservative, allegedly income-producing strategy usually ends up an outright speculation, which means—as the statistics bear out when you speculate in options—that you're probably going to lose money. Tell your salesperson, "Thanks, but no thanks, I'll keep my hand on my pocketbook. You can keep your hand on the options."

"Whether" Forecasting: Economic Forecasting Group

Rounding out the paper pushers of the major wire houses is the economic forecasting group usually made up of a well-recognized economist whom you might even see on the evening news or read about in *The Wall Street Journal*. These six-figure gurus are given the responsibility of nothing less than predicting not just how the stock market is going to do but how the entire United States economy is going to do over the short, intermediate, and long term. Economists are quick to forget about their mistakes and will happily point out to you all of their correct predictions. Because economists make predictions, by mere luck they have to be right some of the time. Also notice that the predictions of the brokerage company economists do not too often contradict those of the research department. It would not sit well to have a pessimistic economist while all other members of the paper-pushing team are recommending that you buy, buy, buy.

Market Makers: Brokerage Firm Bonanza

We've spent a lot of time behind the scenes at your brokerage firm, but there's one more curtain I want to fling open in a quiet little corner of the back stage. In addition to the commission-driven profit center at a brokerage company, there is a division entitled the "market maker," or principal transaction division. This is a department whose sole purpose is to buy and sell stock at a profit. When you buy an over-the-counter stock traded on NASDAQ—the National Association of Securities Dealers, Inc., regulated market— you should be alerted to the fact that the brokerage company may have acted as principal in executing the trade. The brokerage company is required by law to disclose to you that it acted as principal in the transaction.

What does that mean? It means that you are usually making a nice tidy profit for the brokerage firm's trading department and it isn't even sending you a thank-you note.

How does such a thing happen? When your stock salesperson purchases a stock for your account on a principal transaction, you will notice somewhere on the confirmation slip a phrase such as, "We make a market in the security." What that means is that someone in the Over-The-Counter Department has gone through the NASDAQ system and purchased this stock for the *inventory* of the brokerage company, and it's been waiting for you to buy it like day-old bread—at the price of fresh or even above it.

By way of example, let's say the brokerage company acquired an over-the-counter stock on the NASDAQ market at $10 per share. If, three weeks later, the stock is selling on the over-the-counter market, as reflected in the NASDAQ price, at $13 per share, it might sell you the stock out of inventory at $13 per share plus a commission, called a markup. But you will not pay $13 per share for the stock. You will pay $13 per share plus some form of a markup or commission. However, you will not see any commission charged on the confirmation ticket. Why? Because a markup is added to the price of the security. So, while the company might sell it to you for $13, the ultimate price you pay could be as much as $13.65, which includes a $.65 markup. Now, of course, you did not know that the brokerage company acquired the stock for $10 a share and thereafter sold it to you for $13.65, did you? But the market-maker desk knew this.

Remember the Cleavers and that fertilizer stock they got stuck with? What really happened was that the market-maker desk got stuck with the fertilizer stock in inventory. What does that mean? It means that some trader purchased too many shares of the fertilizer company and couldn't liquidate it before he had a problem on his hands. So what did the market-maker department do? It offered a *double commission* to any salesperson who could find a customer foolish enough to purchase the stock. And in walked the trusting Cleavers.

So, remember to ask your stock salesperson whether the company "makes a market in the security" before you buy. Then be careful about buying the stock if indeed they do. Many churning cases involve vast amounts of principal transaction trades because (1) the investor can't determine how much commission is being charged, and (2) the broker often can get stocks out of inventory that no one wants to buy. So don't put yourself in the same position that the Cleavers did and get stuck with a fertilizer company with such a foul stink that nobody will come near it. Let the brokerage company get stuck holding the bag. You don't need to bail it out at your expense.

Invest: Don't Be Sold

Don't misinterpret my denouncement of the brokerage industries sales efforts as a denouncement of investing. There are ways in which you can profit and even beat out inflation over the long term by investing in a diversified portfolio of high-quality blue-chip common stocks. However, if you fall prey to any of the techniques practiced upon you by the major brokerage companies, whether they be a fundamental approach, economic approach, option approach, or technical approach, you will find yourself buying and selling a lot more stock than you need to and making your salesperson a lot richer at your expense.

To navigate around these investment roadblocks, you need information. The more information you have, the more investment self-defense you will acquire and the fewer roadblocks you'll encounter on your way to stock market profits. It is possible to make money in the stock market when you don't have to pay all the middle folks along the way.

How to Spot Others Making a Living Off You

A Proper Introduction

Investors on Wall Street support a gaggle of people whose sole function is to give advice. You've seen or heard about many of them. You may even be using their services right now. Some write market letters while others fill newspaper columns and yack away on the radio or television. You are one of their targets and if they can't grab ahold of you, they're sure to catch the ear of your broker. Why? Because these technical advisors, economists, and timing service operators have something to sell, and the more people will listen to them, the more their pockets will jingle. Some of them—mutual fund managers, stock specialists, and limited partnership managers—are hidden away on the other side of your investment. Sadly, even the people you go to for help when things go wrong—lawyers—can be wasting your money if they are not securities litigation specialists.

Not All Gloom and Doom?
The Common Thread of Success

Such comments don't sit too well with a whole host of mutual fund managers, technicians, and timing services, and it may not make you feel all that comfortable either.

All is not doom and gloom, however it may seem. You do not need a fortune-teller to chart your investment future.

There *is* a solution to successful investing (which I will delve into more deeply in Chapter 7), and it's fairly simple. If you examine the record of successful investors on Wall Street, whether they are fund managers, mutual fund advisors, or individual investors, one common thread runs throughout. The key to success does not lie in subscribing to market letters, following timing services, or listening to economists. It comes from investing over the long term, meaning five years or longer. If you desire to own stocks, then invest in a diversified portfolio of high-quality blue-chip common stocks or in a no-load mutual fund made up of blue-chip common stocks diversified over a broad spectrum of corporations. If, on the other hand, equities don't suit your fancy, then you should consider debt instruments (bonds); and if you don't have enough capital to purchase 20 or 30 different investment-grade bonds, then consider a no-load bond fund made up of U.S. government or AAA corporate bonds. (Incidentally, five years is a minimum holding. You would probably be better off holding investments for a seven- to ten-year duration.) Such sound strategy might not fill your stock salesperson's pockets, but it should fill yours. At the very least, you'll save an awful lot of money in commissions, psychiatry bills, and medical expense from the pain and suffering you'll miss if you resist listening to other people's advice—people such as those you are about to meet.

In past chapters, I mentioned some of the people you should know. In this chapter, I want to introduce you to the rest of the gang who live off your money, the so-called experts that dot the investment landscape.

Sharing the Golden Fleece: Who Are These Guys?

How skillful are these "experts"? Are market newsletters worth the money? Who are these economists and when should you listen to them? Where does the money to operate the mutual funds and limited partnerships come from? What happens if you hire a lawyer who doesn't know the ins and outs of securities law?

You already know the answer to some of these questions by now. The efficient markets hypothesis has shown that the information these people are peddling isn't worth the paper it's printed on. Then why are millions of dollars spent every year in the quest for more and more information? Because investors are generally uninformed about the efficient markets hypothesis and what it means to them. Why else would someone spend anywhere from $300 to $1,000 a year to receive prognostications from a technical analysis guru, market timing service, or professional tape watcher?

Everyone is searching for the ultimate answer—they all want to learn how to beat the stock market. But as you already have learned, no one can predict the future based upon past performance, charts or otherwise. To follow these pundits on their quest for the golden fleece has more to do with being fleeced than anything else.

Actually, the concept itself defies logic. If I really had the key to unlock the mysteries of the future, would I sell my knowledge to whoever was willing to pay for it? Wouldn't I stand to gain far more from quietly applying my knowledge to increasing my wealth? In fact, if I have the ability to predict the future, wouldn't I cause my own *downfall* by revealing the information to anyone willing to pay for it? Obviously, the very act of supplying the information, at whatever price, would destroy my ability to act upon it.

The fact that you can't turn lead into gold was no obstacle to the alchemists who spent centuries searching for the hidden secret. Well, now you have a secret of your own—a secret of knowledge— that will keep more money in your pockets and those "fleecing" hands out of them.

Instant Help . . . By Mail? Investment Letter Writers

Today there are over 100 investment letters written by people who purport to know something you don't—experts with a grasp of the market who will share their insights with you, for a price. The knowledge is so special and up-to-date they offer it by mail, an odd idea. But if you can't wait for the pony express to bring you the news, many of the writers offer you a hotline you can subscribe to for, you guessed it, more money.

If you closely examine the majority of these letter writers, you'll notice that they speak with "forked tongue." They carefully juggle their words using fancy terms to bedazzle. The end result is usually a great deal of information about oscillators, indicators, and moving averages, or gross national product, debt ratios, and foreign currency transactions, all of which leave you with an expanded vocabulary but little else. The subscriber is left with carefully couched predictions that, like astrologers' yearly predictions, can be interpreted in several ways.

One writer became so taken with his own forecasting talents that he began to predict earthquakes. If you had followed his advice at the bottom of the 1982 bear market, you would have lost over 90% of your money. Why? He suggested selling short just as Wall Street put on one of its greatest rallies in history. Where is that man right now? He is still predicting earthquakes, appearing on the "Nightly Business Report," and selling his market letter to all who will buy it.

Yet in spite of overwhelming statistics, market letter writers are enjoying a boom period. While the majority of letters have a technical orientation, there are a good number that are fundamentally based.

It's interesting to note that some letter writers made a reputation, oddly enough, by making a prediction that actually came true. What the public doesn't know about are all of the incorrect forecasts that don't get any attention. Newspapers and financial news stations can't get much mileage out of a pundit's wrong predictions. Only after these fortune-tellers document their one prediction that finally came true can they really start gathering subscribers.

If you closely examine what these soothsayers really have to say, you can readily see that they always, always leave themselves an out. They leave enough alternative decisions or choices so that they can justify almost any position.

One final thought, while we're on the subject: Consider what would happen if one of these gurus was found to have true prophetic powers. The moment he offered an opinion on a specific stock, wouldn't it immediately rise or fall, depending upon what direction he said the stock was going? In other words, the moment his prediction was made public, all investors who had access to his prophesy would immediately act upon it, thus defeating the value of the information they were acting upon. The more one scrutinizes the efficient markets hypothesis, the more one realizes that attempting to predict the future should be a goal of the pundits, not anyone who takes investing seriously.

Numbers to Go: Technicians

I mentioned earlier that many people rely upon technical analysis in order to make market timing decisions. Whether an investor has a short-term, intermediate-term, or long-term horizon, technicians will be happy to offer their opinions upon the duration and direction of the prevailing market move.

What makes technical analysis so fascinating is its link with mathematics and computers. With the advent of the personal computer, the drudgery of performing moving average equations was replaced by the touch of a button, and now everyone has at their fingertips momentum oscillators, relative strength indicators, and moving averages as fast as they can change the screen. Why not devote a chapter to speed resistance lines, gann analysis and the Elliott Wave principle, rather arcane, esoteric principles that all have great followings? But to what end?

It's not so amusing that mathematically bent technicians firmly believe that by pouring over reams of data about the past, the future can be divined; yet they fail to come to grips with the hard reality of statistics that don't bear out their assumptions. I am sure that any technician who sells his services would be happy to offer any number of statistics to support his position. A closer scrutiny of those number crunchers, however, will inevitably reveal a slight push of the pencil in favor of the technicians predictions.

Why? Statistics are only as good as the person playing with them. Computers only work well if they are well-informed. You might have heard the old saying, "Garbage in, garbage out." Well, that applies to statistics as well as computers. If a technician wishes to sell his services, it's probably because he can't make enough money following his own advice. So he'd better have some sort of impressive-looking "statistics" to back up his assertions.

The Good, the Bad, and the Incompetent: Investment Advisors

Well, what about investment advisors? Fee-based investment advisors or financial planners, as they may be called, can perform a legitimate useful service.

Or they can be a financial nightmare. Choosing a financial planner, which you'll learn how to do in Chapter 6, should ordinarily free you from the worry of using a commission-based stock salesperson. Unfortunately, this is not always the case.

Let me tell you about what happened to Ed. A doctor from Texas, Ed turned over his pension account, profit sharing account, and all the other money he made from his 15-year medical practice to a financial planner. A six-day work week was the norm for Ed, who found himself working over 12 hours per day. Fifteen years of such hard work had allowed Ed to enjoy a very lucrative medical practice. In fact it was so lucrative that, early on, he decided to meet with Mike, a financial planner, so that he could focus on his medical practice and let the planner worry about Ed's finances.

Ed's accountant had established a pension and profit sharing trust so that Ed could funnel the majority of his income into a tax-deferred savings plan. But Ed wanted to be sure that the funds were invested properly for an early retirement at age 50, so he sat down with Mike to map out his investment of those funds.

During his first meeting with Mike, Ed informed the financial planner that he wouldn't have time to enter into endless discussions about where to place his money or what type of investments to make. Mike smiled and told Ed not to worry, that he had extensive experience in this area and would invest Ed's money conservatively so that it would grow to such an extent that Ed could easily retire at age 50 with more than enough money to live on for the rest of his life.

Everything seemed fine. As the money poured into the medical practice, Ed consistently wrote checks to the financial planner who, in turn, invested the money for him. Mike, of course, charged Ed for his services. Ed paid three-quarters of 1% of the assets that he had on deposit with Mike. That may sound like a small amount, but ten years after Ed had opened his account with Mike, he had over $1,000,000 on deposit. Ed felt that the $7,500-a-year charge (three-quarters of 1% of $1,000,000) was fair because the statements from the financial planner showed him making 11% a year on his money.

But Ed had made the one mistake that no one can afford to make. He turned over *all* control of his account to another person without ever verifying that the information sent to him was accurate or correct.

Twelve years into the relationship with Mike, Ed received a letter from one of the limited partnerships he had purchased. The partnership was not doing too well. In fact, it might be filing bankruptcy. That was bad news, but Ed took it in stride.

Then, a few months later, Ed received letters from two other partnerships. They, too, were experiencing financial difficulties and had ceased making any further payments to the limited partners. So Ed pulled out his latest statement and was in for a shock. These three limited partnerships were valued at the same prices that Ed had paid *12 years* ago when he purchased them. Naturally, he started to wonder about the stocks and other investments in his portfolio. Might they be doing the same thing, that is reflecting the purchase price when in fact they were worth substantially less. Ed called up his accountant and asked her to take a look at the statement and see if she could make sense out of it. So his accountant enlisted the help of a financial planner and together they perused his statement and made inquiries to determine his portfolio's actual value.

When they were through, Ed was in for another shock. The statement showed that two decades of hard work and 12 years of guidance from the financial planner had ended with disastrous results. The $1,000,000 Ed had invested should have been worth at least $1,500,000, by now, assuming 8% interest rate. But his million wasn't worth a million anymore. The limited partnerships, valued

at $375,000 on his statement, were only worth $75,000—that's if
you could find someone foolish enough to buy them from him.
Ed's portfolio was now only worth $700,000.

Ed called Mike to find out what was going on. Well, of course,
Mike was ready with every excuse in the book. But no excuse could
make up for the worthless stock that Ed had bought from the
financial planner, which turned out to be his *own company's stock*.

Finally, Ed consulted with me to investigate the possibility of
suing the financial planner.

Here is where the plot thickens. Most financial planners do not
have sufficient assets to repay a lawsuit, especially of this magnitude.
In fact, the awful truth is that not only do most financial planners
have limited resources but few carry "error and omissions" insurance or even malpractice insurance of any kind. What that means
is that if you have a problem with an uninsured financial planner,
if he commits an unlawful act or does something that could subject
him to liability for wrongdoing in your account, you probably aren't
going to be able to collect any of the money you have lost. Mike
was uninsured. So Ed was left with the depressing thought that his
six-day work week was going to continue for a lot longer than he
ever expected.

Unfortunately, this is only one of the problems encountered
when dealing with a financial planner. There are an estimated
17,000 financial advisory firms in the United States today. Richard
Bredan, the chairman of the SEC, recently testified before a Senate
subcommittee that because of the explosive increase in the number
of investment advisors, the great majority of investment advisors
will only be inspected once every 30 years—which means, in most
cases, never. With only 46 inspectors to watch over 17,000 financial
advisory firms, chances are that your financial advisor isn't being
watched too carefully.

As I looked over the types of investments in Ed's account, I
was struck by the number of mutual funds that had been bought
and sold. I calculated the amount of commission that Ed would
have paid had he purchased these securities through a retail brokerage company. The mutual fund "buys" and "sells" alone added
up to $125,000 in commissions. Then there was the $375,000 in

limited partnerships and the worthless stock that Ed had bought. I estimated the limited partnership commissions alone at $37,000. When I questioned Ed about the commission structure of his relationship with the financial planner, Ed told me he only paid three-quarters of 1% on his net asset value. However, after Ed asked Mike for a breakdown of the profits and losses from the transactions in his account, he noticed—for the first time—that the *commissions charged for the stock transactions were shown.* Much to his horror, the commissions were in excess of $125,000. Ed had assumed that the commissions were paid to whatever brokerage company was used to execute the transactions on his behalf—not to Mike. But Mike admitted, when Ed questioned him about it all, that he had acted as the broker for the transactions. So what did Mike make from Ed's money? In addition to his annual management fee, Mike received over $125,000 in commissions for security transactions and $37,000 from limited partnership sales, none of which had he bothered to inform Ed about.

The lesson to be learned from this sorry tale is for you to always require full disclosure from your financial planner or advisor in writing prior to turning any assets over to him. Don't be afraid to ask him if he will be compensated for anything he buys or sells in your account, too.

Some financial planners simply charge a flat fee for devising a financial plan for you and then set up annual reviews to determine if any changes should be made. The checklist in Chapter 6 for finding a financial planner will help you search for the Good, in the midst of all the Bad and the Incompetent.

It's Called Limited for a Reason: Limited Partnerships

Of those who make a living off your money, some of the most successful are those involved with limited partnerships.

Limited partnerships are loaded with fees, expenses, costs, and commissions which you rarely find a broker forthright enough to tell you about. Oh sure, the broker may tell you about the commission he is earning by selling you a limited partnership, but even that revelation is an exception to the norm.

Figures, though, speak loud and clear. I'll bet you will be surprised to learn that, on average, for every dollar you put into a limited partnership, between 67 cents and 80 cents actually goes into the investment. That's right. If you invest $10,000 in a limited partnership, between $2,000 and $3,300 of that $10,000 will go towards acquisition fees, start-up expenses, syndicate costs, commissions, and operating expenses.

Now ask yourself this question: If the sales literature says that I am going to make 10% on my money, and I invest $10,000, what do I really have to make in order to earn $1,000 a year? Well, if you simply divide $1,000 by $7,000—the amount that's actually going into the investment—you will plainly see that you need to earn 14.28% to make $1,000 on an investment of $7,000.

But, I hear you say: $7000? Wasn't the figure $10,000? You paid $10,000 but with limited partnerships, you didn't quite "invest" that whole sum you parted with. Remember, only 67–80% is a true investment. The rest goes to that "living" these people are making from your money. So the partnership's general partner must make over 14.25% just to pay you the 10% he has promised to pay to you. Even then you're not going to receive the $1,000 until the partnership has sufficient revenue to pay the general and administrative expenses and the general partner's fee for operating the general partnership.

Don't partnerships have an obligation to tell the investor about such costs? Yes, and they do. I am not saying that these costs are not disclosed to investors, because they are, usually. You will find them in the partnership's beautifully produced prospectus. They are just hidden between the wherefores and notwithstandings. The prospectus, which is required by law to be given to you when you buy any limited partnership, is often over 100 pages in length. And it takes both a qualified accountant and attorney to be able to know where to look to find all the hidden costs. Unless you know where to look, between the whatsoevers and heretofores, you're going to be left with a bunch of gobbledygook.

Brokerage firms love limited partnerships because they produce fees in the huge range. More often than they would like to admit, brokerage firms wear two hats. They act as the selling agent for the partnership—that is, they offer partnership interests for sale to the investing public, for a fee of course—and they act as the managing partner of the limited partnership. Now, why do you think that a brokerage firm would want to be a managing partner? Well, it is virtually standard practice for the managing partner (you know, the guy who makes all the money but bears none of the risk) to charge the partnership (that means you, the investor) a fortune in fees. What kind of fees you ask? How about these: acquisition fee, general and administrative expenses, start-up costs, legal fees, due diligence, a loan processing fee, a commission for obtaining the loan, a management fee, a fee for money invested into the limited partnership, a syndicate fee, and a commission. In some of the more abusive limited partnerships, I have seen as much as 40 cents out of every dollar going to the coffers of the general partner, leaving only 60 cents out of every dollar for the investment. (For an in-depth explanation of how limited partnerships are created and operated, see Chapter 9.)

So the next time your friendly, neighborhood stock salesperson tells you about a great limited partnership, remember that it's great for the general partner and the brokerage company. And when he attempts to convince you that a limited partner only has limited exposure, realize that he is really saying that your loss is limited to your total investment. The more you invest, the more you stand to lose. Limited partnerships might have limited losses, but they usually have limited returns as well. Do you know what is truly limited? Your ability to get out. You are in for the duration, and nobody knows how long that really is.

Mutual Admiration: Mutual Fund Managers

There is nothing wrong with buying mutual funds. As I mentioned earlier, they can be fine investments. If your primary investment goal is capital appreciation through ownership of common stocks, then a diversified mutual fund of blue-chip common stocks is one of the best investments you can make, if you intend to hold the fund for the long run.

Unlike limited partnerships, mutual funds have a ready market, allowing you to get in and out as you please. Of course, a mutual fund might not be worth what you paid for it. But it could also be worth substantially more, if you held it for the long term and allowed inflation and the overall market to carry it higher. One thing you must consider, however, before taking the mutual fund plunge is the cost of owning a mutual fund.

Mutual fund managers, not unlike the general partner of a limited partnership, get paid a fee for managing the mutual fund. But this is not the whole story. Remember the Cleavers and the mutual fund that had no commission? There are many ways in which a stock salesperson can make a commission and you'll never know about it.

Selling Thin Air: New Funds

One way to earn a commission is by selling a *new* mutual fund or a closed-end bond fund that has never traded before. Many of the closed-end bond funds that came to the market in the late eighties started trading between $10 and $12 per share. On a new fund that was offered at $10 per share, between 50 cents and 70 cents of that $10 usually went to syndicate costs and commissions. What does that mean for you? Well, when the fund started to trade, the "smart money," the insiders and professionals, knew that almost 10% of the value of the fund was thin air. And since the stock was trading on thin air, it usually dropped to around $9 per share shortly after the initial offering. What that meant is that the broker made his commission out of that 50 cents or 70 cents, and you were left with an investment that suffered a 10% decline almost before the ink dried on your check.

"Back-Ended": Back-End Loaded Funds

A second way that a stock salesperson can earn a commission that you will never know about is by selling you what is called a back-end loaded mutual fund. It works in this way: The broker tells you that if you buy this mutual fund and hold it for over six years, no commission will ever be charged for your purchase. However, if you liquidate the fund prior to the six-year period, there will be a declining balance of commissions paid upon the liquidation price. In other words, as an example, the commission schedule might be 5%, 4%, 3%, 2%, and 1% in the first, second, third, fourth, and fifth year after you purchase the mutual fund.

What the broker won't tell you is regardless of the time that you liquidate the fund, whether you pay a 1% commission or a 5% commission, he was paid for selling that fund to you the moment that order ticket hit the wire room.

Well, maybe not as soon as it hit the wire room, but as soon as his month-end production run hit New York for his paycheck. That's right. Your salesperson earned a commission even on a back-end loaded mutual fund that allegedly didn't charge you a commission until you got out of it. And the commissions on the back-end loaded mutual funds are usually the highest of all the mutual fund tickets.

It's interesting, isn't it, that—and I know this is a categorical statement, but I will say it anyway—you will never hear a used stock salesperson advise you to purchase a no-load mutual fund. Why? Because the used stock salesperson doesn't make any commission on the sale of such a fund.

I don't expect a mutual fund to manage the fund's assets for free. Nor do I expect a stock salesperson to purchase one of these investments or make a recommendation without getting paid for it. But what I do expect is for the salesperson to fully inform his customer of the cost of making a purchase. If you are fully apprised of the commission charged to purchase a mutual fund then you are a fully informed investor and won't feel that the salesperson is taking advantage of you.

A Class Act? Class Action Attorneys

One "investment" that you should think twice about is the joining of a class action lawsuit. At the risk of offending the class action attorneys whose livelihoods are directly affected by this statement,

I must tell you what I perceive to be the strange-sounding truth: *Class action lawsuits, for the most part, benefit the law firm bringing them and, believe it or not, the defendant—the corporation being sued.*

I can almost see you now, wearing a puzzled look and wondering if I have a screw loose.

I almost wish I were wrong. But my years of experience with this area of law has taught me otherwise. Unfortunately, the sorry state of affairs in our litigation-prone society is that class action lawsuits are a marvelous vehicle for a defendant (corporation) to escape from the majority of damages that would be assessed against it if *individual* lawsuits were to be filed against the corporation. Let me give you an example.

A nationally known brokerage company was recently sued by a class action attorney representing all investors who had made purchases of a limited partnership during the last three years. The suit alleged, in part, that the brokerage company had used deceptive and fraudulent sales practices and had illegally represented a limited partnership to be a safe investment when, in fact, it was a high-risk venture. Investors who made up the class had lost approximately $137,000,000 through their investments in the limited partnership. Investors, whether they knew it or not, became class members in the lawsuit against the brokerage company—even if they did not request to become a member of the lawsuit. In fact, the only way one was able to "opt out" (that is, to withdraw from the lawsuit or not become a member of the class) was to write a letter to a specific agent on or before a specific date, setting forth the case number, the account number, the name and address of the individual, and the desire to opt out of the class action lawsuit. This is one of those strange areas in the law where "silence is deemed acceptance." That's right. Your silence is deemed an approval and acceptance to become a member of the class action.

Well, what does this mean for the individual investor? Unless you opt out of the class action, any rights you have, including the right to commence an arbitration claim or a lawsuit against the brokerage company, would be forever barred because of your failure to exclude yourself from becoming a class member.

If you had been an investor offered the opportunity to join the class action, naturally you might have had your qualms: "Really, I don't know how to file a lawsuit. I don't know how to find an attorney. And I didn't even know that the brokerage company did anything wrong to me."

The moment you looked at your statements, however, and discovered that your $10,000 investment was now worth $4,000, you might have asked the only question truly important to you: "What can I do to get my money back?"

Fortunately, you can do much more than you think you can without the help of the class action lawyers. Each person who was defrauded had a legal right to bring an arbitration claim or commence a lawsuit against the brokerage company for the improper sales practices. Most people aren't even aware that they can bring an action against their stock salesperson, financial planner, or brokerage company for fraudulent sales practices.

Let's take a look at the outcome of this class action lawsuit. The attorneys for the members of the class negotiated a settlement with the brokerage company for payment to all members of the class in the amount of $24,000,000. I'm sure you've already grabbed your pencil and done the quick math to find out the surprising result: The brokerage company was able to wipe out $137,000,000 in liability with the stroke of a pen. Miraculously, it escaped by paying the aggrieved class members only 17½% percent of their overall claim. This, by the way, is not an uncommon practice. Quite the contrary, many class actions are settled for even less money.

But we're not through here. The lawyers have to get paid, don't they? Would you believe that in this particular case the legal fee was close to $5,000,000? That's right. The lawyers that negotiated the settlement of this class action earned themselves a quick $5,000,000. That's almost 21% of the settlement. But what does that mean for the investors? Of course, the $5,000,000 must be deducted from the $24,000,000 settlement, and that leaves the investors with only $19,000,000 to divide up. That's a measly 13.8% of their losses.

It doesn't take an Albert Einstein to figure out that these investors would have done a lot better for themselves if they had filed their own arbitration claims or paid an attorney to file an arbitration claim. What this all means is that the class action attorneys earn one heck of a living by allegedly helping the little guy. But the real help is done on behalf of the wallets of the class action attorney and the coffers of the defendant—the corporation that was the target of the lawsuit. The only losers in the whole transaction are the members of the class.

If there's one common thread that runs throughout this book, it is my belief that as an investor you must take responsibility for your own actions, and that responsibility includes keeping tabs on your investments. If you discover that there is a class action that has been brought or is pending involving one of your investments, you had better make a quick decision about whether it would really serve your best interests to continue to be a member of that class.

Don't forget one important fact I mentioned earlier: You must write a letter to the agent specified in the class action documents, which you should have been served with, before the opt out date, or you will be forever barred from bringing a personal action against the defendant.

"But I was never notified about the class action," you say. Well, judging from the number of telephone calls I've received from investors asking the same question, I believe it is no accident that the notice provisions required by the court often go unfulfilled. *Many* members of a class action do not receive proper notification regarding their ability to opt out. So take some responsibility for your own protection if you find yourself in such a situation. Don't wait for the documentation to take action. Be sure that you're not part of the silent majority who are helping attorneys line their pockets and corporations hang onto their assets all to the detriment of the class members.

Taking Control

A Person Armed with Knowledge Can Take Action

How to Tell If You're Being Cheated

The Warning Signs

For almost a year now, Verna and Harley Cleaver have been receiving their monthly checks from the investments Mr. Newman made with their $100,000. The brokerage company also sends them monthly statements, which at first they tried to read.

"Can you make heads or tails of this, Verna?" Mr. Cleaver asked one day, frowning. "All these different numbers and tables—they don't seem to add up right, but I can't really tell. I work with numbers all the time, but I've never seen anything so confusing."

"I'm sure it's fine, Harley," Verna said, with a wave of her hand. "That nice Mr. Newman would have called us if there were anything to talk about. Now, come and eat. Dinner's ready." At that point, Mr. Cleaver lost all interest in deciphering the statement in his hand and dropped it onto a pile of junk mail already destined for the local landfill.

Which was too bad, considering that nice Mr. Newman had done some not-so-nice things with their funds.

The idea is enough to strike terror into any investor's heart: The person handling our money could be performing a little sleight of hand with our hard-earned dollars. Are there ways to detect such actions early enough to save ourselves from harm or, worse, financial ruin?

Yes. There are early warning signs that can tell you when your relationship with your broker is starting to veer off course. There are common characteristics that can help you spot changes in your account that are not in your best interest and may actually be the prelude to disaster. The American Cancer Society publishes an intensely helpful booklet entitled *The Early Warning Signs of Cancer*. Knowing those signs can literally save lives because early treatment is crucial to effective treatment of cancer. The same is true with your money—seeing the early warning signs of broker incompetence or broker fraud can be just as important for your financial well-being. Most of these early warning signs are simple, and the others are worth learning. All you need to know is what to look for and where to look.

Read Your Mail

Many of the warning signs will come by mail, in your brokerage firm's monthly statement of account.

Many investors who get into trouble with their brokers take one look at their monthly statements and, like Mr. Cleaver, doom them to the landfill, a practice neither good for the health of the earth nor the health of your pocketbook.

That sounds easy enough, you're thinking. Just read the statement, right? The problem is the piece of paper sent to you so obligingly by your brokerage firm might as well be in Swahili. The communique is almost cryptic, it's so undecipherable. I don't know many people who can comprehend their monthly statements without help. In fact, I've had accountants ask me to teach them how to read some of the more complex monthly brokerage statements.

As you might have gathered by now, this is no accident. In the 30 years I've been an investor in the markets, I have yet to come across a statement that reads easily, readily identifying the assets in an account and clearly setting forth what happened in the last 30 days.

Makes you wonder, doesn't it? Such confusing statements for no reason at all? Not hardly. The purpose for such numerical obfuscation is to keep the client unaware of what is going on in his own account. In more than half the cases now on my desk, the clients were unable to understand what the broker was doing with their accounts. That was their first vulnerable step toward becoming victims of fraud or negligence.

Not only are the statements confusing but each brokerage company produces a different form of statement. If you move your account from one brokerage company to another, you're going to have to start all over deciphering the new cryptic code of your new brand of statement.

So the first rule of monitoring your portfolio is to learn how to read that monthly statement. Most brokerage companies publish a booklet that attempts to explain how to read your monthly statement. Give that a try first. But ultimately, if you don't understand the booklet, call your broker and have him explain each and every item on your monthly statement. And for your sanity's sake, I suggest you take a lesson from the schoolroom: Take notes. Better yet, photocopy your monthly statement, and write a definition and explanation of every item on that statement to help your deciphering attempts each month.

The message, then, is this: If you want to be sure that nothing is going wrong in your account, first learn how to read your statement and then spend the time it takes to look at it with a critical eye each month.

Three Things to Look for Monthly

Once you can read a statement, there are three essentials to look for each month.

1. The total net worth of your account.   Most statements from brokerage companies show an *opening total net worth* and a *closing total net worth*. This is what stockbrokers call your *equity*. The opening total net worth is the closing balance shown on your previous month's statement. It should represent the value of your account at the close of the last reporting period for the previous month. So logically, the closing total net worth figure on your current statement will be your portfolio's total net worth at the end of the current month's reporting period.

Obviously you don't want to see the value going down from the opening balance to the closing balance. If you see a loss from the end of the previous month, you should look further into your statement to find out what happened.

2. Portfolio summary or description of investments in your account. The second element to look for on your statement is the value of each of the investments held in your account. Firms will generally show the quantity (that is, the number of shares held), the closing price reported at the end of the reporting period, the total value of that investment, and the estimated income produced by dividends payable to that security. The Cleavers, for instance, should see the Really Good Municipal Bond Fund, the mutual fund, and the synthetic fertilizer company listed on their summary and the figures dealing with the monthly activity of all three.

If you make perusing your monthly statement a regular habit, you'll have a passing familiarity with your previous month's balances and the *portfolio values*. That way, any change should quickly be noticed. It's best to take out your previous month's statement and compare it, item by item, to your current month's statement. It is the easiest way to see if the value of any one investment has gone up or down compared to the previous month.

Now it's time for a little simple arithmetic. Take last month's statement and identify the previous month's *price* for each investment in your account and compare it to the present month's *price* of each investment. Is the product up, down, or the same?

Next, do the same thing with the *values* of the products. Take last month's *value* of each investment in your account and compare it to the present month's *value* of each investment. By doing this simple arithmetic, you can find out not only how the market is treating your portfolio value but whether there are discrepancies in quantity between the two months.

Okay. You have inspected your portfolio's prices and values; you have identified the previous month's equity—your *total net worth*—and compared it to this month's equity. You will now be able to tell if the *closing value* of your equity was less than in the previous statement. And if you're keeping all your statements (which, of course, you are because you are now an informed investor), you can lay them out in front of you and easily identify which item on the statement reduced the portfolio value because it declined in price.

By the way, if you're receiving dividend income, then your tally could be quite different. The total value of the current month's statement will be affected by any dividends that you might have received. If you received a dividend, and if the equity is the same or less than the previous month, then the value of your portfolio must have gone down. Why? Assume you received a $1,000 dividend. If your portfolio was worth $100,000 last month, then it should be worth $101,000 this month because of the dividend. If it is still showing the same $100,000 this month after receiving credit for the dividend, then some position in your account must have gone down in value.

There are a few products that don't go along with the straightforward "decoding" of monthly statements. Don't be fooled by such products as limited partnerships, sold by the brokerage company, which show a constant month-end price and value. Many limited partnerships are not worth the value indicated by the brokerage company on the monthly statement. Some of these limited partnerships might not be doing very well while others, because they are illiquid assets, have no ascertainable market price. But this hasn't stopped the brokerage companies from displaying their purchase price on the monthly statement, even though they may be worth 10 cents on the dollar. Watch out for bonds also. Many brokerage firms display the price of a bond as a "service" to its clients. Don't be fooled by such "service." The price displayed is generally not the price determined in the actual marketplace but that provided by a computer service. The real value of the bond could be substantially different.

How do you handle these products? Quarterly, at least, you should have your broker contact the division of his brokerage firm that obtains pricing in the secondary market on limited partnerships and other such products offered exclusively by the brokerage company. You should then take the true market value—not the value shown in your statement—and incorporate that figure into the overall portfolio value of your inestments.

3. Account activity. This is the area of the statement that people find most confusing. Once you get used to looking at it, you'll see it as one of your best warning signs. In this section you will be able to figure out what happened to your account during the month: what was purchased, what was sold, what dividends you received, what checks went out of your account, what journal entries took place, and what interest charges, if any, occurred. Everything that happened in the account should show up here.

Start on the top left side of the statement section entitled "Monthly Account Activity." Here is where the date that an item was bought, sold, or charged will be printed. Usually the next item will be a transaction description; for instance, "Purchased," "Sold," "Margin interest," or "Dividends."

Here is where your close examination of the account activity section allows you instantly to see any unusual activity that might be occurring in your account. For instance, if you haven't given your broker permission to buy or sell anything, and suddenly purchases and sales galore start popping up in your account activity section, you have a big, bright, blaring warning sign. Something is very wrong.

Now, move to the right side of the account activity section. Here is the area entitled "Quantity." This sets forth the amount of shares that were purchased or sold on the transaction date. If you told your broker to buy or sell something, this is where you should look, scrutinizing carefully. Compare the quantity appearing on your statement to the order given to your broker. Next, find the area entitled "Price/entry." The price at which an item was bought or sold should correspond to the confirmation slips (confirms) that have come through the mail separately. As we will discuss next, confirmation slips are vital pieces of paper that should be saved. Compare the confirms to this entry. They definitely should jibe.

Reading and understanding your statement will not only help you see the early warning signs of problems in your account but can also educate you about the market and what affects it. You can see the fluctuations that occur and the way news and economic events affect your overall portfolio.

If you notice cancellations or "as of" trades (that is, trades done as of a different date), pick up the phone and call your broker, and ask him why they are in your account. Most of the time there is an innocent reason for the "as of" trades or cancellations appearing in the activity section of your statement. But not all the time. Be sure to get a satisfactory answer; if you don't like the answer, speak to the branch manager.

When an unscrupulous broker is performing acts that are not in your best interest, he can use "as of" trades and cancellations to hide his unlawful activity. So don't ever be afraid to ask questions. Always remember who your broker is supposed to be working for—you.

Worth the Time

I realize I'm asking you to carve out a chunk of your leisure time each month to scrutinize your portfolio. Look at it this way: Think about how much time you devoted last month to your favorite TV programs which titillated, entertained, or, in rare cases, enlightened you. Few of them lasted more than a couple of hours and had little, if any, impact on your future.

Couldn't you devote a little time each month to something that has an enormous impact on your future? Spending an hour or two a month with one of the most overlooked and yet important areas of your life—your financial well-being—is surely as important as catching the rerun of your favorite situation comedy, isn't it?

The financial pickpocket, with his fingers in your account, will be glad if your answer is "No."

Confirmation Slips

"Hey, Verna, what are all these little slips we're getting from Mr. Newman?" asked Mr. Cleaver as he looked through the day's mail.

"I don't know, Harley. Maybe it has something to do with that thing Mr. Newman called us about a few months ago, when he talked us into moving some of our money around. Remember?"

"But that was four months ago. This is dated this month."

"Oh, Harley, I'm sure it's nothing. Call Mr. Newman. I'm sure he'll explain it. Have you seen the *TV Guide?*"

Every time you buy or sell anything through your broker, he will send you a confirmation slip, or "confirm" as they are called in the trade. Here is where you can check on the commission earned by the broker from your transaction. In addition, the confirms show the date of the transaction, name of the product, purchase price, number of shares, and total cost. Many of the losses I am attempting to recover for clients probably would not have occurred if those little slips sliding into my clients' homes in the midst of all their junk mail had been read, and read correctly.

One such case is a perfect example. Don and his wife, Ellen, spent the last 20 years working 14 hours a day, seven days a week; they ran a liquor store and laundry in hopes of one day being able to save enough money to retire, move to Oregon, and buy a small Christmas tree farm. Having sold both of their businesses, they decided it was time to seek financial advice on how to make their dream come true. One day they heard an ad on the radio. It was a local stockbroker, who provided a popular radio station's daily stock market reports, telling about a free information seminar he was sponsoring.

They went. After the seminar they introduced themselves to the stockbroker, and he gladly made an appointment to talk with them. After one visit at the broker's office, they decided to wire $250,000—every last cent of their precious savings—to the broker for his management. That was their biggest mistake, the biggest mistake any investor could make. They filled out the discretionary forms that go along with such relinquishing of power, and the broker told them he would provide for their retirement in accordance with their wishes, that all of the investments he would make would be safe ones and would provide them with long-term growth and some degree of income. So they signed the documents, relieved that they were in good hands, and went on a two-week vacation. Because they were unsophisticated in financial matters, especially with stock and bond investments, they were now totally dependent on the broker, not a good position to be in with a trusted friend much less a new acquaintance.

At first, everything seemed in order. As time passed, they would occasionally get a confirmation slip to show that the broker had purchased or sold something.

As the weeks rolled on, though, the volume of Don and Ellen's confirmation slips began to grow. They rarely gave the envelopes more than a quick glance, thinking nothing more of them. But the volume of confirms continued to rise. Finally, Don called the broker and asked him why he was receiving so many slips.

The broker's response: "Don't worry about that. It's normal. I'm just positioning your account so that you can make the highest return possible."

So Don quit worrying. Then at the end of the year he took all of his statements, together with his confirmation slips, and handed them to his accountant to prepare their income tax forms. As soon as the accountant began working on Don's return, he made a frantic call to Don.

"I think you have something terribly wrong with your account," he told Don. "By my calculations, you have lost over $125,000 from an excessive amount of trades. You have had no fewer than 400 trades in the last year! And if these slips are correct, the commissions you've been charged are almost $85,000 of that loss! This can't be right."

It was right. That $125,000 loss was a $40,000 trading loss and an $85,000 loss from commissions the broker made for doing all that trading. In effect, their stock salesperson was losing money for Don and Ellen and charging them for what he had lost. He was "churning" their account just for the commissions. Yet every time he traded, Don and Ellen had received evidence of that trade through the mail—evidence all but ignored.

Read and Save

Most investors are like Mr. and Mrs. Cleaver or Don and Ellen. They don't read those slips, let alone save them.

If there ever was a perfect place to catch a warning sign of broker abuse, this is it. Always read any confirmation slip you receive. If you don't understand it, call up your broker and have him explain it to you.

Every confirmation slip should display the commission earned by your broker and charged to you. On an over-the-counter (OTC) trade, the broker can perform something called a "principal transaction." Principal transactions occur when a brokerage company sells you securities out of its own inventory (that is, securities that have been bought for its own trading account), or when it makes a market in the security and has purchased the security in the open market. In either case, the brokerage company charges you a "markup" (commission) for handling the transaction. Here's how it works.

Suppose your broker purchases 100 shares of an OTC stock selling at $10 per share. The cost should be $1,000, right? Wrong. In addition to the purchase price, the brokerage company charges a markup (a commission). But instead of appearing as a commission on your confirms, the "markup" is added to the purchase price. So rather than paying $10 per share, you might pay $10.37½ or $10.50 per share, making the total purchase price $1,037.50 or $1,050. But what if the brokerage company paid $9 per share to buy the stock for you. Can it still charge you 1⅜ or 1½ dollars per share as markup? It is not supposed to. If it does, it is violating an NASD guideline that usually discourages it from charging more than 5% of the purchase price.

The confirmation slip should disclose the markup (or the markdown in the case of a sales transaction) that the broker charged to make the trade. If the confirmation slip doesn't show a markup, then use that phone again and make that stock salesperson accountable. Ask him to tell you how much the commission for this transaction was and to put it in writing.

Also, remember my suggestion that you compare your statement's cancellations and "as of" trades to these slips. That's because the same amounts should be appearing on confirmation slips, too. The moment you get a confirmation slip that shows an "as of" trade or "cancellation trade," it's another reason to reach out and touch your stock salesperson. He owes you any explanation you ask for.

Exception to the Slip Rule

Once again, there is an exception. Some confirmation slips will show no commissions paid on them. Bonds, limited partnerships, and other products such as back-end loaded mutual funds and new issues do not set forth the commission on the confirmation slip. So when you receive a confirmation slip that does not show the commission, it's time to use the phone again. Call your broker and find out what he is making for handling the transaction.

If he tells you that you are not charged a commission, don't be afraid to ask him what commission he earned anyway. Just because the brokerage firm is not charging you a commission doesn't mean that the broker did not get paid, and paid well, from the other end. Wouldn't the Cleavers have been surprised to know that nice Mr. Sam Newman was making $3,000 in commission to place their money in that Really Good Municipal Bond Fund?

If you ever have an attack of timidity, once again repeat the creed of the informed investor: Whom is your broker supposed to be working for? You have a right to know what he is earning when he makes a recommendation so that you can decide if he is being unduly influenced, conflict-of-interest-wise, in helping you make this important decision. Anytime your broker buys or sells any-thing—even a CD—you have a right to know what he made so that you can decide if he's working for his pocketbook or yours.

If he gets annoyed or refuses to provide the information that you have requested, then it's simple: Change brokers.

Warning Signs: Tricks of the Trade

"Don't worry about that confirmation slip, Mr. Cleaver," Mr. New-man is saying as he quickly scans Mr. Cleaver's account and background information on his quotron screen. "I can see why you might be unduly alarmed, but it's nothing, I assure you. Nothing at all. I made that trade by mistake. Don't worry about it. I sold it out, and it didn't cost you anything."

In and Out: "My Mistake"

Some of the more obvious, well-known tricks used by dishonest brokers have warning signs, too, if you're looking and listening.

One of the many used by the dishonest broker is buying a new offering, and then selling it soon after it was purchased or offered.

That is what our friend Mr. Newman did. A mistake, he told them. Just a mistake.

If a broker can purchase a new issue or other product and quickly sell it before anybody else does, without causing the client a loss, then he gets to pocket the whole commission, a commission that can be as much as 5% of the purchase price.

That is what Mr. Newman pulled off. This is another of those hidden commission ploys that we discussed earlier. He is making money by playing with your money. You have a right to know, don't you think? I mean, the least he could do is take you to dinner for helping him line his own pockets with the contents of yours. Seriously, it wouldn't be a bad idea to have your broker document the total commissions paid from your portfolio per quarter. That would surely help you decide if he is working more for himself than for you.

They're Everywhere: Bait and Switch

Remember that it's not just the stock salesperson handling your portfolio who can trick you. There are plenty of "bait and switch" operators pulling in innocent investors and then slickly parting them from their money.

Donna, a 52-year-old divorcée and mother of two, quit her job over a tiff with the boss. Deciding to go into business for herself, she answered an ad in a local newspaper about a frozen yogurt franchise. A business broker called her and soon she was meeting with him to talk about buying a franchise so she could be her own boss. She explained her financial state and how much money she could afford to spend, making her unemployed status very clear to him. The business broker, all smiles, told her everything seemed fine and he would start working on finding her a store to buy.

For the next three months, Donna suggested one yogurt franchise after another. No matter what location, though, the broker always seemed to find something wrong with it.

However, one day the business broker called up Donna and said, "Have I got good news for you."

As you might have guessed by now, this was Donna's first warning sign. He invited Donna to join him at the office of his partner. There the two men introduced Donna to the Delta Neutral Trading Program. This program, according to the business broker, was a riskless means of making fabulous returns on her investment in a very short period of time and was virtually foolproof. It didn't matter whether the market went up or down, she would do nothing but make money. A statement like that, of course, was Donna's second warning sign.

As the meeting wore on, the business broker's partner explained to Donna how the program was supposed to work, using a "hypothetical trading account" that showed incredible results and enormous return on her investments. This was a golden opportunity for a woman like herself, she was told.

Here is where Donna should have clamped a hand over her pocketbook and run. Incredible results, enormous returns, golden opportunity? Yet Donna, under the spell of words, became so excited that she made an even bigger mistake. She borrowed by placing a second trust deed on her home, taking out all of the equity in it. She then turned over all of the money, $17,500, to the business broker—in actuality, a commodity broker—and his partner.

In three months all of Donna's money was gone. The broker and his partner were doing just fine, though. They generated $6,100 in commission from Donna, a fact Donna only found out long afterward.

This bait and switch, one of the oldest schemes around, is a fraud that occurs daily throughout the United States. It is the same old routine in a slightly different form each time. The clients go in one door thinking they are buying frozen yogurt and come out the other door with soy beans, pork bellies, or frozen orange juice. In this case, The Delta Neutral Trading Program traded everything from gold to Swiss francs—commodities.

The two brokers failed to tell Donna lots of things. The first was the nature of commodity or futures trading, which is speculative at best. The risks can be astronomical, even for the professional trader. You don't have to be victim of a con artist pulling a bait and switch to lose every single cent in seconds. You are just a victim of the nature of the commodity market.

The second thing they didn't tell Donna was that she was wholly unsuitable for the venture. Any reputable broker, whether a business, stock, or commodity broker, would have known this in the first few minutes of meeting Donna. Her financial condition, her lack of capital, her lack of income, her present unemployed condition—all were crystal clear signs. The "risk dollars," money that she could afford to lose without affecting her standard of living, were literally nil. She wanted to buy a small business, hoping to generate income. Instead, she was persuaded to do it without all the bother of a business.

Considering the fact that over one-third of her invested funds went to commissions, it's easy to see why they told her so little. Like the saying goes, if it sounds too good to be true, it probably is. That is perhaps the best warning sign of all when it comes to this trick.

Hypothetical Returns

Most of the warning signs were obvious at the beginning for Donna, if she had just been watching. One warning sign not so obvious is one for you to remember: When any broker talks about the performance of a program, or product, or partnership based upon a "hypothetical trading account," don't ever expect it to be accurate. Anything hypothetical is highly questionable and of little value. That is true for any product, not just one that's a greasy part of a bait and switch. Paper trades and paper profits do not take into account the real world, even when they seem based on paper generated from actual floor trading.

Why? In the real world, there is a time factor between a computer-generated buy signal and the ability of the operator to get that trade executed on the floor of the exchange. With things like slippage, commissions, time lags, computer failures, broker errors, and Murphy's Law at work, you can just about take the results of a hypothetical program and throw them out the proverbial window.

So, anytime you are offered "hypothetical results," whether it is a limited partnership, commodity, stock, mutual fund, or Delta Neutral Trading Program with a "riskless means of making enormous returns on your investment in a short amount of time," that is your warning sign. It's time to clamp that pocketbook shut and travel.

New Issues: Hurry, Hurry

"By the way," Mr. Newman goes on, leaning back in his chair, "since I have you on the phone, let me tell you about this brand new hot product. It's going to go public and once everybody else starts buying it, it will go sky-high. You might want to get in on the ground floor."

Now here's a warning sign coming right over the phone. Mr. Cleaver may not know it but this is a sales technique as old as dirt.

The new issue market is a dangerous game for the uninformed (it's discussed further in Chapter 9). Only the most sophisticated investors can afford to take the chance of purchasing a new issue. The only exception might be the unusual case in which you believe in the product, the management, the company, and the industry, and you wish to buy the stock for a long-term investment. How often does that happen? Don't let your broker convince you that you could buy a new issue, sell it within a few days, and reap a great profit. It is just not realistic.

Just like the situation with hidden commissions discussed in Chapter 2, new tricks are popping up all the time. But you can take heart in the fact that once you train your ear to understand such warning signs as these, you will probably begin to understand the sound of other illogical, unreliable claims. The more informed you are, the more informed you'll continue to become.

Too Much Reach Out and Touch

Most relationships with brokers start off well. As your broker gets to know you better and becomes more personal and friendly, he generally will make more recommendations. You're happy to hear from your stockbroker whenever he calls and as the communication tapers off, you still feel confident that all is well.

But as time goes by, how often does he call you? And more importantly, how often are you okaying the transactions he has suggested?

Strangely enough, this may be another warning sign—any increase in the frequency of calls and recommendations that the broker makes. Because as the broker increases the frequency of his calls and the number of his recommendations, the quality of the investments generally becomes more speculative in nature.

It may sound paranoid or obsessive, but the best way to know the true message of these informal chats is to keep a log of your communication with your broker, even if it's no more than a jotted entry for each call and, specifically, what he is suggesting. Otherwise, if you treat these calls as social instead of professional, you may not notice the changes he is suggesting until suddenly you, like Don and Ellen, find out the meaning of the term "churn and burn" the hard way.

Are you thinking that could never happen? Well, it can. After you have worked with a stock salesperson for as little as six months, he knows which buttons to push to get you to respond. No matter what he may be offering or what buttons he may be pushing, don't let a broker push you into something that you don't want to purchase.

If your broker starts making recommendations that are not in keeping with your objectives or, worse, begins using terms like "buying options" or "short-term trading to generate profits," be on guard. When a stock salesperson presents new and different strategies that you don't understand with the explanation that they are in your best interest, they may be more in his best interest. Why else would he be changing the rules for your portfolio? That is the question to ask.

In the meantime, beware of such phrases as "short-term trading of securities," "options purchases," "low-price, over-the-counter stocks," "new issues," "managed future accounts," and "buy-write programs." If these words are slipped into his friendly chats full of suggestions, it's time to worry. These are all highly speculative, very risky transactions that generate large commissions for the broker and, more often than not, big losses for the client.

"I Guarantee"

"I don't think there's a thing to worry about," Verna Cleaver said with a wave of her hand. "Mr. Newman guaranteed that those bonds were just fine. Why would they give us a guarantee if they weren't going to back it up?"

If you hear the word "guarantee," the sirens should be wailing. Simply put, *a broker cannot guarantee any investment.* From the vast number of cases I have seen that are based on stockbrokers' guarantees, that's not a widely known fact.

Al, a man in his early forties, had been able to save quite a sum of money from his own business. Totally immersed in his work, he felt that financial advice from a stockbroker at a major brokerage company would be a sound business decision. He met several times with a senior vice president and decided that this was the person to work with, turning over all of his accounts to him.

One thing that Al truly appreciated was that each time the broker would make an investment for him, the broker would send him a letter guaranteeing the principal and the payment of interest on the investment. After all of his money was invested, Al had a nice collection of guarantees written on stationery from the brokerage company. Each one repeated the same comforting message: His principal and interest were safe—and guaranteed. Al had nothing to lose, he thought. After all, if the investments turned sour, he had a written guarantee from a senior vice president of a major brokerage company.

Well, the investments did turn sour, and a funny thing happened along the way. The senior vice president was indicted for alleged money laundering and other securities violations. Al, naturally concerned, contacted the manager of the brokerage office.

He found out that his investments were mainly in limited partnerships, almost all of which were of questionable value. Many of them were worth less than 40 cents on the dollar. So Al produced that nice, comforting stack of guarantees on official letterhead and demanded a return of his initial monies. The manager's response? "We are not guarantors of your investments," he told Al. "You should know that brokers are not in a position to guarantee their clients' investments."

So now Al is left with a lawsuit or an arbitration proceeding to recover his funds.

Guarantees are worth nothing more than the paper they are printed on. In any lawsuit in which a broker made a guarantee to a client, the brokerage firm's compliance and/or legal department will respond with something very near what Al's manager said: "The client must be gravely mistaken—the firm does not guarantee the assets in your account as to market loss. We are not a guarantor of your investments."

There is no such thing as a guarantee from a brokerage firm. All of those comforting, written guarantees were really just warning signs from the senior vice president, warnings that Al could have seen if he'd known to look.

Used stock salespeople, caught up in the "sale," sometimes will say anything to make a deal. Above all, they certainly know they cannot guarantee anything in the investment world. So if a broker guarantees anything, whether you won't lose a penny or whether you will make 10% on this wonderful investment, stop him in mid-sentence and ask him who backs up that guarantee. Better yet, ask him to have the branch manager put that guarantee in writing. And then after all that, question seriously whether you want to have anything to do with him or his guarantee, since you know something he doesn't: You are not seeing a guarantee, you are seeing a warning sign.

Financial Planners/Money Managers

So you've decided not to waste any more time with these used stock salespeople. You've found yourself a financial planner.

It may be hard to believe, but that could be worse. The field is almost devoid of regulation. Remember in Chapter 4 you learned that there are only 46 SEC agents assigned to oversee 17,000 financial advisors. That amounts to one inspection every 30 years. That's right, one every 30 years. Basically it means that most smaller investment advisors, financial planners, and money managers will never be inspected. There is an International Board of Standards and Practices for Certified Financial Planners that sets standards for those who choose to be members. But not all choose to be members. Not all want to be members of a regulating board for the obvious reason that they don't want to be regulated. And "financial planner" is an easy title to bestow on oneself. As one investment professional put it in a recent *Chicago Magazine* article, "A financial planner can be an insurance salesman in disguise."

We'll go into the pitfalls and problems of this new wave of "financial planners/financial advisors/money managers" later in the book. For now, here are three of the most blatant warning signs you should be on guard for:

1. Is he a member of any of the reputable professional associations? Is he a member of the NASD or any other self-regulatory organization? Is he registered with the SEC as an investment advisor? Is he certified?

   If not, think again. Because even being certified is not enough. "Certified" can sometimes mean that the financial planner has taken a few courses, some legitimately helpful, some not. Your financial planner should be a professional member of the main organizations of the investment world. If not, ask him why not. If he is a member of the International Board of Standards and Practices for Financial Planners, check to see if he is in good standing with a call to its headquarters in Denver (303-830-7543).

2. Is the financial planner insured? This is one warning sign you do not want to ignore. Whether or not this person who is advising you is covered by errors and omissions insurance, generally known as malpractice insurance, is a very important question. Don't be afraid to ask him. As always, if he

takes offense to your questions, then he's not the right person for you. You are entitled to know whether this person offering financial advice that may have a dramatic impact upon your well-being is covered by insurance, in case he makes a grossly incompetent mistake.

3. Did he ask you to make your checks out to him? If so, stop and listen. Can you hear the bells and whistles going off?

Your job in your own investment self-defense is to be in control, remember. So when you make a deposit, it should be deposited into a segregated fund in your name. Ask him to help you set up such an account.

Maybe he wants to make investments in the stock or bond market for you, to keep you from the bother.

Maybe he also thinks you're stupid, not wise to all the commissions that can be made doing just that.

If you do want him to make investments for you in the stock or bond market, then you should open an outside, independent brokerage account with a discount broker and make sure that the financial planner does not participate in the commissions generated from buying or selling items in your account. If he balks, there is always another certified financial planner around the corner.

Stay in Touch

"Verna, I'm calling Mr. Newman."

"I don't know, Harley. We shouldn't be bothering him. He's a busy man."

"Well," Harley grumbled, fingering the confirmation slip, "I'm calling him anyway. There's something funny about all this."

Earlier, when Mr. Cleaver continued to get strange slips in the mail, he had phoned Mr. Newman. Mr. Newman talked his way around them and then tried to sell Mr. Cleaver something else. But when Mr. Cleaver received this new slip, he suddenly smelled something underhanded. He had turned down Mr. Newman's suggestion to buy that hot new issue, even though Mr. Newman had been quite persuasive, so what was this slip for? Actually, the only reason he'd turned Mr. Newman down was because Verna's bursitis had flared up again, and they had some unexpected medical bills. Maybe he should have told Mr. Newman about it. Maybe he should have been talking to him all along because here is another darn confirmation slip. What did it mean?

It meant Harley was right—he should have been calling Mr. Newman all along. The Cleavers had only talked to Mr. Newman a couple of times since that day a year ago when they first took that elevator ride and landed themselves and their money into Mr. Newman's plush office. Except for that one phone call from Mr. Newman asking them if he could trade one of their accounts, the Cleavers wouldn't have known that Mr. Newman was there anymore. That is only one of the things that can change as the months go by. For instance, Verna's bursitis and its accompanying billable woes is a change, and a change that affects the Cleavers financial status. Harley really should be informing Mr. Newman of Verna's bursitis bills, as strange as that sounds. Any change can affect your money and what a stockbroker should do with it. Your changes are integral to your investment self-defense.

When you open an account with a stockbroker, you provide him with information regarding your suitability, tolerance for risk, and investment objectives; this is the information upon which he should rely in making recommendations to you. The problem is that six months or a year later your suitability requirement may change. What if you suddenly find yourself in a bit of a financial strait? Or battling an expensive illness? If you don't regularly talk to your broker and inform him of changes in your financial condition or objectives, then he will be unaware that he might be making an incorrect recommendation based upon outdated information.

So even though you might not want him calling you all that much, you should be calling him regularly, giving information as well as getting it. You owe it to yourself and your family to treat this area of your life—your financial health—at least as well as you do your physical health. You think enough of your teeth and your body to get yearly checkups. You should think enough of your financial future to get a broker checkup. Because things can happen daily to affect your investments, your checkup call should be a monthly habit, at the very least. Some people, those with a large monetary commitment, should speak with their broker at least once a week.

Consider this: In the best of situations, you and your money manager—a stock salesperson or a financial planner—are attempting to make some sort of prediction about what is going to happen in the economy. That is how your investment money is made or lost. Personal change is a given in your life. *Change is the only constant in the financial world.* His guesses on what those changes will be, unlike yours, are educated ones; that is what you are relying upon and why you are paying him. But how can he help you adjust to meet your new financial goals if you don't speak with him and inform him about your financial needs, objectives, and desires? The more you know, the better you can safeguard the contents of your pocket. The more he knows of your needs and expectations, the more he can serve you the way he should. So if you must trust him, the warning signs you're learning, coupled with your regular habit of conferring with him, will help you maintain that trust. As I keep reminding you, he's working for you. Keep in touch.

Maintain a Telephone Log

As mentioned briefly before, whether you are talking with a financial planner, certified financial analyst, or stockbroker, one basic operating premise for your investment self-defense should always be followed: Keep a telephone log of all conversations with your broker. Although it smacks of a spy novel or a bit of Watergate, this is one seemingly paranoid idea that may one day save you a fortune.

Here's how to do it. If you have the equipment available, tape-record any orders that you give your financial planner or broker. All you have to do is inform the other party that you will be recording all of your telephone calls with him; that way, you are not violating the law. If you don't have the equipment to record calls, or if you find the whole idea so distasteful you might forget to do it, then at least make a simple memo in a date book of each conversation showing the date, time, and content of your conversation. That will give you a record of your orders to the broker and his acknowledgment of what he was required to do.

Think about it. If you were a stockbroker and you knew you were being recorded, would you suggest anything questionable, much less dishonest?

Put It in Writing

How much of your communication is down on paper? Verbal commitments and promises are worth little, if worse ever comes to worse. We all know that many court cases come down to one thing—evidence. You may know your broker has fleeced you, and he may know it. But he's walking around free with your money jingling in his pocket instead of yours. Why? Because you have no evidence. It is your word against his. Yet bring in one little note with a few words on it from that sticky-fingered person and suddenly your possibility for justice has just increased a millionfold.

What's the point? Put things in writing. Anytime you talk with your broker, sit down and scribble out what you decided and mail it to him—after you have made yourself a copy. Things in writing have weight. Words spoken evaporate as quickly as they are uttered.

Here are a few more specific suggestions:

1. If you have an open order, an order that will not be executed on the day you give it to the broker, send a short letter to the broker setting forth your exact instructions so that you have proof that you placed an open order with him.
2. Also, if you go on a vacation, take a moment and call your broker and give him express orders for the days you are gone, even if your order is to do nothing. Then take a little more time before you finish packing the station wagon and write your broker a letter setting forth what your instructions were and what should be done if something important happens, whether it is calling you at the cabin in the woods or abiding by the emergency instructions you gave him.

3. As the parting words for this chapter of warning, if you notice that there is something unusual going on in your account, make that call to your broker for an explanation, just as I've suggested. Then promptly sit down and write that used stock salesperson a letter about it, also sending a copy to the branch manager. Put it all, put everything, in writing.

If you make these precautions a natural habit of your investment life, I'll hazard a guarantee that you will thank yourself for it later and very possibly save yourself a future of worry and tears.

If there ever was one, that's a guarantee worth believing.

How to Pick a Stockbroker or Money Advisor

Three Checklists

I hope at this point you have decided to take ultimate responsibility for the management of your investments. The cardinal rule of investment self-defense is, remember, *never relinquish control of your account to anyone.*

Even the most self-reliant investor will still seek the investment advice of a broker or money manager. So that leaves you with an important dilemma: How do you choose the right stockbroker or financial planner to aid you in your investment decisions?

There are specific, practical essentials you must know about your own needs and about the qualifications and attitude of any person helping you. I have gathered the relevant information previously discussed and added many others, to compile them all in one place for you—right here. This chapter includes three checklists of questions every investor should examine, and examine again, before taking the first step toward that elusive professional help. The checklists include:

1. questions to ask yourself
2. questions to ask when choosing a broker or advisor, and
3. questions to ask after you have an ongoing relationship with a broker or advisor

Before you sign on the dotted line with that stock salesperson, you already know one basic fact: there is a built-in conflict of interest between you and your broker. What is in your best interest often differs from what is in your broker's best interest. Why? You already know the answer: The investment best-suited to your goals and financial resources are probably not the investments that earn the highest compensation for your broker.

Most brokers are honest, but many succumb to the temptation to place their own interests ahead of yours. That's why before you meet with a financial planner or stock salesperson you must use a road map to guide you through this hazardous journey. You certainly wouldn't get into your car and drive from Los Angeles,

---

Checklist No. 1: Preparing Your Own Profile
Questions You Must Ask Yourself Before Meeting with a Broker

1. Why am I seeking financial help?
   a) Decide your financial goals
      Basic investing goals:
      * Safety of principal
      * Income with safety
      * Income with risk
      * Appreciation
      * Appreciation with risk
      * Speculation
      * Amusement
   b) Jot down your financial condition
   c) Ask yourself the "R word" question
2. Am I expecting any changes in my financial condition over the next few years?
3. Is this a long-term investment or do I want the ability to pull my money out at any time?

California, to Dallas, Texas, without a road map. If you did, you almost certainly would find yourself off the beaten track or, even worse, downright lost. Who can afford to get lost when it comes to one's savings and finances? With the high cost of living, taxes, and that unforeseen emergency that always seems to arrive, it's hard enough just to save a few dollars. You certainly don't want to lose what you have saved because of someone else's negligence or outright fraud.

So what I am going to do right now is give you a road map. If you will follow this map without deviating from the correct course, then the money you invested in this book will save you from needing a courtroom, a psychiatric couch, or, even worse, a hospital bed along your financial journey.

As a point of reference, I give you the basic outline of each checklist first, then offer a detailed explanation of each outline's points.

Why Am I Seeking Financial Help?

Decide Your Financial Goals

Before you embark upon this financial journey, have a good idea of where you want to go. You are not going to pull out a map of California to help you plan your trip from Arizona to Texas, are you? As obvious as this might sound, you would be amazed, or maybe just amused, by how many people walk into a brokerage office without having a clue of where they want to go, how they are going to get there, or what they want their broker to do for them.

So before you pick up that telephone, pick up a pencil and paper and jot down the reasons you are seeking financial help. The Cleavers, you might remember, wanted to be sure—even if they didn't know it—that they had enough money to live out their retirement years. They weren't trying to build a nest egg. They already had one and really couldn't afford to lose any of it. On the other hand, a young couple in their early thirties with two young children wouldn't have the same goals as the Cleavers. They might be more interested in building a nest egg and trying to save enough money to invest for their future.

No two persons' financial circumstances, goals, or conditions are the same. Everyone has his or her own particular needs and desires. You can't seek financial help or guidance unless you can describe your ultimate goal to your financial planner or stock salesperson.

Why are you seeking help? What is the destination of your journey? You might say it's to be rich. Well, we all want to be rich but there is no magic formula (no matter what others might tell you) to making money in the stock market, or any other market for that matter. So be specific. Take a deeper look into the mirror and try to discover your financial goals.

Are you planning for your retirement? Or is the funding of your children's education the foremost question on your mind? Maybe you want to add on to your nest egg with the hope of making it grow large enough to retire before you reach retirement age. What if you're one of those lucky few that already has a lot of money or is about to receive an inheritance that will take care of you for the rest of your life? Your goal should be preservation of capital and safety rather than trying to build your assets for the future.

By now you probably have an idea of what your goals might be. You must, in order to have a handle on what you are trying to accomplish. The reason understanding your goals is so important is because your goals go hand in hand with the type of investment you should be making to meet them. This all revolves around the basic suitability question of matching your financial goals, circumstances, and condition with a suitable product.

Remember, too, there is no guarantee that you will obtain your goals, no matter who you choose as your consultant. What you can do is try to make the probability of achieving your goals as favorable as possible.

So, you say your goal is still just to be rich? If your desire is to make a fortune in the stock market, I don't want to dissuade you but let me say that although it can be accomplished, it can't be done without assuming a great deal of risk. You have already learned that risk and reward go hand in hand. We know that the investing journey you are about to embark upon is one of speculation. It's all right to speculate as long as you know the risks involved and the amount of money you can afford to lose. You must clearly know your specific investing goal.

Here is a brief list of what I perceive to be some of the basic investing goals, described in as clear and understandable words, risk- and reward-wise, as I can give you:

1. *Safety of principal*: I can't afford to lose any of my money and therefore it must be maintained in a safe investment with no possible risk of loss.
2. *Income with safety*: I am satisfied with the assets that I have accumulated and wish to live on the income I can generate from my investments without any risk to the principal. I realize that to have safety of income I must be willing to sacrifice some of the higher yielding investments available to someone willing to choose the next category.
3. *Income with risk*: I am willing to assume some additional degree of risk in order to achieve higher income than would be available in a riskless or relatively risk-free investment.
4. *Appreciation*: I am not satisfied with my present assets, or I believe the future will require more assets for me to maintain my standard of living, and therefore I am willing to accept some degree of risk in order to realize the gains associated with a growth-oriented investment. My desire is to achieve capital gains, not income.
5. *Appreciation with risk*: While I desire to increase my assets, I am willing to assume more than a minor amount of risk in order to achieve more than a moderate amount of growth (capital gains) of assets. By choosing this category, I am willing to subject my portfolio to more substantial losses in the hopes of achieving more substantial gains.
6. *Speculation*: I truly want to make a fortune in the stock market, and I am willing to assume the high amount of risk commensurate with such a goal. I realize that by choosing this category, I could possibly lose a substantial portion, if not all, of the money that I am willing to speculate with.

7. *Amusement*: I would like to make good profits from whatever strategy I utilize in the stock market and, although I would like to make money, my primary goal is to enjoy applying my intellect against that of everyone else's in the market, and thereby commit time, energy, and money to a pursuit that is both amusing and may be lucrative as well.

None of these categories are set in concrete, of course. Any financial planner or broker that you will ultimately work with will have no problem understanding your goals if you use such clear-cut, no-nonsense language. And you will have no problem understanding it yourself, either.

If you take a close look at these categories, you'll see that questions about each of them should have already been asked of you by your financial planner or stock salesperson. If he hasn't asked you questions entailing some of the above, it may be a first warning sign that he just might not be the right broker for you. Why? Because answers to these questions are the very minimum a broker must know in order to comply with the suitability requirements of the New York Stock Exchange and NASD.

Overlapping Goals: Frances and Rick

It is also possible for some of your goals to overlap without such clear-cut understanding and that can create problems. Unless your stock salesperson has a very strong hand, one goal can overtake another, and, before you know it, your goals and objectives have changed; what was once a conservative portfolio could become a stockbroker's dream—a speculative, high-turnover trading account.

Frances and Rick, a couple in their early forties, unfortunately know all too well what can happen, first, when a broker gets the better of your account, and second, when goals and objectives change from those specified when your account was opened.

Frances worked as a medical technician at a hospital, and Rick worked as a real estate sales agent for a local real estate company. Frances made about $27,000 a year, while Rick, because of the depressed real estate market, wasn't able to make much money for the past couple of years. Frances, however, had inherited from her

mother a considerable sum of money which had remained her separate property throughout the marriage. Rick and Frances often
discussed what they should do with the money and one day decided
to meet with a broker to map out a strategy to provide an education
trust fund for their three young children.

After several meetings the broker gave them a game plan that
seemed conservative enough. Following the broker's recommendation, they purchased three limited partnerships and took the
remainder of the inheritance and invested in a diversified portfolio
of quality blue-chip common stocks. Sounds great, doesn't it? They
thought so too. Everything went along just fine for the first two
years. But at the beginning of the third year, the broker decided
that to increase their portfolio's income, she should start a call-
writing program, a risky strategy using options we discussed in
Chapter 3. The broker suggested selling calls against each of the
stock positions so that Rick and Frances could take in the premium—the price the call was selling for—as income to the portfolio.

"What's the worst-case scenario?" they asked. The worst thing
that could happen, the broker assured them, was that the stock
would be "called away"—that is, the stock would all be sold—when
the call was exercised. And if that happened, they'd just buy another
stock with the profit.

After much discussion, Rick and Frances decided to go along
with the broker's idea. The broker's timing wasn't quite right, however. The stock market put on an enormous rally and their entire
portfolio was called away. Not to worry, said the broker. They'd
just reinvest the money they made in a whole new portfolio.

That seemed all right. But, as you might have guessed, it wasn't.
Unfortunately, Rick and Frances paid four separate commissions.
That's right, four commissions: (1) a commission to sell the option,
(2) a commission when the option was exercised and the stock was
sold, (3) a commission to buy stock to replace the stock that was
sold, and (4) a commission to sell an option to replace the option
that had been exercised. Rick and Frances were also stuck with a
whopping capital gains tax to pay. This went on for quite some
time, and the more transactions that took place, the more Rick took
a hands-on approach in helping the broker make decisions about
which stocks to buy, which options to sell, and the ultimate decision

of whether to cover the option, sell another option, buy back the stock, or buy new stock. Sound confusing?

Rick got so caught up in the decision-making process that he lost sight of his original investing goal. Fifteen months later, when their accountant was preparing their income tax returns, Rick and Frances were in for a surprise. The accountant called them to ask what the heck was going on with their account. They said, "What do you mean?" That's when the accountant dropped the bombshell. He estimated they had paid $72,000 in commissions and their portfolio had declined by $100,000 in value over the last 15 months. And believe it or not, Rick and Frances thought they were making money. They were so confused with the buys, the shorts, the sells, the longs, the exercises, the strike prices, the calls, and the buy-writes that not only did they miss the money that was trickling away from their account but they also missed the commissions that the broker made on the transactions—and worse, they also forgot about their children's education fund.

While this might seem an out-of-the-ordinary case, sadly enough it is not. Many people originally open an account with safety, income, and appreciation as their goals. Unscrupulous stockbrokers or honest ones who succumb to the temptation to push their clients into high-turnover transactions (trading) do so by gaining the trust and confidence of their clients over many months before they lead them down the primrose path. A common thread that runs through most churning cases is the trust and confidence reposed in the broker by the customer—so much so that the customer doesn't bother to look at his statements any longer or wouldn't even think of calling the broker because it might interfere with the broker's concentration or work habits.

Jot Down Your Financial Condition

Having answered as best you can the questions regarding your financial goals, the next thing to do is to jot down your financial condition on paper, or better yet, go to your friendly banker for help. If you don't have a friendly banker, then go to any bank in the neighborhood and ask for a loan application. Take it home, sit down, and fill it out as completely as possible. What will this accomplish for you? It will immediately give you a thorough understanding of your present financial condition, including your income, expenses, savings, assets, debts, life insurance—all of those items that make up your overall financial portfolio. Why is this important? Because once you fully understand your financial condition, you will take along the loan application to use during your first meeting with whomever you are considering to help you manage your assets. No . . . on second thought, change "meeting" to "interview." Lest we forget, this process is an *interview process* whereby you ask the questions of the broker, not the other way around. You have plenty of time to answer the broker's questions, after you are convinced this person is the one with whom you want to do business.

Ask Yourself the "R Word" Question

But hold it. You're not ready to meet with that broker just yet. Probably the single most important question has not yet been asked, and it's a question that most brokers are either afraid to ask, or don't want to ask, because your answer might take them out of the commission loop by sending you down to the neighborhood bank to purchase a Certificate of Deposit. What is that question? *"How much money can I afford to lose without affecting my standard of living?"*

If you can't answer that question, don't call a broker or a financial planner. Because if you don't know how to deal with the "R word," I can promise you that your broker certainly doesn't. The R word—spelled R-I-S-K—is the most misunderstood and least-talked-about term in the stockbroker's jargon and in the scam artist's dialogue.

You know there is no free lunch, and you have already learned that there is no reward without risk. Your job is to define your own risk tolerance, not an easy task. One way to do this is to ask yourself, "Can I sleep at night if I lose XX% of my money?" If you can't pass the sleep test (whether your reason is emotional or financial), then you know you can't afford to lose any of the money you are about to turn over to this person. If on the other hand you say to yourself, "Well, I'm young, I'm just starting out, I can afford to lose a small percentage of my money," then you must identify what that small percentage is. You might think 5% is a small number. Your broker might think 25% is a small number.

So once you have that R word down to a point where you can make a numerical value out of it, write that at the top of the financial statement. Indelibly. Put it in writing to anyone you're about to interview.

When a broker knows that you know how much you can afford to lose (if anything), then the broker has a responsibility to follow your goals and objectives. Furthermore, once you show him your financial statement, be sure you're not withholding anything, because he has an ethical and legal responsibility to follow your goals, objectives, and desires. For instance, you tell the broker: "I've got $100,000 to give you; if I lose 7% of my money, we're closing down shop." But you have also put it in writing and made sure he has received it. That broker better take whatever steps are necessary to ensure that if you get close to that magic number, he's on the phone with you discussing what the next step should be.

Are you now ready to set up that all-important interview? Not just yet. Before you pick up the phone, you have two more questions to ask yourself.

Am I Expecting Any Changes in My Financial Condition over the Next Few Years?

Now, obviously no one can predict the future, so this is not an easy question to answer. But I can tell you this: If your children are starting college in three years, or your spouse is going to need an operation in the next nine months, or you are about to retire and that $65,000-a-year income won't be there anymore, these are obvious changes that will affect your financial condition over the next few years. So stop, think, listen, and ask yourself what might possibly happen that could influence your investment decisions today.

Is This a Long-Term Investment, or Do I Want the Ability to Pull My Money Out Anytime?

The stockbroker jargon for this question is liquidity. Do I need to be able to draw upon any of these assets at a moment's notice? Can

Checklist No. 2:
Preparing Your Relationship with Your Broker
Questions You Must Ask Brokers Before Doing Business with Them

1. How long have you worked with this securities firm?
2. What training and prior experience do you have that will make you able to manage my portfolio or give me professional advice?
3. Have you ever been the subject of a lawsuit, NASD complaint, or an arbitration proceeding?
4. How much risk is involved?
5. How long will my money be tied up? Is there a liquid market?
6. How much compensation will you receive if I buy this product? Better yet, what's in it for you?
7. What makes this an appropriate investment for my objectives?
8. What is your investment philosophy?
   a. Do you advise the use of options?
   b. Do you suggest commodities or financial futures for your clients?
   c. How long is the average holding period for your investment recommendations?
   d. Do you invest any of your own money?
   e. How many clients do you have?
   f. May I have a profile of your professional track record (audited statements, a list of other clients)?
   g. Do you follow the firm's recommendations, or do you come up with your own ideas?

I get by with 50% of my portfolio invested in a long-term investment that I know I can't touch for the next few years? Do I need cash readily available as quickly as I can lift the receiver and call my friendly broker?

Have you answered them? Okay, then. Now you're ready to talk to your potential financial planner or broker.

"Boy," I can hear you saying, "if this guy has this many questions for me to ask myself, I can't wait to find out what he wants me to know about the broker."

Well, you're right. You and I are now ready to give that broker the third degree. All kidding aside, I don't mean that you are going to grill him with white lights and a rubber hose. But I do mean you are going to shine that hot, white spotlight of truth through his office, across his desk, and into his eyes so that he knows that you know . . . and if he knows you know, then he knows he can't fool you.

The order that these questions are asked is not important. What is important is that you ask them—and are not *afraid* to ask them. If your broker does not want to respond to any of these questions or is unwilling to provide information because he says the information isn't readily available (or any other such excuse), then you probably are talking to the wrong person. Within a matter of minutes, you have saved yourself a lot of grief and aggravation and maybe much, much more. Place your hands firmly around your pocketbook and find someone who will answer these questions, and answer them the way you want them answered.

How Long Have You Worked with This Securities Firm?

You'll notice I didn't ask the broker how long he has worked in the securities industry. I asked the broker how long he has worked with this securities firm. There is a reason for this. Brokers get paid a lot of up-front bonus money by jumping from firm to firm and taking their clients with them. Why? Because they get paid handsomely for the commissions they produce, and other brokerage companies are willing to pay them to leave and bring those commissions to them. Unfortunately, many brokers who jump from firm to firm do so by burning their bridges and leaving burnt clients behind. If I am a broker working in Atlanta making $400,000 a year while I am dialing for dollars, and I get an offer of $80,000 to leave and work for a brokerage firm in Los Angeles, I am not only leaving behind all the clients whose money I have lost, I'm getting paid $80,000 to burn my bridges and make a fresh new start. Hollywood, here I come.

The *Los Angeles Times* recently featured a series of articles on brokers who jump from firm to firm to firm leaving behind a regulatory nightmare without a compliance officer ever raising an eyebrow. That's right. Production is what counts on Wall Street, not clients' portfolios.

As long as you're asking the broker how long he has been with this firm, you might as well go ahead and ask him how long he has been in the securities industry, which brings up the rest of the questions.

What Training and Prior Experience Do You Have That Will Make You Able to Manage My Portfolio or Give Me Professional Advice?

You would be surprised by the amount of unqualified stock salespeople offering professional advice to clients who believe every word that comes off of their golden tongues. Or maybe you wouldn't after being introduced to Tom, Dick, and Harry in Chapter 1. As I mentioned before, a lot of this has to do with the mumbo-jumbo jargon the stockbrokers espouse on their attentive audience. Don't let the smooth-talking jargon fool you. Get the facts straight from the horse's mouth. Find out what university the broker attended and what prior line of work he was in that enabled him to become a professional, well-trained, and knowledgeable stock salesperson. Tom, Dick, and Harry, as you recall—three of the "best" stock salespeople that I ever met—were a used car salesman, a surf reporter, and a disc jockey.

Have You Ever Been the Subject of a Lawsuit, NASD Complaint, or Arbitration Proceeding?

This question might throw your interviewee into a retreat or, better yet, he might be affronted that you should ask such a dastardly question. Don't let that dissuade you from your appointed task. Look him straight in the eyes with confidence and say, "I don't mean to assault or attack your integrity but I am dealing with my money, and I want to know that it will be safe, secure, and protected from unlawful activity."

If that sounds too harsh, you could phrase it in a kinder and gentler way. Being the cynic that I am after all the abuse I've seen, I sometimes tend to come off a little harshly. So pass the buck if you must, but ask. Say, for instance, "I've been told to ask this question by my attorney," and leave it at that. That would serve two purposes. First, it will let the broker know, once again, that you know what you're doing. And second, it will let him know that you have an attorney shrewd enough to ask that kind of question so that if he does do something wrong, he is going to pay for his dishonesty.

How Much Risk Is Involved?

This is a pretty self-explanatory question, but I can't wait to hear the answer from the broker. Obviously it is a generic question, but what I really want you to do with it is be sure the broker understands the risk/reward relationship and especially the risk of any particular investment proposed.

How Long Will My Money Be Tied Up?
Is There a Liquid Market?

I have enough horror stories about limited partnerships to fill an entire book so I won't bore you with them now, but what I will tell you is that many brokers have sold limited partnerships under the guise of an active secondary liquid market for the limited partnership. Don't be fooled by that ruse. An active market means the New York Stock Exchange, NASDAQ, or the American Stock Exchange. It doesn't mean a stock that trades 50 shares a day either. So when you ask about liquidity, be sure you understand how you are going to get out of a product, what you might lose if you get out early, and what is the broker's idea of a long-term commitment.

How Much Compensation Will You Receive if I Buy This Product? Better Yet, What's in It for You?

No one expects a broker or financial planner to work for nothing. That wouldn't be fair or right. On the other hand, because this person is working for you, you have a right to know how he is going to be compensated, how much he is going to be compensated, and how often he is going to be compensated.

When you hear a broker start to offer investments with no commission, turn the question around and say to him, "I'm not asking if I am paying any commission for this purchase. I am asking what compensation you will be paid or you will receive if I buy this product."

What Makes This an Appropriate Investment for My Objectives?

This is the question that will let you see how the broker thinks or what the financial planner believes will be suitable and proper for your goals and objectives. If you tell the financial planner that you want absolute safety of principal and you can't afford to lose any money, and he suggests stock options and over-the-counter speculative stocks, you will know something isn't right.

What Is Your Investment Philosophy?

Here are seven short questions that require no explanation but will round out your understanding of this person with whom you are about to do business.

1. Do you advise the use of options?
2. Do you use commodities or financial futures for your clients?
3. How long is the average holding period for your investment recommendations?
4. Do you invest any of your own money?
5. How many clients do you have?

6. May I have a profile of your professional track record (audited statements, a list of other clients)?
7. Do you follow the firm's recommendations, or do you come up with your own ideas?

Well, now that you and your proposed broker are well-acquainted and you have decided to invest with him, you are two-thirds through your checklists.

Here now is Checklist No. 3.

Checklist No. 3: Protecting Your Investments
Actions You Must Take to Protect Your Money

1. At least every quarter tell your broker about any changes in your financial condition.
2. Read and understand your statements, and keep a copy of all documents you receive from the brokerage firm.
3. Keep a log of your conversations with your broker.

At Least Every Quarter Tell Your Broker About Any Changes in Your Financial Condition

In order for your broker to do the best possible job he can for you, you must keep him informed. This means that if any changes occur, you should notify your broker and let him know what's going on. Why? Because if you lose your job, your goals and objectives have probably changed. Suddenly, you cannot afford to lose any of the money that you have saved. If your broker doesn't know you've lost your job and he is working under the mistaken belief that speculation and appreciation with risk are your primary goals, when they no longer are, then he is not working in your best interests—and it is not his fault. Therefore, you have a responsibility to let your broker know that you have lost your job so that he can alter the way in which he transacts business for you. With price appreciation and speculation no longer your primary goals, changes to your portfolio will probably have to be made.

There's another important reason for calling your broker at least quarterly. In addition to changes in medical condition, investment objectives, or financial circumstances, it's important to let your broker know that you are staying in touch. After all, your broker is only a phone call away. Incidentally, don't just call up your broker and say, "Hi, Fred, how are you doing today?" I have found over the years that the majority of conversations between a broker and his client do not center around the client's investments.

Here's an interesting fact: On a recent survey conducted to determine how a client ranks his broker, performance was at the bottom of the list. More important items were: Is he friendly? Does he talk to me? Will he immediately answer my telephone calls? Does he treat me nicely? So don't get sidetracked by gossip, the latest football scores, or a discussion about your favorite movie last week. Stick to the subject and discuss the meat and potatoes of your account.

Don't be afraid to ask how you have been doing. Of course, since you already have the statement in front of you, you know how you have been doing. By keeping your broker informed that you are informed, you will be performing preventive maintenance on your portfolio. It's very difficult for a broker to abuse an account when a client knows what's going on.

Read and Understand Your Statements and Keep a Copy of All Documents You Receive from the Brokerage Firm

Although this might sound like a routine responsibility, you'd be amazed at how many people file their statements, confirmations, and account documents in their garbage cans. Every item you get from a brokerage company is important, no matter how trivial it may seem. Later, if something should go wrong in your account, those new documents you signed when you opened your account, especially the ones dealing with your suitability—those all-important investment goals and objectives—will be critical in determining whether you may or may not be able to win a lawsuit.

Especially important are any communications between the branch manager, compliance department, or other supervisory personnel. If somebody is writing you a letter discussing your account, you had better get on the phone as soon as you open that envelope to find out why this person is writing.

You'll notice I said "read and *understand* your statements." I am constantly surprised by the vast amount of investors who do not understand their statements but are reluctant to ask their brokers to explain the statements to them. Chapter 5 discussed deciphering those essential monthly statements. If you can't comprehend either the terminology on a statement or what all the numbers mean, it is your responsibility to call your broker for an explanation. Most brokerage companies publish a pamphlet or sheet explaining each of the terms contained within a statement, what they mean, and how to use them. If your broker won't help you learn how to read a statement, maybe you've got the wrong broker. Call the branch manager or the operations manager instead, and have that person sit down with you and go over your statement item by item.

One thing you should do every single month: Compare the previous month's statement with the present month's, paying special attention to the equity (the net account value) and the transactions that occurred during the month.

Keep a Log of Your Conversations with Your Broker

This can be a written list with notations of the conversations. I use a calendar, otherwise known as a Day Timer, and whenever I have a conversation with my broker, I record the terms of the conversation on the specific date; I even put the time of day I spoke with the broker. If you want more details about keeping a log, refer back to Chapter 5.

If you follow the checklists outlined, then you probably are not going to need the services of an attorney to recover losses from activity that your broker committed in your account. The reason is obvious: You are now informed enough to watch out for his bag of tricks and to keep a watchful eye on any sleight of hand he might try.

One Last Note:
A Couple of Phone Calls Worth the Time

Before you sign on the dotted line, there are a couple of phone numbers I want to give you so that you can be sure your broker has told you the truth, the whole truth, and nothing but the truth.

I advise you to contact the following agencies to find out whether there have been any disciplinary proceedings, regulatory violations, or arbitration proceedings commenced against your broker.

Certified Board of Financial Planners: (303) 830-7543
    To obtain information on financial planners

NASAA (North American Securities Administrators Assoc.):
    (202) 737-0900
555 New Jersey Avenue, N.S., Suite 750
Washington DC 20001
    To obtain the department in your state responsible for
    registration and licensing of brokers and broker dealers

NASD (National Association of Securities Dealers):
    (800) 289-9999
33 Whitehall Street,
New York, NY 10004
    Verify broker registration with the NASD and obtain
    disciplinary record of brokers

You also might want to know the history of the brokerage company with which you're about to do business. This is especially important in a small regional company that might not have the capitalization or net capital requirements to withstand a major error by a broker or a lawsuit filed by an aggrieved customer.

A sad illustration on this point concerns a case that I recently settled for $156,000 against a small regional brokerage firm that doesn't have sufficient capital to pay my client the settlement. Our fingers are crossed because the settlement we entered into provided for payments over two years at $6,000 a month, with a lump sum settlement at the end of the two years. Our hope is that the firm will stay in business long enough to pay off the debt.

Don't find yourself in the same position. Be sure the company you are doing business with has high net capital requirements and a sufficient asset base to pay you should something go wrong in your account. And of course, you want to be sure they have SIPC insurance which provides insurance protection in the event that the company becomes insolvent.

Armed with all this new knowledge, you are now ready to think about making some of your own investment decisions. And that's what we'll talk about in Chapter 7. Let's take a look at some rules to live by if you want to survive investing or trading in the market on your own.

How to
Invest Alone

An Investor's
Commonsense Rules

"Should* I invest in the stock market?"
After reading the preceding chapters, you just might be asking yourself that question. And maybe you should.

The question is personal; so is the answer. I cannot and will not attempt to answer it for you. Personal questions are like that. To answer them you have to take into account all sorts of information: What are your financial circumstances? Inner desires, goals, tolerance for risk? Your willingness to take risks? You may desire to plan for your children's education, your retirement, or just to stay ahead of inflation. Others may need liquidity to be able to draw upon cash or assets immediately. There are so many variables. Few people possess identical financial needs and goals.

Hundreds of books have been written on the subject of investing, and I am not presumptuous enough to claim that I can tell you all you need to know in one chapter.

This is what I can do: I can help give you the freedom and the self-confidence to begin your journey toward financial independence with six simple rules that apply to most situations, be they investing or trading. Of course, the application of these rules will vary from person to person. An individual with $10,000 to invest will not necessarily make the same allocations as an individual with $100,000. A 70-year-old widow living on income from a $300,000 portfolio is certainly not going to invest in the same way as a middle-aged career woman or a young couple preparing for a family. But there are some characteristics common to all investments, regardless of an individual's suitability, goals, or tolerance for risk. Putting your money into a savings account, Certificate of Deposit, or real estate is also making an investment, but for the purposes of this chapter, we'll stick with the securities market and its role in your portfolio.

You'll recognize the first two of my Investor's Commonsense Rules. They are the basic rules of investment self-defense and financial independence we've already discussed—taking responsibility for all your investment activities and understanding the risk inherent in any investment. They are first because they are the heart of this book's message and the firm foundation for any investing strategy based on "common sense." After a reminder of these basics, we'll sail into the rest of my Commonsense Rules. Then, in Chapter 8, I present my Dozen Rules of Trading Survival, taking time to discuss each one in the detail it deserves and you need.

I think you'll find this is time well spent. If you invest your time before you invest your money, the results can be dramatic. The rules are listed first, followed by the explanation of each in detail.

The Investor's Commonsense Rules

1. Take responsibility for all your investment activities.
2. Identify the risk before counting the profit.
3. Know how much you can lose by understanding risk/ reward.
4. Diversify to avoid a financial wipeout.
5. Do nothing: The best advice of all?
6. Understand the basic difference between price and value.

Take Responsibility for All Your Investment Activities

Maybe a better question than "Should I invest in the stock market?" is "*Why* should I invest in the stock market?"

The question reminds me of an older fellow who appeared in my office one morning seeking representation about a stock market loss he had suffered. Ed believed he was not responsible for the losses that had occurred in his account, quite convinced that everything that had happened to him was the fault of his broker—a discount broker, no less—who had "allowed" him to proceed down a path of self-destruction. The first time that I laid eyes on Ed I knew that he was an accident looking for an excuse. Maybe that's a bit presumptuous of me to say, but you get a feeling about certain people when you first meet them, and this guy immediately left me with the impression that he felt the world owed him something and his responsibility in life was to make sure that he cashed in on what was owed him.

After years of working with people, especially those who have painfully suffered monetary losses that have dramatically reduced their standard of living, I've come to realize it is in a potential client's best interest that I determine, as quickly as possible, whether or not he has a viable case. An attorney has a moral and ethical responsibility, I believe, to do so.

So I've devised an evaluation process that, I hope, causes the least amount of pain to a potential client, but at the same time provides me with enough information to properly evaluate the case and make an informed decision about the merits of a proposed lawsuit. (Of course, no one can ever make a *guarantee* regarding the outcome of a case; we already know what a broker's guarantee is worth. And I strongly suggest that any attorney who makes such a guarantee is either unqualified to do so or is in need of some of your cash.)

The evaluation process partially consists of a fairly sophisticated "client questionnaire" I ask potential clients to complete before meeting with me, which not only saves several hours of interview time but also provides the prospective client with a checklist not unlike Checklist No. 2 in Chapter 6. It enables the potential client to take a deeper look at his relationship with the stock salesperson and more particularly with the surrounding circumstances of his loss.

Ed refused to fill out such a questionnaire. When potential clients respond this way, I've found it usually spells trouble in one of two ways. Either they are too lazy to fill it out, considering the questionnaire to be an intrusion into their precious time, or they don't want to disclose all the information requested because it might have a detrimental impact upon the outcome of their proposed claim. Ed's reason was that he was too busy to "waste his time" fiddling around with such an "intrusive" document. Rather, he decided to save time by showing up at my office and telling me the story of what happened.

Financial Suicide: Ed's Revelation

So Ed sadly rattled off the facts about his case—the "facts" as he saw them—and before he was halfway through with the chronology of events I stopped him. "In other words," I said, "you committed financial suicide, didn't you?"

There seemed an eternity of silence until, with a sigh full of emotion, Ed looked at me and said, "I never really thought about it like that, but you could put it that way. I didn't stop to think if what I was doing was in my best interest. I thought all my decisions were right, especially since my broker never rejected an order I gave him and never offered any advice contrary to my opinions. Now I find myself, at 72, having lost most of the money I spent my entire life trying to save."

Harsh as my statement might have been, I felt compelled to hone in on the precise issue that was at the very center of Ed's case.

It's very disheartening to look at the history of a relationship in which the broker sat back acting as a mere order taker and watched his client self-destruct. But that's exactly what happens in a financial suicide case. Ed had no business trading in the stock market. In fact, Ed had no business being in the stock market. He had enough money, at his stage in life, to live comfortably for the rest of his life without exposing any of his capital to risk. Why then did Ed commence a journey down a black hole into which he poured his life savings, both monetarily and emotionally? Even now, why was Ed unwilling to accept any of the responsibility for his own actions and instead sought to push them onto his broker's shoulders?

Financial Doctors of Doom

Financial suicide cases are very ugly. They involve deep emotional needs, the source of which are rarely shared with family members, let alone strangers. To make matters worse, it is a new and evolving area of the law that changes from district to district, and state to state, and has no clear guidelines or rules upon which to act.

I have successfully fought and won financial suicide cases. I am very selective about the cases I choose to accept and the clients with whom I will work. There is one common thread intertwined throughout them all: In each of those cases, the broker did *more* than just take orders; he played an integral part in assisting the investor down his suicidal path. Not unlike the doctors of death who have assisted terminally ill patients in committing suicide, these "financial doctors of doom" actively participated by encouraging the investors to continue down a ruinous path or by taking an order that was, on its face, irresponsible, self-destructive, and irrational. Your broker has an ethical responsibility to categorically reject an unsuitable order and to inform you that placing such an order would be exposing you to a risk you would not emotionally or financially be able to bear.

Incidentally, Ed lost $1,100,000. That's right, $1,100,000; and yet I rejected his case and told him that, in my opinion, he would not be successful were he to pursue his case against the broker or the broker-dealer. Ed never stopped to ask himself why he was investing in the stock market and to this day has refused to accept any responsibility for his own actions.

Before you decide whether or not you belong in the stock market, ask yourself if you can take responsibility for your own investment activities. If you can't blame others, you'll be more careful in your decision-making process, won't you? Realize that the buck stops with you. If you start to take ultimate responsibility for all of your investment activities, you will force yourself into a better understanding of what you are trying to accomplish, whether you do it alone or with the help of a financial advisor or stockbroker.

Recreational Investors

Some people, in fact a lot more than wish to admit it, are *recreational investors.*

That is, whether they know it or not, their main reason for investing or trading is the pleasure they derive from being a recreational investor, pitting their wits against those of all the other combatants in the marketplace. This intellectual game has been around for as long as man has bartered or exchanged goods and services with one another.

I'll bet if you dig below the surface, virtually all brokerage accounts throughout the United States involve some form of recreation for the investing public. The problem arises when the broker, as well as the client, has never isolated the true purpose for the client's stock market endeavors. Brokers should spend time with their clients and determine the main purpose for their account. If they acknowledged their clients' desire to pit their intellect and their will against those of others in the marketplace, they would do a far greater service to their clients and to the brokerage industry by preventing the disastrous losses that occur throughout the United States every day.

I find no fault with recreational investing, but I find great fault with those who believe that their primary investment purpose is the preservation of capital, when in reality it's pleasure. It is great fun to butt heads with a billion dollar portfolio manager whom you never meet face to face, but if you can't tell the difference between recreational investing and serious portfolio management, the serious "fun" can end with disastrous results.

It's okay to risk 5% or 10% of your assets for recreational purposes, if you so desire; it is not okay to risk 50% or 75% of your assets toward the same end.

What's the answer? If you already are a recreational investor or wish to become one, I suggest that you mentally, as well as physically, isolate a portion of your portfolio and leave it segregated and *permanently separated* from the rest of your portfolio. Make it very official: Any of the funds you intend to use for this recreational investing should be kept in a separate account bearing a separate account number. If investors could limit their recreational accounts to a small portion of their overall portfolio, and, in fact, if brokers would suggest this approach, then the abuses that are widespread and rampant would quickly diminish. The act of segregating your recreational account and specifying the amount of capital invested in it will help you make sure you are never confusing your recreational decisions with those affecting your overall finances.

By not comingling the assets of your recreational account with your "serious account," you will have come a long way toward preserving your asset base while still allowing you the fun and opportunity of being a recreational investor.

Do Your Homework: Read, Study, Ask

Make a contract with yourself. Once you have agreed to accept responsibility for your investing, you'll find it a lot easier to do your homework; that is, to study, read, and ask questions. Remember, don't be afraid to look stupid. It's always better to appear ignorant and inquisitive than smart and knowledgeable. You won't get hurt too often if you know what you're getting into. But if you are afraid to ask a question because it might cast a shadow over how much you really know, then you're just asking for trouble. Don't forget, Mrs. Cleaver never wanted to bother her broker with silly little questions. She thought that he would take care of everything. And if you remember, he certainly did. He took care that the Cleavers' "everything" took care of *him*. Being the cynic that I am, I ask questions until I run out of questions to ask. I might not like hearing some of the answers, but it's better to hear a negative answer now, before the money leaves my pocketbook, than to sit in silence watching my money disappear because I left a question unasked.

Don't Expect the Government to Protect You

While we're on the subject of responsibility, don't make decisions by relying on governmental agencies to protect your interests. It simply doesn't work that way. If you've ever had the opportunity (if you want to call it that) to ask the SEC to investigate what you believe to be an investment fraud, then you know what I'm talking about. The SEC's common response to such an inquiry is, "We are not responsible for recovering investor losses, even if they are due to fraud committed on the part of a broker or a broker-dealer." In fact, in most cases, the SEC will not even launch an investigation unless the complained-of activity has been ongoing for quite some time or many other investors have complained about the same types of activity.

We have already learned in Chapter 4 that the SEC does not have sufficient personnel to investigate the 17,000 financial plan-ners currently giving advice to investors throughout this country. It doesn't even have the personnel to investigate thoroughly formal complaints against brokers launched by aggrieved investors. What this all means is that you're left on your own. You're back to the first rule of financial self-defense, the responsibility rule. Once you learn that the government, whether it is local, regional, or federal, is not going to help you get your money back if something goes wrong in your account, you'll be a heck of a lot more careful when you transact business with a financial planner or stock salesperson.

Communicate with Your Broker: A Final Reminder

Responsibility begins here, it doesn't end here. As you learned in Chapter 5, that means if you work with a stockbroker or financial planner, *you* are going to take the responsibility to establish regular communications with your broker. Regular doesn't mean once a year, it means as often as time allows, but never less than once every three months. And don't forget: When you pick up the phone to reach out and touch your broker, you're not making a social call. You're not calling to talk movies or football but to discuss your financial condition, paying as much attention to detail as is required to update him so that he is thoroughly informed about your needs, desires, and goals. The proper investment of yesterday, remember, just might be the wrong one today.

If you've discovered something that doesn't look quite right in your monthly statements, which you are now reading and comparing each month, you'll have the questionable statement in front of you so that you can refer to it during this important phone call.

Ask Others: Get a Second Opinion

Don't be afraid to get a second opinion about your quarterly review with your broker or about any recommendations he may wish to foist upon you. Treat your financial health in the same manner as you would treat your physical health. You'll be amazed how much you can learn by simply asking questions and getting a second opinion from someone who is not a party to the transaction and has nothing to gain by delivering the right answers. Your accountant might be someone to contact for a second opinion, or, if you don't use an accountant, you might seek guidance from another financial planner or stockbroker.

Financial health and financial responsibility go hand in hand, just like physical health and physical responsibility. Eating the right foods, drinking plenty of water, and getting the appropriate amount of exercise can literally make the difference between life and death. Taking responsibility for your own actions and establishing a regular checkup with your broker can do the same for your financial health.

Identify the Risk Before Counting the Profit

There's an even more crucial element, however, to staying financially healthy: identifying the risk before you mentally pocket the profits.

With all due respect to such best-selling books as *Wealth Without Risk*, I take great exception to authors, late-night television commercials, and audiocassette gurus purporting to tell the public that they have the secret to wealth without risk. It simply isn't true. There is no wealth without risk. There never has been and never will be. Those who believe that following a cash flow system or a real estate program can make them millionaires without ever risking a dime had better take a closer, clearheaded look before they plunk down 500 bucks for the audiocassette program or $1,000 for the latest seminar and accompanying video cassettes. After all, haven't we already learned that if these "financial gurus" really had all the answers, they wouldn't be selling their secrets? They'd be off on their yacht in the Bahamas counting all of their riskless money instead of offering the secret to you.

Every investment has a degree of risk. You may recall from previous chapters that *risk* is the most understated and least-talked-about word in the stockbroker's lexicon. On the other hand, many economics professors have devoted their life's studies to the determination, analysis, and evaluation of risk. The evaluation of risk is not a static event. Rather, it's not unlike trying to hit a moving target. Why? Because when you enter into a transaction, you've only begun the journey; not until you come to the journey's end—when you've received the financial benefit of that for which you have bargained—can you actually know just how much risk was in the investment.

That's not to say you can't try to determine the relative degree of risk. You should *always* try to identify and understand the risk.

But how is that done?

Determining the Risk/Reward

Trying to compute risk/reward is not an easy matter. But that should not dissuade us from undertaking our mission.

Many books have been devoted to the subject of risk, so I would be shortchanging you if I attempted to provide you with a simple solution. What I can do is provide a few simple guidelines that you can use to make a comparison of the risk—that is, to try to determine the "relative risk" of an investment.

Risk is a lot easier to understand if you compare the risk inherent in one investment with the risk inherent in another. So let's do that.

Most financial experts would agree that 90-day United States Treasury Bills are just about the least risky investments on earth. Why? They are a very short-term investment that matures in only three months and can be immediately converted into cash. They are backed by the full faith and credit of the United States government and are a direct obligation of the United States Treasury. The payment of principal and interest is guaranteed by the Treasury so the default risk is about as close to zero as you are ever going to get. Not only are Treasury Bills extremely popular with institutional investors seeking a temporary home for their funds but they are especially popular with foreign investors seeking investments in a country with a stable political process. So the liquidity of the market, combined with its size and the government's safeguards, make Treasury Bills the safest investment for the security-conscious investor at home or abroad.

Should I go out and only buy Treasury Bills? That's a good question. The reason we're discussing Treasury Bills is that in order to understand risk one must first understand what is virtually a risk-free investment. Since we've determined that United States Treasury Bills are virtually risk-free and are probably the safest investment on earth, we can now use Treasury Bills as a sort of "barometer" with which to gauge the relative risk of other investments. (Incidentally, in addition to 90-day Treasury Bills, the Treasury also sells six-month and one-year Treasury Bills.)

Now, before I suggest how to use Treasury Bills as a risk "barometer," you should also be aware that the United States government sells Treasury Notes and Treasury Bonds as well as Treasury Bills. United States Treasury Notes are issued with original maturities from two to ten years, thus making them appropriate for intermediate-term investors. Those individuals seeking longer-term investments might be interested in United States Treasury Bonds, which are issued in either 20- or 30-year maturities. Remember, though, that both Treasury Notes and Treasury Bonds, because of their longer maturity periods, are not risk-free.

"Not risk-free?" I can hear you asking. "How can a United States Treasury Note or Treasury Bond carry any risk with it?" The risk is not the default risk; that is, the risk that the government will fail to pay the bond when it matures or the interest when it becomes due. Rather, it's the interest rate risk. An investment that is kept for five years or longer will most probably be held during periods of fluctuating interest rates. As with any interest-sensitive investment, if interest rates should rise during the time in which you are holding a Treasury Note or Treasury Bond, the price of that note or bond will decrease. If your intent was to hold the note or bond to maturity, then you would ultimately not be harmed by the increased interest rate structure. However, if you needed to cash in your note or bond before its maturity date, you could end up with a total return that is substantially less than you thought you were going to make from your investment. Other than the interest rate risk, however, United States Treasury Notes and Treasury Bonds are virtually as safe as a United States Treasury Bill.

Now, let's find out how we can use our Treasury Bill barometer to gauge our investments. (By the way, you can substitute a Treasury Note or United States Government Bond in place of the Treasury Bill for our "barometer" purposes, if your time horizons are intermediate or long-term in nature.)

The first thing to do is to open your newspaper and find the current Treasury Bill rate. Finding the right Treasury Bill rate for your personal barometer depends on your time horizon. If you are looking for an investment of approximately one year, the time frame we'll use in this example, then use the one-year Treasury Bill for your starting point. You can find the one-year Treasury Bill rate in *The Wall Street Journal, Barron's,* or the financial section of most local newspapers. If you have an insatiable desire for numbers, you can write to the Federal Reserve Bank of St. Louis, Post Office Box 66953, St. Louis, Missouri, 63166, and ask for *U.S. Financial Data,* which is published weekly by the Research and Public Information Division of the Federal Reserve Bank of St. Louis. For those who are so inclined, the publication not only provides a thorough breakdown of the interest rate structure but also provides such arcane information as the money stock (M1), adjusted monetary base, and the money multiplier (to name only a few).

Relative Risk Barometer

With the newspaper in front of you, turn to the business or financial section. The one-year Treasury Bills, you notice, are currently yielding, say, 3%. Armed with this 3% Treasury Bill barometer, compare it to the anticipated return of the proposed investment. What is the difference between the two rates? If you remember the greater the return, the greater the risk, you will be able to very quickly determine just how much more relative risk the proposed investment carries when compared to the Treasury Bill.

Now let's see how we can put this valuable information to use. You've just looked up the Treasury Bill rate when your friendly neighborhood broker calls you with a terrific idea. He wants you to buy a stock currently selling at $30 per share with a dividend that pays $3; or, to put it another way, a stock whose current dividend yield is 10%. The 10% dividend yield is about three-and-one-third (3.3) times greater than the virtually risk-free Treasury Bill rate.

You should *immediately* be aware that in order for an investment to pay you more than *triple* the Treasury Bill rate, there has to be a substantial increase in the risk to your investment. In other words, you might be able to get 10%, but for how long? And even more importantly, how safely? How safe is this stock? That's the question to ponder. While it would be nice to earn more than triple the current Treasury Bill rate without any increased risk, it just can't be done. You have to look at the total return on your proposed investment.

What do I mean by total return? I mean the amount of dividend income you receive plus or minus the value of the security when you sell it. The broker might tell you, "Well, the dividend is so good you'll never have to sell the stock because the dividend will make up for any price decline." But you are already aware that with a 7% differential, you are speculating that the stock is not going to decrease in value. This is a risk that you might not be able to afford. Because if that stock does decline, it could wipe out the 7% interest premium you are receiving over the Treasury Bill.

Risk and reward go hand in hand. You just can't escape this essential point. You are now aware that either the dividend is in jeopardy or the stock might go down in price, or even worse, both might happen. So you tell your broker that you're not interested in a stock with such a high risk. Does he have anything else to recommend?

"All right. I have a more conservative investment," he responds, "a utility company that is currently yielding 5½%."

Now you're in the ballpark on the risk/reward ratio. You have a difference of only two-and-one-half (2.5)—a far less risky investment. By using the relative risk barometer, you can make decisions on whether investments are in keeping with your ability to suffer possible loss by knowing more about their risk.

Beta Power

If you wish to examine more fully the study of risk, you might want to pay special attention to modern portfolio theory, market allocation models, and the efficient markets hypothesis discussed in Chapter 3.

But I have one more secret for you to think about: consider determining the beta of any particular stock prior to its purchase. With the widespread use of the computer, virtually all major brokerage houses compute the beta of all stocks in their universe.

What is beta? Beta can be expressed as a ratio of the volatility of a particular stock as it relates to the volatility of the market taken as a whole for that type of asset. As an example, using the Standard & Poor's (S&P) 500 Stock Index as a base, one might compare the beta of a particular stock to the S&P 500. For example, our famous XYZ stock has a current beta of 1—that should mean that its stock would move in the same proportion, either up or down, as would the S&P 500. A stock with a beta of 2 should be two times as volatile, both to the upside and to the downside of the S&P 500.

On the other hand, a stock with a beta of .5 should be half as volatile as the S&P 500. So, say you were to anticipate that the stock averages, as measured by the S&P 500, had the potential for a 10% price increase, and you were to buy a stock with a beta of 2. If the S&P 500 were to rise 10%, the stock with a beta of 2 should rise 20%.

Although the concept of beta might sound complex, it's really nothing more than one more tool in your arsenal to help you evaluate the risk of assets in your portfolio as they relate to the overall market.

Why is beta important? If you are a risk-averse person, then you probably would want a stock with a beta of 1 or lower. If, on the other hand, you are looking for volatility and the possibility of a large price movement, then you might desire to buy a stock with a beta of greater than 1 so that if you are correct in predicting the market's direction, you can get "more bang for your buck."

Be sure you do not mistakenly believe that because the beta of a stock is low, the stock is less risky than a stock with a high beta— a stock with a .5 beta, for instance, versus a stock with a beta of 2. A beta of .5 only means that a particular stock will usually move half as much as the overall market in which it trades. Obviously, if you place all of your capital in one stock with a beta of .5, you have not eliminated the risk of that stock going out of business and wiping you out.

So ask your broker (or prospective broker) about the beta of any particular stock that he recommends. If the broker doesn't know what beta is, or he doesn't know how to find out what the beta of a stock is, then you had better find another broker.

Know How Much You Can Lose by Understanding Risk/Reward

Can I afford to lose any of my money, and if so, how much can I afford to lose? What percent of my total net worth does this investment comprise?

The answers to these key questions are vital for your investment survival. You must always determine the amount that you can afford to lose *before* you try to determine the amount you want to make. If the amount you desire to make isn't more than the amount you are willing to lose, then maybe you should take a closer look at CDs, because the mathematics of the risk/reward ratio will be working against you.

It is of the utmost importance that, in any investment undertaking, *the amount you are willing to risk be far less than the amount you are trying to gain.* Why? Because no one's perfect. You are bound to have investments turn sour; they might not have been poor investments when you made them but they just happened to turn out that way. If you allow for a potential return that is far greater than your potential loss, you will be using the risk/reward ratio to your advantage.

Stop Loss Orders

After you have decided how much, if any, you can afford to lose, you must determine your "maximum negative return point," the maximum price decline you can sustain before you reach your capital loss limit.

For instance, if you buy 1,000 shares of a stock at $10 a share, and you have decided that the most you can lose on this transaction is $2,000, you have thus determined that the stock cannot go below $8 a share. Why? Because if it goes below $8 you will lose more than your agreed-upon limit. Once you have established your maximum negative return point (loss limit), my advice is to enter a "stop loss order," if allowable, at that price. So if your stock were to trade at $8 per share, your stop loss order would be executed and, depending on the size and liquidity of the market, you would generally sell your stock around the stop loss price.

All too many times I've watched investors consistently remove stop loss orders only to replace them at lower prices. Once I watched an investor initially place a stop loss order on a stock at $40 per share. By the time the investor was finally "stopped out" of his position at $12 per share, he had replaced the stop loss order no less than ten times. So be honest with yourself. No matter how painful it is, once you have determined your maximum negative return point, don't change it. You might not like taking a loss, but it could save you from a disaster later.

Another Look at Suitability

While we're on the subject of risk, don't forget to compare the inherent risk of the investment with your goals, to determine if the recommended product is suitable. Remember, your broker is supposed to help you match your risk tolerance, present financial condition, and investment goals with a product that meets those needs. If, as was Ed's case, you really can't afford to take any chances, then almost any investment in stocks would be unsuitable for you. If you know what you can afford to lose—your risk/reward ratio—and you've clearly communicated it to your stockbroker, you still should perform a "suitability check" on each of his recommendations.

Do You Need to Stay Loose and Liquid?

Liquidity is an element of suitability you should definitely add to your risk checklist. Let's say that you are investing in a start-up company, a limited partnership, or a long-term bond. You might not be aware that your money is going to be tied up for a long time; that is, until the bond matures, the start-up company succeeds, or the limited partnership dissolves. As we have already learned, it's very difficult, if not impossible, to get out of a limited partnership before it is dissolved. If you decide to sell a bond before the maturity date, you might have to sell it for a loss if interest rates have gone up. And as for that start-up company, it might not have gotten off to such a good start. If you do have to sell your stock before the company ever shows the possibility of earnings, you could also suffer a considerable loss. What is the point? Be sure you know whether or not you can get out of an investment before you get into it. *Never make an irrevocable decision hastily.*

Be sure you know how long your money is going to be tied up. By understanding the duration of the investment before you commit your dollars, you will be giving yourself a road map to guide you for the foreseeable future, paying special consideration to any major expenditures that might interfere with your time horizon.

I strongly urge you to develop a more comprehensive understanding of risk and how it relates to all of your investment decisions. A working knowledge of risk and reward will enable you to develop a more objective viewpoint in your decision-making process. It has been my observation that when people fall in love with an idea, or become married to a stock, their objectivity flies out the window. They work from hope rather than reason.

If your decision-making process is based upon a foundation of reason combined with a thorough understanding of the risk/reward relationship, then you will have come a long way toward financial independence and eliminating the potential for disaster.

The Psychology of Investing: Don't Buy Emotionally

No one is immune to the psychological element of investing. It is well documented that markets of all types and descriptions (whether stock, bond, art, gold, or real estate) oscillate from periods of high prices to periods of low prices. All one has to do is to look at the roaring stock market of the 1920s, the 1987 stock market crash, or the precipitous drop in California real estate to understand this concept.

A major element, if not the primary element, of these wild gyrations from extreme optimism to utter depression is the psychological component of the parties making up the market. Euphoria and hysteria are not limited to geographic regions, nor are they bounded by economic parameters. History is replete with stories of crowds hysterically caught up in the moment. The crowd members lose all ability to reason and act upon their most primeval emotion. The Salem Witch Trials, the Spanish Inquisition, and the 1950s McCarthyism are only a few examples of reason losing out to crowd psychology.

The bottom line of my message on investment psychology, then, is: Don't let your ability to think logically and rationally be overtaken by emotion and hysteria. Stick to your game plan even if those about you have lost theirs. It is no accident that the news at a market top is most bullish and at a market bottom is most bearish. So don't let the actions of others influence your course of conduct.

Diversify to Avoid a Financial Wipeout

Every surfer has suffered a wipeout or two; but surfers have one overriding conviction: to avoid getting crunched on the head by a surfboard. You too must avoid a financial wipeout, and the simplest and yet most effective method is to diversify your portfolio. Diversification substantially alleviates the possibility of an economic catastrophe befalling you.

By spreading the risk across a broad spectrum of assets, you can protect yourself from the wide swings known to exist in all marketplaces. Diversification is not limited to an asset type. In other words, by spreading your investments across a wide range of investment quality blue-chip common stocks, you can reduce the risk of one particular stock causing a major loss in your portfolio. Let us say, for example, that you own 100 shares each of 30 different quality blue-chip common stocks. Through diversification, you have reduced the risk of one stock impacting to a major degree your financial well-being, but you have not eliminated the risk of a major market decline in which *all* of your stock portfolio is subject to a downward-trending market.

Therefore, diversification involves more than owning a wide range of one particular asset. Diversification is really a hedge against unknown economic conditions.

While no two portfolios will be the same, generally speaking a well-diversified portfolio would include stocks, bonds, real estate, Certificates of Deposit, gold, savings accounts, cash, and possibly foreign currencies (assuming that stocks were in keeping with the suitability requirements of the investor). By diversifying your portfolio across a broad range of assets, you are attempting to reduce the risk of the overall portfolio to economic uncertainties. In times of deflation, portions of your assets will go down while others will maintain their purchasing power. In times of inflation, those portions of your portfolio best suited to profit from an inflationary trend will increase.

You don't have to be rich to spread the risk. Many people feel that diversification is limited to people of great wealth. This is simply not the case. The main problem with diversification is that by spreading the risk across a wide portion of your portfolio, you also reduce the opportunity for substantial profit in any one position. You can never elude this basic premise: If you reduce the potential for risk, then you also reduce the potential for reward. You can't have one without the other. But there is one solution to this dilemma.

Recreational Option

While I don't generally advocate the use of futures or options for most individuals, there are some people suited to the use of these speculative vehicles.

If you are a recreational investor with a separate recreational account—and you wish to increase the opportunity for reward without substantially increasing the *amount* of money you have to risk—you can do so through the use of options. By purchasing an option, you can limit the amount of money at risk without limiting the potential for reward.

Commodities, or "futures" as they are now called, can also accomplish this goal, but with one important caveat: My suggestion is to trade options on futures rather than to trade futures. Just as you would with stock options, you are limiting the amount of capital at risk without placing a ceiling on the potential for reward.

Do Nothing: The Best Advice of All?

All of these rules—understanding the risk/reward ratio, using beta to manage the volatility of the assets in your portfolio, and diversifying the risks across a broad spectrum of assets—are valuable tools in your quest for financial independence.

But sometimes, *doing nothing may be the best advice of all*. In times of extreme economic uncertainty, as we have experienced for the last few years, people seem compelled to do something, to take advantage of the economic dislocations or to protect themselves from future events.

Don't feel compelled to act. Instead be prepared to react. Many people would be better suited keeping their money in United States Treasury Bills, savings accounts, Certificates of Deposits, or even cash rather than jumping into investments with questionable economic viability. Economic transitions have resulted in extreme dislocations throughout history. Many people have heralded the great accomplishments of the Industrial Revolution, for instance, but few mention the countless thousands of people who became unemployed when the great factories replaced workers with industrial machinery. These historical episodes of rebuilding foster political unrest, wide fluctuations in currency values, and great swings in markets throughout the world.

Does that sound like the time to be taking unnecessary risks? Only if you're financially able to withstand the losses associated with taking such huge risks. Most of us can't afford to enter into high-risk transactions during periods of transition. Therefore, sometimes the best advice is to do nothing . . . unless you want to be one of those great risk-takers who is willing to make or lose a fortune in the pursuit of his enterprise.

Understand the Basic Difference between Price and Value

While at first glance the two may seem inseparable, throughout history people have held a difference of opinion about the value of an item and its relationship to the price that is ultimately paid to obtain it. For centuries, philosophers have argued about price and value.

And the argument is not limited to philosophers. It occurs every day on the trading floor of every market in the world. To grasp the difference between the two concepts, let's take a look at how the dictionary defines price and value. The *Random House Dictionary of the American Language* states that "price" is ". . . the sum or amount of money or its equivalent for which anything is bought or sold."

The *Random House Dictionary*'s definition of "value" is: ". . . relative worth or importance; estimated or assigned worth; equivalent worth in money, material, or services."

Although these two definitions appear to be very similar, let me give you my understanding of the two. Value is an idea expressed in terms of some monetary unit. That monetary unit when paid is its price.

In other words, the worth of an item is the opinion of one or many minds. One only need look at the attempts by a real estate appraiser to place a value on a piece of land.

Reasonable minds will differ as to the true value of any piece of land. It's only at the instant that the land is sold for a "price" that one can readily identify the true "value" of that land. So, therefore, price is the monetary value—"dollars" in the United States—at which the exchange of money has actually taken place.

Price

The distinction between the two concepts is *not* a trifling matter. Price, correctly used, always denotes a completed exchange. Before there has been a transaction, there can be no price—only estimations of the item's value. Up to the instant of consummation, there can only be bids and offers.

In an auction market, every exchange is the result of an agreement between those willing to make a bid on an item (buyers) and those offering to sell an item (sellers). There can be no price until the agreement has been reached.

So price is the rate and money at which an exchange has been made.

In an auction market at any given moment, the last trade, whether it be a stock, commodity, or art object, establishes the price of that item.

For that one moment in time the price and the value of that object are the same.

Value

But moments before and moments after the exchange, ideas about the value of that object will necessarily change. Yet in the whole world of economics and everyday life, no one word is more important and no one word is tossed about more indiscriminately. I believe one of the greatest obstacles to success in any auction market is the *erroneous assumption that value is fixed—that value remains constant while price fluctuates.*

The only time value remains fixed is at that already-mentioned moment a buyer and seller come together at a price by consummating an exchange.

Value then is an abstract idea, a kind of theoretical estimate by experts that, of course, is subject to constant change. Put very succinctly: *Value is an opinion of what price should be.*

By now you must be asking yourself, "Well, fine, but really, what does this philosophical argument concerning price and value have to do with me?"

The answer is that differing opinions about the value of a stock necessarily result in some investors making a profit while others sustain a loss. Participants in auction markets such as the stock market believe if they are buying something, its true value is not reflected in the price they are willing to pay for it. Otherwise, they wouldn't make such a purchase, would they? On the other hand, an investor who desires to sell a particular stock believes he is getting full value—maybe even more than full value—for the stock that he is selling. The buyer has an opinion and so does the seller.

All auction markets are based upon the difference of opinion concerning what is the ideally correct value. And because opinions change constantly, values as well as prices must likewise change constantly. At the moment of the exchange between a buyer and a seller in the stock market, the price and the value of a stock are the same. Yet the buyer's opinion about the value of that stock and the seller's opinion about the value of that stock are not the same, are they?

Here is the basic point: *Do not confuse price and value.* If you look back at the efficient markets hypothesis, you will notice that it's just another way of saying that the current price of a stock is the only known method of establishing its value. Therefore, unless you have some information unknown to the general public that would lead you to believe you know something about the theoretical value of a stock that no one else knows, your opinion about value is merely theoretical and cannot be acted upon with any assurance that you could profit from it.

So if you wish to theorize about the value of a particular item, whether it be a stock, commodity, or a piece of art, do so with the understanding that your opinion about value and your ability to profit from it is more of an amusement and less of an investment opportunity.

It's all right to trade, speculate, or invest based upon such opinions *if* you do so with the understanding that it is recreational in nature and should not be applied to the management of your overall portfolio.

C H A P T E R 8

How to Trade Alone

A Trader's Dozen Rules for Survival

It's a lot of fun to be a recreational investor; it might even be more fun to be a recreational trader. Speculation has been an integral part of every auction market throughout history. It is the great speculators that make all the headlines concerning the tremendous profits they're able to garner from the markets. Stories abound about individuals who have turned $1,000 into $100,000 and $10,000 into $1,000,000 or more.

But for everyone who has "made it" in the market, there are thousands who have been wiped out. Those that have fallen by the wayside exceeded their capital or their emotional limits . . . and most probably didn't have a game plan to follow.

Easy Way to Make a Living?

I'll bet you didn't know that even the professional floor trader who buys and sells solely for himself has a hard time making a living. Visit the floor of any major exchange and you will see that there are few middle-aged traders down there. Trading is a young person's game because it's a combat zone with money as the ammunition. I've seen hair pulling, chest shoving, and knockdown, drag-out fights on the jam-packed trading floors—pure survival reflexes at their scariest. It is not a pretty sight. The tension is high. But these traders believe that the few seconds' edge they gain by "being in the pit" can make the difference between winning and losing.

Many professional traders, however, work away from the floor, often in offices surrounded by sophisticated computers running $100,000 software, trading with millions of dollars. Yet even they don't know what the next moment might bring.

The amateur trader has none of these advantages. Trying to trade through a broker is like having two strikes against you before you even get the first pitch. The professional floor trader, because he's doing his own brokering, doesn't have extraordinary commissions to overcome before making a profit, and he certainly has better access to information.

If you do want to trade, you can eliminate some of the obstacles. But first you should learn about the advantages and disadvantages of going it alone as well as the high risk of this specific game.

I have been there. I even invented my own stock index arbitrage trading program and traded it for years. I know the rewards but I am painfully aware of the deep pitfalls.

So, for the rest of this chapter, I'm going to examine personal trading in a brutally honest way for you, and then I'll offer my trader's dozen, 12 rules of survival for those hardy souls who still want to venture into the investing combat zone.

Are You an Amateur? Do You Want to Become a Professional?

What separates the professional from the amateur? A professional simply makes fewer mistakes than an amateur—that's why he's a professional. During my years as a professional trader, I became well acquainted with many of my peers, some of whom are still down on the floors of the futures exchanges in Chicago. As I talked with them, I attempted to piece together a profile of a successful trader so that I could mimic the attributes that separated the

---

The Trader's Dozen Rules for Survival

1. Have a plan and follow it.
2. Manage your money.
3. "Where am I wrong?"
4. Learn to cut your losses.
5. Don't add to a loser.
6. Don't overtrade.
7. Learn from your mistakes.
8. Don't try to catch a falling knife.
9. Don't seek the advice of your broker.
10. Know when to do nothing at all.
11. Let your profits run.
12. Learn your stress point.

---

winners from the losers. I kept trying to discover the single distinguishing element that allowed only a privileged few to make a good living at trading, while all the rest stumbled or fell by the wayside.

Not until I approached the question aided with the gift of hindsight was I able to achieve an objective viewpoint clear enough to reach a conclusion.

The answer was so obvious and simple in nature, I'm almost embarrassed to share it with you: *The professional trader is superior because he has trained himself not to make mistakes.* Many professional traders, I noticed, had far less ability or God-given intellect than their compatriots, and yet the intellectuals, the business people, or the computer engineers (with gobs of software and glorious trading programs) were routinely on the losing end of a trade. They simply hadn't learned how not to make mistakes.

Do you want to be a professional? Are you willing to make the sacrifices? Can you reach down and determine just how much resolve you have to not beat yourself up by making mistakes?

Train yourself to act in a manner that will avoid mistakes . . . couple it with the exercise of extreme discipline . . . and apply it to a well-devised game plan . . . that is the way, the only way, you can succeed in this most difficult enterprise. Still want to try? Then it's time to talk "survival rules."

So here they are—my trader's dozen. I'm sure that other professionals may wish to add a few rules of their own; any trader worth his salt, if put to the test, however, would include most of these rules in his own rule book. My goal is to provide you with a starting place to build your own rules as you expand your knowledge base.

Have a Plan and Follow It

Without a well-developed set of rules that you never violate—a system of procedures that allow you to always identify the basic strategy of every trade—you will be doomed to failure. I have seen traders enter a position only to second-guess themselves and reverse the trade they felt so strongly about only a few moments earlier. They obviously had no game plan, or, if they did, they were unwilling to follow it.

If you cannot identify (1) the reason you are entering into a trade, (2) what you expect to gain, (3) how long it will take to achieve that gain, and (4) how much you are willing to lose if you are wrong, then you have no business entering the trade in the first place. I am not going to provide you with a game plan because a plan is a very personal matter; each individual has his own ideas, his own philosophy, and a particular market in which he desires to speculate. What I can tell you is that every plan should include these items:

- An entry point
- An exit point
- A computation of the risk/reward ratio
- Some method of calculating the probability of success and the possibility of failure
- The reason for the trade, whether it is technical, fundamental, news-driven, seasonal, or market psychology

I have found it advantageous to post your trading rules in a conspicuous place and read them every day. While this might seem silly at first blush, it will prove indispensable, especially as you begin.

Why? With an established game plan, you will probably violate at least one rule the first day you put the plan into operation. Having your game plan always before your eyes will help you through small accidents. If your game plan can become an integral part of your thought process so that you go down your checklist before, during, and after every trade, you will have come a long way toward improving the outcome of your trades.

The Battle Between Reason and Emotion

Having a trading plan is one thing. Following it is another matter. It is very difficult, indeed, to separate the intellect from the emotion. Most traders (even professionals) have the tendency to allow emotion to replace reason just when they should be acting on intellect and not out of fear or greed.

This continuing struggle between intellect and emotion weighs heavily on the psyche of all traders. One does not have to be on the trading floor to be consumed by it. It is a well-documented fact that market panics have occurred across broad geographic areas, and yet they involve the psychology of a crowd that is not gathered in one place. Witness the international market crisis of 1987. A crash in one market touched off a crash on many other markets around the world.

Once the average person is caught up in the bedlam of market speculation, he becomes more or less mesmerized, and at critical moments his resolutions and game plans all take flight. As the herd psychology weighs more and more heavily on a person's psyche, his perspective becomes distorted, he becomes incapable of calm reasoning, and he's likely to do precisely the opposite of what he had intended to do in the beginning. He is much like a piece of driftwood caught in a swirling ocean, his actions controlled more by the currents about him and less by his free will or the game plan he spent so much time devising.

The difficulties attendant to the application of an operating plan are no small matter. Just think how difficult it must be to follow your game plan to buy stock at the bottom of a bear market when practically every other participant is selling. It's no small comfort that your game plan tells you the market must go up while the newspaper headlines, radio commentators, and latest gurus are all calling for nine more months of a bear market.

If you can stick to your game plan when all other participants have seemingly gone mad, you'll have a far greater opportunity to achieve success.

Do You Believe? Testing Your Strategy

One major brokerage house has a slogan that goes something like this: "Invest your time before you invest your money." I have a slogan also, and it goes something like this: "Test your strategy prior to risking your money."

Simple enough, isn't it? If you don't want to follow my suggestion and would rather dive right in to see if your trading plan works, I have another suggestion: Send your money to the charity of your choice—it will do a lot more good fighting cancer or helping the homeless than going down the investment drain, which is where it's destined to go, without testing.

Here is one way to test your plan: Keep a log of your score so that math determines the success or failure of your strategy, not your subjective opinion. "Paper trading," as it is called, can help you fine-tune and further define your trading strategy so that when you invest your money, rather than just your time, you'll have had some experience operating your trading program. By keeping a log and knowing your score, you can, hopefully, seek to eliminate any possible errors that might increase the possibility of loss.

Murphy's Law Is Forever

Remember, though: Paper trades do not account for order execution problems, mistakes, and Murphy's Law. I wish I had a dollar for every order execution I missed. Too many times I've believed a sharp rally was about to ensue, placed my order, and then watched the market take off on its intended course only to have the floor broker tell me, "Sorry, we missed the market. Your order never got executed."

On the other hand, I'd be even happier to have $5 for every order that was filled the moment the words left my lips. It seemed like my mistakes were never missed. Whenever I was wrong about the direction of the market, my order was always filled immediately, but when I had correctly predicted the direction of the market—I had to wait to see if my order went through.

No matter how wonderful your paper trading looks, once you enter into the real world of trading, you'll be amazed by how many things can go wrong that you never predicted.

So keep a watchful eye out for Murphy's Law, because if something can go wrong, it will. And even if it can't go wrong, it will still go wrong.

I remember one incident back in the early days of stock index futures when I was trading the S&P 500. My computer program indicated that the market was about to break out to the upside, a move from which I would profit handsomely. I was waiting for the right moment to enter the market—that moment being the point in which I had the least risk and the greatest potential for reward. As the minutes ticked by while I was waiting for the computer to generate its buy, I started to wonder why the market was trading so slowly considering only a few minutes earlier it had been very active. After 35–40 minutes, I decided to call the data distribution company to find out if there was anything wrong with their transmission. When I inquired about the current price of the S&P 500, I was calmly informed by a programmer that it was 400 points higher than my computer indicated. Well, this cost me a small fortune in lost profits, to say nothing of my frustration over the breakdown in communications. What was the reason my computer was not showing the correct price? A snowstorm had dumped too much snow into the satellite dish, and it was interfering with the data transmission.

I could go on giving you countless stories of the oddest ways in which my orders didn't get executed, or worse were simply bungled. Brokers bought when I wanted to sell or they sold when I wanted to buy. Errors are, unfortunately, a part of a trader's life. The noise, stress, and physical hardship of the trading floor make the occurrence of errors a fact of life, something that cannot be avoided. All you can do is try to keep errors to a minimum.

If, after careful analysis, your system proves successful, follow your plan. Don't change your rules as you go along. If, however, the system does not work in the real world as planned, stop trading and redefine your game plan.

Manage Your Money

I have observed that most authors of books addressing the subject of investing (or trading) devote the bulk of writing to strategies they believe will lead to success, if you will only follow them.

Unfortunately, I have found that chapters in such books devoted to the management of your money are scant, or even worse, nonexistent. Without the establishment of a basic profit-and-loss model (one that you never violate), you'll find it just about impossible to be a successful investor or trader.

If you establish sound money management skills at the onset of your trading venture, however, you'll be far ahead of most traders, who are directed more by their whims than by a prudent and well-thought-out money management plan.

Know Before You Go

You should always know how much you intend to risk and how much you are willing to lose on every trade *before* you enter it. Even though I was working from a computer-generated trading program, I always filled out a trade sheet before I entered a trade. The first item I would write down was the level (price) at which I desired to enter the market (whether it was long or short); next to that level (entry price) I would write down an entry range showing the maximum I was willing to pay to enter the market. After writing my entry point, I would jot down my exit point. And, just as I established an entry point range, I would also establish an exit point range. Why? So that I knew, within a few degrees of certainty, just how much I stood to gain or lose on each trade. Next, I calculated the profit as a percentage of my invested capital and the loss as a percentage of my invested capital.

By having a clear understanding of my trading power (capital), I was always in a position to objectively evaluate the sensibility of the proposed trade.

My money management analysis didn't stop there. I tried, as best I could, to identify some percentage between 0 and 100 that I could assign as the probability of success for that particular trade. For example, if a market was extremely "oversold" (that is, an indication that most of the willing sellers had already established their losses or put on their shorts), then the probability for the market to rally (even a short counter-trend rally) could be high, depending on the level of oversold. This oversold condition could present a trading opportunity that I might assign a probability of 70–85%. These are only estimates, but there are statistics that can show that a market is due for a rally. (The problem, of course, is that "due for a rally" does not guarantee that this rally is going to occur in the next minute, hour, day, or week. I'll leave that to the statisticians and get back to my example.)

Now, assuming, for whatever reason, you believe as I did that there is a 75% probability of the market rallying, you might be willing to establish a trade in which the risk and reward are more evenly disbursed. In other words, you may be willing to risk losing the same amount of capital as you're trying to make—because you perceive the probability of success to be very high.

On the other hand, if the probability of success is 50% or lower, it would not make economic sense to risk losing the same amount of capital as you are trying to gain. To do so would be to invite economic ruin. Why? Well, one reason is that the losses you suffer will not be limited to trades in which your market predictions don't turn out quite right. You must account for commissions (both on winning and losing trades), poor executions, missing the market, unavoidable events, broker and floor errors, and the inevitable Murphy's Law.

You Can Lose and Still Win/You Can Win and Still Lose

It is possible to lose on more trades than you win and still achieve success. That's right. If you are correct in only 35% of your trades but achieve far greater profits from those successful trades while limiting the incorrect trades to much smaller losses, you can be quite successful.

On the other hand, it is very probable that without proper money management techniques you can be successful 80% of the time and still lose money. Why? Because the eight trades that were correct were wiped out by the two trades that were wrong. *The single greatest area of failure that I have observed is the inability of the trader to control his losses.*

Just as you must always control your losses, believe it or not you must also learn how to control your profits. What do I mean by "control your profits"? *You must always know how to get out of a profitable trade with a profit.* This rule might sound quite simple. But once you have entered the market, you will become a combatant—with all the attendant emotional, psychological, and financial strains. Unless you have a prearranged game plan (that is firmly entrenched in your mind) with the *exact exit point* for your trade, you will find taking profits to be far more difficult than you ever imagined. If you have established a prearranged exit point, then there is no thought process involved in the matter—you have already determined the profit you wish to make and the price at which it will be accomplished. If you use a stop order to set a prearranged profit, then you won't violate this rule.

So the one cardinal rule that if violated will destroy you is *allowing a profit to become a loss.* Profits are hard to come by (if you don't already know), and no one can afford to allow a profit to become a loss. You will never get hurt by taking a small profit, but you will go broke by allowing a profit to become a loss. Knowing when to get out of a trade is probably more important than knowing when to get in. You can't let the currents of the market control you like a piece of driftwood. You must take action; don't be acted upon.

"Where Am I Wrong?"

Self-Evaluation Rules

When I first moved my trading operation from the office in my home to the bull-pen at a major brokerage company, the transition was more psychological than physical. I was seated among all the traders in the local office. I don't know if it was an accident or purposely designed but the office manager had cordoned off this group of speculators from the rest of the stockbrokers. Seated to my left was our one-and-only commodity trader, and seated to my right was Don, a stock trader who followed the Elliott Wave principle. His one ambition in life was to be right. He was totally obsessed with beating the market—pitting his intellect against all the other combatants in the arena. He always arrived before the market opened and usually turned out the lights at the end of the day.

I enjoyed Don's company, and we spent many hours discussing each other's technical approach to the market. But for all the years Don spent in "being right," he had little to show for it. I'm not faulting his effort; in fact, no one made a more gallant effort than Don. The moral of this little story is that Don was more concerned about being right than he was about making money. I'll never forget a breakfast conversation we had. We were discussing why it was so difficult to beat the market. I blurted out a comment that had far deeper meaning than I ever imagined: "I'm not here to be right," I heard myself saying, "I'm here to make money." Now I know we all want to make money, but the fact of the matter is that recreational traders are more interested in beating the market, "being right," than they are in making money. Unfortunately, you just can't be successful trying to beat the market. Success is not measured by how many times you were right or wrong; success is measured, as one cynic wisely observed, by how much money you make.

Accept Losses Gracefully

Don't let ego get in the way of the facts, or else you'll lose a lot more than your ego. Don's ego, even if he didn't make any money on a trade, refused to allow for the possibility that he might be wrong. All traders will be wrong a lot of the time. Don't confuse being wrong with making a mistake. If a trade doesn't turn out the way you anticipated, and you were wrong about the direction of the market, it's okay. The question is: Can you deal with that reality? If not, don't trade.

During my early days of trading, it was a great insult to my ego to suffer a loss. What separates the professional from the amateur is that professionals accept losses—they know losses are part of the territory. This is one of the reasons why they can be successful at trading. It is the amateur who does not expect to suffer losses. He will allow this condition to prejudice his judgment and allow emotions rather than reason to guide him.

Learn to Cut Your Losses

Survival Instincts

Whenever you enter a trade, you always believe that you perceive something in the market that others do not. You are predicting that something—whether it is technical, fundamental, seasonal, or a news event—will cause a price change. But there is always a chance of being wrong. So, can you change your mind? If you enter a trade and thereafter decide that the reason for the trade no longer exists, will you be afraid to get out and take an early loss?

I hope your answers are yes: Yes, you can change your mind. And yes, if the reason for a trade no longer exists, you'll know enough to get out and take an early loss. Don't box yourself into a corner with a preconceived idea of what the market is going to do and a bullheaded notion that, by golly, no matter what happens, you are going to see the trade through to the end. The end just might mean the end of your capital and your ego. So when you're wrong, do something about it. Don't operate on hope because hope turns into fear, and fear ends in disaster.

Your First Loss is Your Least Loss

If you can learn this one lesson, you can save yourself a heck of a lot of money. As all traders know, taking losses is part of the game. What separates the professional from the amateur is the size of the loss that is taken, not the quantity of the loss. When you are wrong, the sooner you can get out, the less you will lose. If you let a trade get away from you because you believe that it will turn around, the loss has the potential to go from a small mistake to a devastating disaster.

No Time to Brood

The primary difference between a successful professional trader and the amateur is the ability of the professional to take a loss immediately, without emotion and without damage to his ego. You must learn to admit when you are wrong and quickly eliminate the potential for any further losses. Exit from your position gracefully and control any emotional desire to blame yourself, or even worse, someone else. If you will take time to reconsider the reasons and judgment that led you to the decision to establish the trade, you might be able to avoid a similar loss in the future. I can tell you from my own personal experience that beating yourself up and brooding over your losses will not allow you to be ready for the next opportunity.

Don't Wait for a Bounce

Be willing to lose, so you can gain. If you are afraid to take many small losses and a few large gains, then you will soon lose your capital and your ego. Once you realize you're wrong, don't wait for a bounce. When a market trade goes against them, it's a common practice for traders and investors to wait for a correction to let them get out of the market. Waiting for the correction could cost you a fortune. The market has a mind of its own—it waits for no one.

Subordinate your will to the will of the market. Learn how to enter and exit the market on its terms, not yours.

Don't Add to a Loser

As simple as the rule sounds, it is surprising how many amateurs and even many professionals violate this basic rule. If you have a loss, then something is wrong relative to your prediction of events. Your timing is incorrect or the market doesn't see things the way you do. Either way, adding to a losing position is one of the surest ways to ruin.

I remember the rip-roaring silver market of the early eighties. I was trading the S&P 500 in those days, but the broker seated behind me had a silver trader who was hooked into believing that the market had no place to go but up. As we have already learned, news is always most bullish at a market top. And the silver market was no exception. As the market made its first major break to the downside, the client, who already had a small loss, kept adding to his position—adding to a loser. He felt, like many brokers feel, that "averaging down" was a prudent game plan. Even when the trade had all but wiped him out, he still believed he was doing the correct thing.

"Averaging down" (also called averaging against the market) is just another way of increasing your losses. Averaging down is accomplished by increasing your position as the market continues to move against you, thus producing greater and greater losses. The more you buy or sell, the larger your losses become. Oddly enough, most amateurs will readily add to a loser but fail to add to a winner. When you add to a winner, you are increasing a profitable position.

For example, let's say that you buy a stock at $10 per share, and it goes to $12. Most amateurs would say to themselves, "Why should I buy the stock at $12 when I could have bought more at $10?" The professional will say, "My prediction that the stock is going higher seems to be correct. Therefore, the opportunity for success is even greater than I originally thought, and I will add to a winning position." I have never been able to understand why an amateur would add to a losing position. Especially considering that the value of his purchase is going down, which would seem to be confirming that his prediction was wrong.

For those of you who are day traders (buying and selling your stock or futures contract the same day), I would strongly advise you *not* to take home a loser. If you are day trading, or even holding positions overnight, don't keep a losing trade past the closing bell. If the stock or future contract is going down, why expose yourself to overnight news events when you have no control over them? There is a reason that the price is declining against you. It's better to get out while you can and take a fresh look the next day. There is always another opportunity around the corner.

Don't Overtrade

Each trade is an opportunity for more losses and more commissions. Amateurs and even professionals develop "trade-itis," a dangerous and devastating disease that can wipe you out. I have heard it said that a person afflicted with trade-itis is no more capable of reasonable and self-composed action than one who is in the delirium of typhoid fever. The volatile action of price movements produces a sort of mental intoxication, which blurs a person's vision, causing involuntary submissiveness to momentary influences. Trade-itis—overtrading—eventually leads to reliance on hope rather than reason. We have already learned that hope does not belong in your game plan.

So don't find yourself in the position where you are afraid to stop trading for fear that you will miss a chance to make a big profit. Because if you become a compulsive trader—one who is afraid to stop trading or to take a vacation out of fear that something important is going to happen—you'll be a great asset to your commission-driven broker, but you will be leading yourself down the path toward financial ruin. That's the time to take a vacation from trading and give your mind a rest.

Learn from Your Mistakes

Making a mistake comes with the territory. Repeating a mistake is asking for a disaster. The first mistake is not usually the one that kills you—it's the second one that will do you in. We have already learned that taking losses is part of the game. So is making mistakes. The professional not only makes fewer mistakes but he doesn't repeat the same mistake twice.

Keep a logbook and record all of your mistakes. It's a great learning device. If you find yourself making the same variation on a theme (committing the same mistake in different ways), do something about it before it's too late.

Keeping a positive attitude about your trading is of primary importance, too. We know that taking losses is part of the game, so we realize that it's all right to be wrong. When asked what it was like to repeat a grade during his primary education, Winston Churchill remarked that "making a mistake is just another way of giving you the opportunity to do it right."

Don't Try to Catch a Falling Knife

Trying to pick the bottom of the market is all but impossible. If you are right, you could make a fortune; if you are wrong, you might not have enough capital to come back and try it again. You never know how much lower a market can go, and you could get ruined if you try to find the bottom. The same advice applies to market tops. No one can tell you where a market top is until after the fact. You simply can't trade on hindsight. The best that you can do is *make sound, educated assumptions, predicated upon conditions known, allowing for events unexpected and fashioned toward a future uncertain.*

Don't Seek the Advice of Your Broker

If you are asking your broker what to do, then you don't know what you're doing. Remember, if your broker's advice was so good, then he wouldn't need your business. We're talking about trading— not investing. If you have a trading plan, you must live or die by following that plan. Once you start asking your broker or any other person for advice, you are second-guessing your plan. If your plan doesn't work, then fix it, change it, or get a new plan. Asking your broker for help will not only give him the opportunity to increase your trading but, even worse, it will give you the opportunity to blame your losses on your broker. Not only is it unfair to blame your broker for your incorrect predictions but using him as a scapegoat will take you away from the self-evaluation process that is so necessary to be successful in this most difficult game.

You should be able to rely on your broker's ability to efficiently and quickly execute your orders. So don't allow your broker to second-guess your opinion, or even worse, change your mind. A well-trained broker might be able to help you solve some of your problems, such as money management or even trade selection (if he has a particular specialty). But if you start relying on the broker instead of your plan, then you really have no plan at all. A broker can be an important part of a trading team. But remember, he is only one part of the team.

There is one area in which the broker might be of great service to you—information. If you are trading from your home without access to Reuter's, Dow Jones' News Services, or any of the other news information bureaus, your broker can be your eyes and ears for news events. In that case, by all means, make sure that your broker is aware of any trade that you are about to enter into so that he can inform you of any news events or information that might affect the successful outcome of your trade.

Let Your Profits Run

Letting your profits run helps you achieve greater success. In one of my earlier rules I suggested that it was possible to be successful, even if you had eight losing trades out of ten. As long as the two winning trades were large enough to make up for the small losses you sustained from the other eight trades, you could be very successful.

It is the big move that makes it possible for most traders to come out ahead. If you constantly take small losses and small profits, it doesn't take a mathematician to figure out that by the time you pay commissions and cover your losses, you'll be left with very little trading capital. The ability to let your profits run, to overcome all of the commission costs and losing trades, is essential if you are to succeed on a long-term basis.

You must be emotionally and mentally prepared for the big move. If you have trained yourself to consistently take small losses, that's okay. But you can't train yourself to consistently take small profits. You must incorporate into your game plan the ability to let your profits run so that when the big move does come, you can capitalize on it.

Know When to Do Nothing at All

There are many times in which markets are impossible to trade. If you study statistics, you will learn that in any given market there is a percentage of time when the market is generally trending up, and there is a percentage of time in which the market is generally trending down; the rest of the market's actions are devoted to oscillating in a narrowly defined trading range. The professional trader always has an opinion about the general trend of the market and, with that in mind, then formulates a game plan to trade against that backdrop.

Most professionals will not waste their time or money trying to enter a trade if the market is in a narrowly defined trading range. Conditions are too uncertain. Other factors may also influence a trader's decision to remain on the sidelines. Seasonal considerations, option expiration periods, and unforeseen crises may wave a cautionary flag that most amateurs aren't able to see. Many of the professionals that I competed against when I traded the S&P 500 stock index refused to trade during the two weeks leading up to the expiration date. They did this because it was impossible to unravel all of the contrary forces at work in the market.

So during those periods of uncertainty, it is better to go on vacation or read a book than to trade. Not trading could save you more money than you could possibly imagine.

Learn Your Stress Point

Heart specialists have been quick to point out that a Type A personality is more prone to suffer a heart attack. You know that kind of person—the hard-driving, never-stopping, compulsive high-achiever. Do you want to suffer from a heart attack? The answer is obviously no. Well, trading can cause a market attack. If you trade beyond your stress point, you could be asking for more trouble than you ever want to encounter. What is your stress point? It's different for each person. Some people are stress junkies. Doc, my mentor, has testified in more arbitrations than anyone I have ever met. His doctor told him that if all of his patients were like Doc, he'd have to close down his medical practice. Doc is just about the only person I have ever met who thrives on stress. In fact, he seeks it out. If he is not testifying at an arbitration or writing a book, you'll find him trading his commodity account or playing in a poker tournament. The more stress the better.

Most of us, on the other hand—and probably even Doc—have a stress point. If you trade beyond your stress point, sooner or later it is going to end in disaster. You might find yourself mentally unprepared to do the right thing at the right time, or even worse, do precisely the wrong thing at the wrong time.

I remember a trade I put on in United States government bond futures. I was long ten contracts, which for me was a lot of money, and the market had turned against me for a couple of days. It was during my early days of trading, and I was just beginning to write my book of mistakes. This trade was one of the first entries. My broker, either out of ignorance or greed, encouraged me to add to a losing position, telling me that it was okay to average down. Halfway through the trade I was the not-so-proud owner of 20 contracts of U.S. government bonds. This exposed me to a far greater loss than I could afford. In fact, it represented so much money that I found myself lying awake in the middle of the night worrying about what tomorrow might bring. Stumbling into my broker's office at 5:30 in the morning one day, I was greeted by an old salt of a broker who could tell from the expression on my face that all was not well. After discussing my plight with him, I'll never forget what he said: "Why don't you sell down to the sleeping level?"

Hearing those words was like being struck by a bolt of lightning. That day I liquidated *half* my bond position and felt the weight of the world come off of my shoulders. That night I had the first good night's sleep I had experienced since I had added to a loser. The trade eventually turned out to be a profitable one, but that's not the purpose or point of this story. Through that experience I had become well acquainted with my stress point.

I have found that the easiest way to reach your stress point is to trade either more than you can afford to lose or to have too much money riding in one position. The stress from the thought of an enormous loss, or even worse, one that is more than you can afford, invariably clouds your judgment and substitutes fear for reason. That is why money management skills are so important—especially in dealing with your stress point. If you can find your stress point and always trade below it, you will have a great advantage over your other adversaries in the combat zone.

When to Say "No"

Investment Products
Most Misused

Remember the Cleaver's synthetic fertilizer investment? One day Mr. Cleaver, now well-versed on how to read his monthly statements, noticed that his $10,000 investment in this new company stock had suddenly taken a sickening turn downward. In fact, by the time he had caught up with Mr. Newman to ask him about it, the company was no longer in existence. The futuristic fertilizer had finally hit the fan, and the investors' money, along with the dummy dung, was gone with the wind.

"What can I say, Mr. Cleaver?" Sam Newman whines over the phone. "Most investments are risky. Surely you knew that." Blah, blah, blah. "I remember distinctly telling you that the synthetic fertilizer was an idea ahead of its time. Perhaps that was the problem . . ." Blah, blah, blah. "It could have made you a rich man . . ." Blah, blah. "But there was no guarantee on a stock, you know . . ." Blah, blah, blah, blah, blah, blah.

Mr. Cleaver, teeth clenched, blood pulsing through his temples, slammed down the phone. The conversation didn't make him feel any better.

Many years ago, the only products brokerage firms offered for investments were stocks and bonds. That's all. Your portfolio was made up of one or the other; that was all you talked about when you planned your investment strategy.

Today there are all kinds of new products—limited partnerships, closed-end bond funds, options, mutual funds, real estate investment trusts, unit trusts; and as you might have guessed by now, new isn't necessarily better. A good, honest stockbroker will take these products and, according to your needs, attempt to fashion a healthy portfolio from the growing group of alternatives.

In their never-ending quest to generate more commissions, used stock salespeople prefer to hype certain products and new variations on old products, which you should reject completely or purchase aware of the inherent risk. The thousands of lawsuits pending over the mishandling of these products demonstrate that there are many stock salespeople hoping you will keep your eyes closed. Let's take a close look at these products, at what your stockbroker will not tell you about them, and why you should cast a doubtful eye their way.

Limited Partnerships

Jack was a building inspector for the city of Los Angeles. While inspecting a building, he fell off the scaffolding and was forced to take an early retirement on disability. Jack, in his early sixties, was a high school graduate who had never attended college and was not a reader of financial publications such as *The Wall Street Journal*, *Forbes*, or any other business-related publications. A conservative person, Jack had always kept his funds in a savings account or a Certificate of Deposit. Scrimping together what he could, he managed to save enough money to buy a small apartment building (in which he lived), and from the rents in the apartment building, together with the money he received from his savings account, he was able to live a modest existence. Later he sold the apartment, made a good profit, and put the money into his bank account.

Then when a teller at the bank informed Jack that he was paying too much income tax on the $225,000 sitting there in his bank account, Jack decided to seek professional guidance from a major brokerage company. Telephoning a local office, he was assigned the "broker of the day." He met with the stock salesperson and explained his conservative investment nature. He wanted to take no chances with this money, he firmly stated, yet he wanted to earn more than he could get in a bank.

"I think I understand," the stock salesperson told him. "You want no risk, and income is your primary objective. I believe I have the perfect investment for you. As you may know, stocks and bonds can fluctuate in value, and it is therefore possible to lose money in a stock or bond investment. But I can put you into an investment with a guaranteed income of 12% for at least the next ten years. After that, you'll get all your money back."

"Sounds great," Jack responded. How could he get in on something like that?

"All you have to do is invest in two or three of the limited partnerships I am now going to recommend for you." The salesperson handed Jack some glossy pictures depicting beautiful buildings, lot locations, and well-dressed, happy folks walking in and out of the buildings. Taking out his pen, the stock salesperson circled the words "Guaranteed 12% return on your investment," printed boldly on the second page.

So, Jack invested the $225,000—all of his life's savings—into three limited partnerships and went happily on his way. During the first two years of the investments, everything was fine. However, at the beginning of the third year, two of the partnerships ceased making any payments to the limited partners, one of which was Jack. His income cut by two-thirds, Jack contacted the brokerage office to speak to his stock salesperson.

"Well," the stockbroker replied, "we didn't anticipate the unforeseen problems in the real estate market, the higher interest rates, and the higher-than-expected vacancy factors."

"But what about my guarantee of 12% per year?" Jack cried.

"I'm really sorry to say I have no control over what the partnership does in terms of payments to the limited partners," the broker answered.

"How do I make my monthly payments on my mortgage? You guaranteed this! Doesn't anybody back up the statements that you gave me?"

The broker did not respond.

The Legendary Secondary Market

As Jack became numbly aware that he was not going to receive more payments from the limited partnerships, his mind turned toward ways to recover his money. After taking several days to calm down, Jack telephoned his stock salesperson and asked him for the present values of his limited partnerships. The broker's response was another shocker: "Well, there is really no means of selling your limited partnership interests at the present time. Right now even the secondary market has no bids (no buyers) for your partnership interests."

"But," Jack stammered, "you told me there was always a market in which I could sell my position."

The secondary market was, in reality, an internal market, as with all limited partnerships—a market made up of other stock salespeople. And they were not going to buy Jack's shares now that it wasn't doing well. The assets of his limited partnerships were illiquid.

The liquidity problem that Jack just discovered is inherent in almost all limited partnerships and is one of the major reasons why limited partnerships pose such a high risk for the investor. It is a rare case, indeed, when a limited partnership liquidates its holdings earlier than anticipated; as for resale, that's fairly rare, too—unless you are willing to give your investment away for next to nothing.

Golden Egg/Rotten Egg

Limited partnerships sold through brokerage firms, one of the most abused product areas in the investment landscape, have been around for a long time. During the last 20 years, Wall Street has sought more commissions. But with less stock sales and higher overhead, brokerage firms have turned to the limited partnership as a major source of revenue. As we have discussed in earlier chapters, limited partnerships also offer the biggest incentives for the stock salesperson—so big they are hard to ignore.

It takes an unusually ethical person to offer you a two- or three-year CD knowing that for his efforts he will receive no brownie or contest points, no free trip to the Caribbean, and little or no commission and that he *could* earn all those goodies by selling limited partnerships. For the stock salesperson, limited partnerships are golden eggs. For you, too often they are just plain rotten eggs. It is one thing to purchase a limited partnership aware of the risks and prepared to wipe the egg off your face if it comes to no good; it's another, like Jack, to have the sky-high risks kept from you by the stock salesperson on his way to padding his own nest.

How It Works

What exactly is a limited partnership? Here's how it works.

In a typical limited partnership, an outside organization will find a product or piece of real estate that it wishes to acquire—for instance, a real estate deal that has great potential. A group of businesspeople create a limited partnership. The partnership intends to raise $50 million to purchase strip shopping centers throughout the Northeast, currently depressed because of economic conditions. The shopping centers are to be rehabilitated, allowing them to operate profitably and sold for a nice gain.

The general partner goes to a major brokerage firm to persuade the upper management to help him raise the $50 million through the sale of limited partnership interests in the firm's retail brokerage system—in other words, through the firm's stock salespeople. The general partner will manage the assets and operate the business of the partnership, and the brokerage company will raise the $50 million through the sale of limited partnership shares that are distributed, marketed, and sold through the retail brokerage system.

The responsibility for marketing and sales rests with the brokerage firm. It will create internal office memoranda and scripts on how to sell the limited partnership (much like the cold-calling scripts), attach them to glossy brochures, and mail them to all their stock salespeople across the country.

When your stockbroker opens his morning mail, there is the neat little package. The first thing he will probably look at will be the commission payout page, setting forth contest points, gross commission for each unit sold, and all the other incentives. This specific limited partnership offers any broker who sells over a million dollars' worth of the product a free Sony television set. Anyone selling $2 million wins a VCR and a Sony television set. Anyone selling over $3 million gets a free trip to Las Vegas for the weekend. And anyone selling over $5 million gets a free cruise in the Mediterranean. In almost all of these situations, the risks are always downplayed and the reward substantially overstated—even to the brokers.

What brokers generally fail to do is to advise the investor that these limited partnerships, as previously mentioned, usually require an investment period longer than expected and usually do not live up to the projections contained in the partnership statements. Why? Because the projections are merely figures put together by accountants and pencil pushers who sometimes have no reasonable basis for making their projections. They, like economists, cannot accurately predict what the economy is going to do and what effect it might have on the investment. Therefore, they should not be making those projections without also mentioning that this is all one large set of assumptions, rooted in "guestimates" and chock full of risk.

The illiquidity of the product multiplies the gamble into the stratosphere because you cannot "get out" early without losing your shirt—or more. With stock, you can always turn to the financial page in the newspaper or call your stockbroker for a quote to see the price. But when you buy into a limited partnership, you're basically in for the duration, and the duration might be 10 or 15 years. Many of my clients thought they would be in and out of their limited partnerships in 1 or 2 years, and they are in the 11th year of owning them with nary a prospective buyer in sight.

Who Do You Trust?

Too often we think we can rely on the reputation of a company backing one of these partnerships. If the partnership is a company's own product, how objective can the company be? It is the same conflict of interest issue we have talked about before.

A *Business Week* article tells of a Prudential Securities real estate limited partnership fiasco already on its way to court. Prudential has been accused of improperly investigating VMS Realty Partners, the group behind a limited partnership Prudential sold. The partnership was to buy 28 Holiday Inns; after 26 found their way into the partnership, VMS had piled up such debt in the fund that the debt far exceeded the market value of the hotels. The suit filed under the Racketeer Influenced and Corrupt Organization Act asks damages for more than 600 investors who invested a total of $80 million to be limited partners in VMS. "They prided themselves on their special expertise in evaluating limited partnership investments," said the attorney representing the group suing Prudential.

One of the "partner/investors," who invested to the tune of $500,000, was quoted as saying, "I was misled by Pru-Bachè's reputation and the representation that they would investigate everything thoroughly. It looks like I'm going to lose it all." This is only one of several losing products Prudential has backed. The same article quoted a former executive as saying that the sales force itself was livid about the poor quality of products coming from the New York office. These brokers, No Brain Bills obviously, are guilty of trusting their company's investigation of new products and are now the ones the clients want to throttle. Prudential is, sadly, not an exception to the rule—it's the same at most brokerage houses. Many of the product suggestions received by brokers throughout the industry are of the same poor quality.

Of course, with these products a lot of upfront money went to stockbrokers, general partners, and brokerage firms' executives. But not to the investors.

Talk about conflict of interest. If your broker offers you a limited partnership, ask your broker what's in it for him—and for his firm. Then sit back and ask yourself if you feel like a big gamble—a long-term one, at that.

Closed-End Bond Funds

"Diversification!" the stock salesperson is telling his client. "You can't have all your eggs in one basket. Your $10,000 shouldn't go into just one bond. What if the company issuing that bond has a problem? You might lose your entire principal!"

"However," he continues, "I have a closed-end bond fund which owns two or three hundred bonds and if one bond should fail—let me reassure you that less than 1% of all the bonds fail—you would not be hurt because the other bonds in the portfolio would make up for that!"

One of the biggest disasters of the 1980s market was the proliferation of bond funds. As stated before, Wall Street's commissions from the equity business have been shrinking for 20 years. The same problems that caused Wall Street to turn to limited partnerships for more revenue has pushed them into the invention, marketing, and sale of closed-end bond funds, and they come in all flavors—municipal, U.S. government, corporate, and junk.

A Hybrid Animal: A Bond That's a Stock

Bond funds are a sort of hybrid animal that have been unleashed on the public. A closed-end bond fund is different from a mutual fund in that a mutual fund constantly takes in new investors. There is no limit to the number of outstanding shares that a mutual fund offers. A closed-end bond fund, though, offers a finite number of shares on its initial public offering, and thereafter those shares will trade in the stock market. So, instead of the closed-end bond fund being treated like a real bond fund, which would be impossible considering its lineage, it will be traded on the stock market. To buy into a closed-end bond fund is to buy into a portfolio of bonds that trade like a stock.

The differences between a bond and a bond fund are simple enough. A bond's worth fluctuates based on two elements.

1. It trades on the basis of the risk involved. If you have an investment-grade bond issued from AT&T, for instance, the risk on that bond is minimal, so the yield on your bond will be lower. Remember—the more the risk, the higher the return rate you will be offered to entice you to take the risk. The lower the yield, the lower the risk; the higher the yield, the higher the risk.

If you own a bond issued from a company in trouble, the bond's price is going to be depressed because of the doubts circulating over whether that company will meet the interest obligation of the bond. This could be a company experiencing financial difficulty because of falling sales and a declining market share, or a leveraged buy-out victim of the eighties with more debt than it can handle. If you read the financial section of the newspaper, you will notice that the price of a poor-quality bond is lower than that of a high-quality bond, such as AT&T. And the yield—the amount of interest to be paid—will be higher to compensate for the "known risk factor."

2. It is influenced by the current level and the perceived future level of interest rates.   The higher that interest rates appear to be headed, the lower the price of a bond will go in anticipation of those higher rates. The reverse is also true. So when you buy a bond, the price of it will generally go up and down, depending on what interest rates do, or are perceived to do.

Not so with a closed-end bond fund. A bond fund's value is subject to all the vagaries of the stock market, just like a stock. The moment the bonds in your fund are perceived to be a bad risk, the bond fund will go down in price. Add to that the (stock) market perception of higher interest rates ahead, and watch out—you and your closed-end bond fund are headed for a fall.

A longer term bond—15–30 years—is going to be more volatile (fluctuating in price) than short to intermediate bonds—three to ten years. Generally speaking, as the time to maturity date increases, so does the volatility. In addition to the interest rate structure, the price of the bond is always influenced by its maturity date.

So if you are "risk-adverse"—that is, if you want to have as little risk as possible—then short-term maturities would be your ticket. Therefore, if you want to reduce your exposure to loss when you buy a bond fund, you have to shorten your time horizon by sticking to short or intermediate bond funds.

When the Cows Come Home

There is another big difference between a bond and a closed-end bond fund. Usually bonds have a definite end period. That means, for instance, if you buy a $1,000 General Motors bond that matures in the year 2000 and hold it until that year, you will get your $1,000 back, and you'll have been paid interest on the bond throughout the period you owned it.

This is not true with a closed-end bond fund. Unlike purchasing a bond directly from the issuing company, the investor may never get his principal back. The closed-end bond fund is made up of a great number of bonds contained within the portfolio; the maturity of one bond in the portfolio may be paid back to the principal of the overall fund and not directly to the investor.

Once you purchase a bond fund you have no guarantee that any of the maturing bonds will be paid directly to you. You could own the fund until the cows come home, while each individual bond in the fund has matured or been sold. The bond fund might not even go back to the price that you paid for it. Be aware, then, that when you buy a closed-end bond fund, there is no certain date in the future at which time you will get all of your money back.

Lose Before You Begin

Don't forget about the "no commission" statement. Stock sales-people, as you now know, may use the line that there is no commission charged to you for the purchase of a new bond fund. Here's what they don't tell you: (1) They might earn 5% or more for selling the fund to you (as well as a very high payout), and (2) soon after the issuance of the stock, the bond fund almost always trades down, quite often 10% of the fund. Why? Because the insiders and traders on Wall Street know that 10% of the fund was spent—either to cover syndicate, underwriting, or commission costs or to cover a loan taken out to pay these expenses—thus causing a 10% debt against the overall value of the bond fund. Therefore, as soon as the fund opens for trading, professional traders immediately sell it. Believe it or not, many of these funds have sold down by as much as 30%.

Closed-end bond funds are not good investments unless you are willing to assume the risk—the risk you now know all about.

Stocks

Although I might incur the wrath of every stock salesperson, I feel an obligation to let you know that stocks are not suitable for everyone. That includes AT&T, General Motors, General Electric, and Southern California Edison as well. Whether or not you should purchase a stock is a very personal matter. There are many individuals who are simply not suitable candidates for the purchase of stocks—even the bluest of the blue-chip quality stocks. Are you one of those people? Should you say no to your broker when he advises you to commit 40% of your portfolio to common stocks?

I cannot possibly answer such a specific question by jotting down a bunch of generalities applicable to all investors. What I can do, though, is advise you to read over Chapter 6's Checklist No. 2 on how to choose a stockbroker and Chapter 7's commonsense rules so that you are able to make your own determination of whether stocks belong in your portfolio.

It isn't simply a matter of whether you should own stocks. You should also be concerned with the quantity as well as the quality of stocks in your overall portfolio. While one person might be a suitable candidate to have 10% of his overall assets invested in stocks, another's needs or financial conditions might require a 40% commitment to stocks.

If you determine, based upon your tolerance for risk, financial circumstances, and investment goals, that stocks should constitute a substantial part of your portfolio, then you have to make a determination of what types of stocks belong in your portfolio. Just as no two people possess exactly the same suitability requirements regarding the ownership of stocks in a portfolio, so too do the suitability requirements for the types of stock differ from person to person. Some investors might feel comfortable with speculative, low-priced securities, while others might only be able to sleep at night if they own utility stocks.

So just because a broker recommends stocks to you doesn't mean you should rush in, where only fools dare go, and embrace his recommendation. Stop and think first about whether you can afford the risk involved in stock ownership.

One caution: Don't let a broker convince you that through diversification you can eliminate the stock ownership risk. If you own 30 different stocks, the likelihood of one stock severely impacting the portfolio will be reduced. But if *you are only invested in stocks*, no matter how diversified your portfolio, when the stock market goes down, your portfolio is going to go with it.

Commodities: Financial Futures

For all but a few, commodities—financial futures—do not belong in a portfolio. I am not saying that a recreational trader or speculator shouldn't own financial futures in a portion of his portfolio. What I am saying is that unless you are fully aware of the extreme high-risk nature of future trading, you shouldn't venture into this arena. And that's what it is, by the way: trading. Your broker may wish to call it investing but I have found that because of the short-term nature of the contracts and the high volatility of the markets, it's more like trading than investing.

For the speculator, trader, or recreational risk-taker, financial futures can be both exciting and rewarding. Unfortunately, most who venture into the game lose money. In fact I have heard it said that 98% of futures traders lose money and 2% win. I have never documented that saying, but it probably isn't far from the truth. It has been said that a speculator who dies rich dies before his time.

The art of speculation, and it is an art, should not be left to the uninformed or naive. It's okay to risk a small portion of your assets with the hope of making a fortune. Just remember that you might well lose all of the capital you are willing to risk, and, therefore, you should not venture into the water so far that you might find yourself drowning.

If it is your intent to genuinely hedge your portfolio against the risk of some unforeseen consequence such as depression or inflation or economic dislocation, and you believe that some commodity—and I mean the commodity, not a commodity contract—belongs in your account, then, by all means, go ahead and make that commitment. Some "gold bugs" believe that a portion of gold belongs in every portfolio. My warning doesn't center around the ownership of a commodity but rather the trading of commodities through the futures market.

New Issues

Groucho Marx once remarked that he never wanted to join a club that would have him as a member. The same is usually true of new issues. A stock about to go public that has not traded before is, to say the least, a high-risk transaction. You had better ask yourself, "If this is such a great deal, why is the broker calling me?" If you're on some cold-caller's list, or your friendly neighborhood broker (whom you haven't heard from for three months) is calling to tell you about this great fertilizer company that's going public, you're probably the last one down the information pipeline, and you know what that means.

You don't want new issues whose shares are easily available. On the other hand, you want *all* of the shares of a new issue that you can't get. That's right. You want to get your hands on all the shares of new issues that are not available to you. Why? Because the syndicate participants and the brokerage companies try to obtain all the shares they can get their grubby little hands on when they believe that a particular new offering is going to do quite well. It's the ones they don't want that you end up with. If you look at the history of new issues, you will see that many of them never make it past the first couple of years, and some of them experience price declines the moment the paper hits the street.

Options

Stock salespeople routinely sell options as a risk-limiting mechanism. Used properly, one can, to a minor degree, reduce the risk of loss on a particular stock through the use of options. For example, if you own a stock and you believe the market is about to decline, you could either sell a "call" against your stock position or buy a "put." The problem is that most brokers are not sophisticated enough to have a thorough and meaningful understanding of the application of option principles as they relate to stock hedging techniques.

To make matters worse, not only are most brokers ill-trained in this area but the primary reason for a stock option program recommendation may be, once again, the generation of commissions—*not* the proposed safety net or insurance premium that the broker is espousing.

If one truly felt that the market was about to enter into a declining phase, in most cases it would be far more prudent to liquidate your stock holdings than it would be to write a call against your position or purchase a put. Why? Well, firstly you would be avoiding the possibility of double or triple commissions on the transaction. Secondly, in the case of call writing, should you be incorrect and the market continued to rally further, there is a strong likelihood that the stock you love so dearly would be called away from you, and you would then be forced into the position of having to buy back your call at a loss, pay the commission from the sale of your stock, or enter the market and repurchase your stock at a higher price with yet another commission. If you are the buyer of a put and the market continues to rally, you will, of course, lose the cost of purchasing that put.

Most major retail brokerage companies have option departments whose major function is to dream up new ideas for their retail brokers. Swaps, buy-writes, butterflies, spreads, strangles, and every other kind of concoction known to man have been sent down the pipeline to the retail stock salesperson who usually doesn't understand the strategy. In fact, I'll bet if you called your friendly neighborhood broker and asked him to explain to you why it would be prudent to sell a put at the price you wish to purchase a stock, you will be surprised about his inability either to understand your question or give you a proper answer.

Although options are sold—that is, marketed—as a risk-limiting mechanism, they are rarely used in that manner. Precisely the opposite is what usually occurs.

I have heard it said that 87½% of the buyers of options lose money on the transaction. That's right; 87½% of the market participants who are buyers of options lose money on their trades.

But this is only the beginning. Inevitably, I have found the use of options in over 70% of the churning cases brought to my attention. Options by their very nature increase the turnover ratio of the portfolio. Let us say, for example, that you have a portfolio with an equity worth $50,000. If, at the end of the year, you have made purchases totaling $200,000, you would have turned over your portfolio four times—that is, four times the value of your equity. More turnover in a portfolio means more trading, and that means more commissions are generated. So it's not hard to understand that in churning cases, commissions and turnover go hand in hand.

The problem is that even if your account is not being churned, the distinction between the use of an option as a risk-limiting mechanism (or a hedging device) and that of a speculating tool can become indistinguishable. Even professionals routinely cross this line only to wind up getting themselves into a lot of trouble. What starts out as a conservative option program ends up as outright speculation to the detriment of the overall portfolio.

The amateur investor, on the other hand, with less understanding about the option market, can be even more prone to cross the line between hedging and speculating. In fact, brokers often encourage their clients to engage in more option transactions. The commissions charged on option transactions, especially low-priced options, are among the highest in the industry. That, coupled with the high turnover in an option account, can provide a broker with a heck of a lot of commissions.

I recall a case in which a client originally entered into a conservative call-writing strategy in which she wrote calls against all of the stocks in her portfolio. Fourteen months after she started the strategy not only had she lost all of her stocks—because they were called away when the options were exercised—but she began to speculate wildly using options, in the belief that she had come up with some formula that would protect her whether the market went up or down. By the time she caught on to the fact that her broker was making a lot of commissions while she was losing a lot of money, the client and her money had parted company. Of the $200,000 loss the client suffered, $125,000 was commission.

So my best advice to you is this: Don't get caught up in the option frenzy and become your broker's best source of income. It's okay to buy an option now and then . . . as long as you limit the amount of money you invest and realize that the odds favor you losing on the transaction.

Principal Transactions: Market Makers

Whenever your broker recommends a stock in which his brokerage company "makes a market in the stock," ask yourself the question, "Is the brokerage company stuck with the stock in inventory, or is this really as good a deal as the broker claims?"

Principal or market maker transactions, as we called them in Chapter 3, are transactions in which the brokerage company sells you stock that it purchased in the open market or sells you stock out of its own inventory. These transactions are quite a source of income for the brokerage company.

We have already learned that a broker-dealer might purchase a stock at $10 per share and sell it to you out of inventory at $10.50 or higher. But what happens if the brokerage company gets stuck with a stock that nobody wants to buy—one whose value is declining faster than a brokerage company can get out of it? You might end up, like the Cleavers, buying that fertilizer company that truly stinks.

Principal transactions provide a profit center from inventory sales as well as a profit through hidden commissions. Don't forget, the price you pay includes the commission (the markup), and unless you ask the broker how much commission or markup he made on the transaction, you just might not know how much you're really paying. Like option transactions, I have found principal transactions to be another source of commission revenue in churning cases, too. Not all principal transactions are in and of themselves improper. Just be sure that you're not getting stuck with a stock that nobody else wants to buy.

Foreign Stocks

The purchase of foreign stocks, whether ordinary shares or American Depository Receipts (ADRs), can involve high degrees of risk.

The main reason is the limited access to information concerning the foreign securities. Furthermore, the listing requirements in foreign countries can be significantly less stringent than those found in the United States. You would be surprised by how many foreign stocks trade in our secondary markets, either over the counter or out of brokerage houses' inventories—where practically no active market exists. While some foreign stocks might be a great investment, many of them trade on poorly managed exchanges, or even if they've traded on a nationally recognized market, they do not have to meet the capital requirements or other reporting requirements set forth under the United States' securities regulations.

If you can't gain access to information—information that might be crucial to your investment decisions—then you better think twice about investing in foreign stocks.

I recall a case in which a client purchased a foreign security that encountered innumerable problems in its home country, none of which were brought to the attention of the client. Had the client known the true circumstances surrounding the foreign stock, he never would have purchased it in the first place, or he certainly would have gotten out of the stock before it went into a tailspin and took his money down with it. Only sophisticated investors, capable of comprehending the risks involved in foreign securities, should engage in such activity.

While we're on the subject of foreign securities, I would like to mention the Vancouver stock market. Unlike the United States' stock markets, the Vancouver stock market has registration requirements that would make even the bravest speculator nervous. There are countless stocks trading on the Vancouver Exchange with no proven track record of earnings, let alone assets. These "shells" have been passed from person to person through boiler room-type operations in which telemarketing experts are dialing for dollars. The Vancouver Exchange has tried to "clean itself up" in recent years but has seen more than its fair share of scandals, leaving investors with nothing more than the worthless stock certificates for which they paid so much money.

Junk Bonds

The term "junk bond" is used to define those bonds that are below investment grade; they are often called "high-yield" bonds. The junk bond or high-yield market is composed of all bonds rated below investment grade by at least one of the major rating agencies.

Actually, the term "junk bond" covers a wide spectrum of corporate bonds and includes all bonds rated "BB/Ba" and below. Some experts describe high-yield bonds to be anything at or below the higher rank of "BBB split." (A split occurs when Moody's and Standard & Poor's give and issue different grades. This happens for only 20–30% of the issues rated.)

Although the origin of the phrase "junk bond" is unclear, its use in common business journals can be traced back as far as 1974. The speculative nature of junk bonds has long been recognized. In 1974, *Business Week* magazine acknowledged that the market considered the solvency of junk bond issuers as "highly suspect." In the late seventies, an article in *Forbes* magazine noted that junk bonds had been "all the rage for the last few years," but called them "chancy securities." Even back then, experts were pointing out that the boom in junk bond sales was happening because investors had become "less cautious" and "willing to take gamblers' risks."

But it wasn't until Michael Milken ushered in the junk bond era that junk bonds became fashionable and Wall Street got caught up in the junk bond fad.

Wall Street Fashion

Wall Street is just like the fashion industry in one chief respect: Both the fashion industry and Wall Street jump from one fad to another almost as quickly as a model changes an outfit during a fashion show. In fact, Wall Street fads are much like fashion shows— Wall Street is always putting on a pretty face and trying to sell the investing public the latest hot new product.

This year's long dresses might sweep the garment industry; next year designers might bring back the mini-dress as the latest new sensation. It's funny how fashions of the past reappear with only a few alterations to usher in the new "fashion era," isn't it? For those of you who are students of history, you can easily define fashion eras on Wall Street as well. Remember back in the early seventies when the nifty-fifty era was in full swing? Money managers focused primarily on 50 blue-chip stocks, disregarding thousands of other companies. How about the limited partnership craze during which investments from windmills to airplane equipment leasing were packaged with all the glitz of a Hollywood movie and sold to the unwary public?

While I'm on the subject of Hollywood movies, let's not forget that Hollywood came to Wall Street, and many investors rushed to snap up limited partnership shares on film production deals. Do you want to talk about risky investments?

Unfortunately, when Wall Street gets caught up in a fad, commonsense rules of investing seem to fly out the window. The herd instinct overtakes even the most conservative professional, and everyone stampedes to the feeding trough. You already know what happens if everyone wants to get ahold of the same investment. It reaches overvaluation levels, or, even worse, it becomes an economic nightmare.

Well, this is precisely what happened to the junk bond market of the roaring eighties. Michael Milken ushered it in, and then he was ushered off to jail. But his jail sentence didn't help the thousands of investors who lost over $100 million as a result of being left holding the junk bond "bag," which had literally deflated in value. Losses from the default of junk bonds increased staggeringly in the years 1985–1989. Yet, in spite of overwhelming evidence to the contrary, investors, both individual and professional, just couldn't get enough junk bonds to fill their portfolios. James Grant, author of *Grant's Interest Rate Observer*, stated that "high yield bonds are not suitable for most investors." In his many articles, Grant has been consistently critical of the junk bond market since the mid-eighties.

Junk Bonds' Sky-High Risk/Reward Ratio

Simply put, the relationship between risk and reward, even in the best "junk," doesn't augur well for the purchaser of a junk bond—

unless the purchaser is willing to bear the risk of loss. This risk of loss not only relates to the interest payments on the bond but can also be quite meaningful if the bond goes into default and its value drops by 70% or 80%.

The overleveraging of America has already been the subject of many books, but the consequences to every citizen and every investor will reverberate throughout the economy for years to come. Corporations, which had no other means of borrowing, sold billions of dollars of junk bonds to unwise investors, wiping out the life savings of countless thousands.

Junk bonds have been clearly defined and recognized by the investment industry as inherently risky. Because they are below investment grade and defined as predominately speculative, investors should be advised to buy these bonds only if their goal is speculation for profit or they've been advised of the substantial risk and are willing to assume this considerable risk in return for a higher yield.

The Packaging of Junk Bonds

It's the broker's responsibility to adequately inform the investor that the purchase of a junk bond will expose the investor to a high risk of principal loss and the possibility of temporary or even permanent cessation of the bond income. However, the large retail brokerage companies, as well as their stock salespeople, did not package junk bonds in this manner. Many older investors flocked to junk bonds, believing that the higher yield was sustainable and there was really no risk involved in attaining this higher yield—no doubt because a broker told them so.

One way in which Wall Street packaged junk bonds was through junk bond mutual funds in which the investor was led to believe that by diversification he could "diversify away the risk" and get substantially increased rewards without substantially increased risk. This, history has shown, has never been the case. There is no way to escape the risk/reward relationship.

So the next time your broker tells you that with low, long-term interest rates, for example 6% or 7%, you can earn 10% without any increased risk, you had better take a long, hard look at his investment proposal and be sure it doesn't carry any high-yield bonds—you know, "junk bonds."

Bond Principal Transaction: Watch Out

While we are on the subject of junk bonds, I want to call your attention to a potential problem that applies not only to junk bonds but to the purchase of any bond that you buy from a brokerage company.

Remember our discussion about principal transactions in stocks? The brokerage company sells you a stock out of its inventory and then adds the commission to the price of the stock as a markup? The same situation applies to bonds. Always be careful when you buy a bond from your friendly neighborhood stockbroker because you never know at what price he took that bond into his inventory. What do I mean? When you call your broker to get a quote on a bond—whether it's municipal, corporate, or government—he doesn't tell you what commission he is going to charge you on that bond. Nor does he tell you at what price the brokerage company took that bond into its inventory.

There could be significant hidden commissions included in the price of a bond, and you will never know about it. When you buy a bond, always ask your salesperson what the commission or markup charge is to purchase the bond. It's one more piece of information to help you make informed decisions about your investments.

So now you know when to say no or, at the very least, what questions to ask as you proceed with caution. Sooner or later you will probably be offered most of these investments. When they are misused, they can injure, or, as in the case of the junk bonds of the 1980s, they can mortally damage. Have you fallen prey at the hands of an unscrupulous broker? Have you ever wondered if you can recover your losses? Well, I've saved the best for last. The next chapters—the remainder of the book—will help you determine whether you have been the victim of fraudulent or negligent acts and what specific steps you can take to do something about it—to make Wall Street pay you back.

Making Wall Street Pay You Back

A Person Armed with Knowledge Can Beat the System and Recover Lost Money

When You Can Recover Your Losses and Why

Negligent or Fraudulent Acts Explained

Harley Cleaver has just broken the news of the synthetic fertilizer loss to his wife Verna. She isn't taking it well.

"But, Harley," Verna cries, "he guaranteed . . ."

"Forget the guarantee, honey," Harley grunts. "That was a lie. And the rest of our investments? Well, I hate to say this, but I'm not sure they were good choices, either. But we can't pull out of those funds right now without a big loss. At least I can get our savings out of Sam Newman's paws, though."

"Why, that . . ." Verna swallows down an uncharacteristic curse as she plops into a dinette chair. "Can't we get any of the money back?"

"Don't know," Harley mumbles. "But I'm going to find out."

Your stock salesperson has lost your money. To add insult to injury, you are convinced it was his fault.

Did he goof?

Or did he just outright defraud you?

Either way, if certain rules of law have been violated, you might have a chance to see that money again.

We have just looked long and hard at the major areas in which stock salespeople take advantage of the investor. Now let's scrutinize what a stock salesperson does that can subject both him and his brokerage firm to liability.

Incidentally all of the following deeds are governed by a federally regulated act or rule, the majority of which often fall under Section 10(b) and 20 of the Securities Exchange Act of 1934 and Rule 10B5 of the Securities Exchange Commission. Various state corporations' codes and other common law state actions are also relied upon by lawyers when they commence civil lawsuits against a brokerage company. Today, however, most cases will be resolved through arbitration, not the courtroom. So, in this chapter, we will only discuss the violations normally addressed in arbitration. (An overview of how one prepares, commences, tries, and concludes a claim through the arbitration process is the subject of Chapters 11 and 12.)

Rules of Suitability

Suitability: Three Cases

Do the Cleavers have a case against Mr. Newman? If they do, it most likely would be based upon fraud, negligence, and a violation of the suitability rule.

What is suitability?

The NASD defines suitability under Article III, Section 2, Recommendations to Customers:

> (a) In recommending to a customer the purchase, sale or exchange of any security, a member shall have reasonable grounds for believing that the recommendation is suitable for such customer upon the basis of the facts, if any, disclosed by such customer as to his other security holdings and as to his financial situation and needs.
>
> (b) Prior to the execution of a transaction recommended to a non-institutional customer, other than transactions with

customers where investments are limited to money market mutual funds, a member shall make reasonable efforts to obtain information concerning:
  (i) the customer's financial status;
  (ii) the customer's tax status;
  (iii) the customer's investment objectives; and
  (iv) such other information used or considered to be reasonable and by such member or registered representative in making recommendations to the customer.
  [Sec. 2 amended May 2, 1990, effective for accounts opened and recommendations made after January 1, 1991.]

The New York Stock Exchange "know your customer rule" (Rule 405) states that:

Every member organization is required . . . to
  (1) Use due diligence to learn the essential facts relative to every customer, every order, every cash or margin account accepted or carried by such organization and every person holding power of attorney over any account accepted or carried by such organization.

Suitability standards can be violated in quite a few ways by stockbrokers—careless ones as well as devious ones. Let me tell you three true life stories to illustrate:

Michael: Reach Out and Pinch

One day, Michael, a construction worker, was in his boss's office when he overheard a phone conversation between his boss and his boss's stockbroker. They were discussing how much money they were going to make on this hot stock deal. The boss handed Michael the phone, and in ten short minutes the broker had convinced Michael to take most of his savings, $40,000, and go for a pop in this stock. It was a sure thing. A deal was going to take place in a couple of weeks and the stock would go from $14 to $25, making Michael quite a chunk of money. The broker never asked Michael any of the normal questions about suitability that, by law, a broker must ask prior to making an investment for a new client. The broker didn't bother to ask basic questions, such as did Michael have any savings, what he could afford to lose, or how much money did he make. The deal was everything. Michael was just part of the deal.

As soon as the stock salesperson put the order in, he sent a messenger to the boss's construction office to pick up a check from Michael and to get Michael's signature on the paperwork necessary to open the account.

Then, against everything the stock salesperson had predicted, the stock began to spiral down. As the stock went ever lower, the stockbroker kept telling Michael to buy more stock because if it was good at $14, it had to be a lot better at $10. Michael purchased another $40,000 of stock on *margin*. What's margin? It's a device whereby the brokerage firm lends you money against the value of your stock, and you buy more stock with that borrowed money.

Sounds dangerous, doesn't it? Well, it is. When the stock goes down, guess what? The brokerage firm will ask for more money, a "margin call," because the value of the stock used as collateral for the loan is disappearing—just like your money.

The hot stock, at this writing, is trading around $1.50 a share. Michael's life savings were wiped out.

Alice: De Facto Control

Alice at least knew her stock salesperson but, ultimately, it didn't help matters. Alice received $100,000 from her mother's estate after moving to this country. Fearful of the stock market because she witnessed her mother lose money in it years ago, Alice still needed help with her money. She met with a highly recommended stock salesperson but made it clear how she felt, telling him pointedly of her mother's experience in the stock market. With absolute safety as her first and foremost goal, she wanted to invest her funds conservatively. She could not—repeat, *not*—afford to lose any of the money since it was all she ever hoped to have. The stockbroker assured Alice he would follow her wishes, taking no risks with her money. Alice trusted him and turned over her $100,000, giving him "de facto control."

Turning over control of your account to a stockbroker, granting him discretion to do as he pleases in the purchase and sale of securities, is an act that requires your signature authorizing the stock salesperson to have such authority. In most cases, however, the stock salesperson gains control through establishing a special relationship in which the client essentially trusts the broker with every little decision. De facto control occurs when an investor doesn't sign a specific discretionary account authorization form but nonetheless allows the stock salesperson to do as he pleases. Alice's stockbroker had it. As soon as the money was transferred into the new brokerage account, he began to place the funds into two limited partnerships. A limited partnership, as you know from Chapter 9, is one of the riskiest investments available but one that pays the highest commission. Alice's specific limited partnerships' returns did not even compete with that of a savings account, and its liquidity was nonexistent.

By placing Alice into illiquid limited partnerships of questionable economic viability that produced little or no income and exposed her to grave risks, Alice's trusted stock salesperson clearly violated the suitability requirement that a stock salesperson must meet prior to making any investment for the customer.

But that's not all he violated. In this case, these limited partnerships contained eligibility requirements that had to be met for the state in which Alice resided. Later, Alice found out that she didn't meet the income levels, overall net worth, or virtually any of the requirements set forth in the limited partnership prospectus itself.

Yet this trusted stock salesperson wasn't through. Given Alice's previous history, he should only have invested in the highest quality, most conservative bonds, such as AT&T or government bonds. Yet the next thing he did was to place Alice in high-risk stocks. All the investments he made violated her suitability requirements.

What this stock salesperson was thinking is anybody's guess. Whether his acts were intentional or whether he truly didn't understand how unsuitable those recommendations were for Alice, the result is the same. Alice lost all her inheritance almost as quickly as she received it.

Sheldon: Who's Calling the Shots?

And then there was Sheldon, who had been calling his own shots in the stock market for quite a few years. Sheldon, age 73, was a

self-made man. He had worked as a salesperson for a major manufacturing company and, through the company's retirement program, had saved quite a bundle. He moved to California following
his retirement and invested his money in second trust deeds and
Certificates of Deposit. Six or seven years after his retirement, Sheldon became bored with his sedentary life-style and decided to invest
in the stock market.

He began slowly, by purchasing quality blue-chip stocks of big-
name companies.

Sheldon's relationship with his broker remained consistent for
over two years—the broker was just an order taker and Sheldon
called all of the shots. When Sheldon originally opened his account,
he told his broker about his desire for two things: (1) secure income
upon which to live during his retirement years, and (2) long-term
growth to keep up with inflation. These were his investment objectives during the first two years of his relationship with the broker.

One day all of this changed. Sheldon's broker called him up
and told him that he had information that a "buy-out" was im-
minent for a Federal Savings and Loan. The stock was currently
trading around $14 per share, and the buy-out was going to occur
between $18 and $22 per share. Sheldon wasn't sure. He told the
broker he was leery of purchasing such a stock, because the savings
and loan crisis was currently making national headlines every day.
The broker assured Sheldon that this was a safe investment, and
besides, it would only be a short-term trade. So Sheldon purchased
10,000 shares or approximately $140,000 worth of stock.

Soon the broker advised Sheldon of another buy-out. Sheldon
purchased a total of 25,000 shares of stock at $11 per share, for
a purchase price of approximately $275,000. Sheldon now held
$415,000 worth of shares in only two stocks—highly speculative,
high-risk, over-the-counter stocks which were clearly unsuitable for
him. Sheldon had not requested the broker to make the purchases;
the broker had solicited Sheldon to purchase the stocks based on
his recommendations. Clearly Sheldon could not afford to take such
a gamble with his savings. He had been clear about his objectives
with the stockbroker long ago. He thought that was obvious. Shel-

don didn't understand the risk in the stock salesperson's suggestions, and the risk was certainly not spelled out to him.

To make matters worse, the broker had allowed and encouraged Sheldon to purchase the stock on margin.

The bottom line was this: Allowing Sheldon to over-weight or concentrate the majority of his investment dollars in only two stocks was clearly an unsuitable recommendation and a violation of the prudent rule of diversification any stockbroker is expected to follow—especially with stated goals like Sheldon's.

When the dust settled, Sheldon was wiped out. Losing all of his life's savings in only two stocks, Sheldon is now left with an arbitration claim against the brokerage company.

Alice, Michael, and Sheldon all lost their money because their stock salespeople either ignored or didn't understand their needs, and their money went into investments totally unsuitable for them.

Think about Michael. In learning about the suitability of a customer, a broker should, at the very least, inquire about the financial capacity of the customer. What is the customer's tolerance for risk? How much can he afford to lose? How much money does he have to invest? Michael's stockbroker sold him on a hot deal over the phone, without asking him any questions.

Alice's stated investment objective was no risk, but risk is what she got. And although Sheldon was somewhat more sophisticated an investor than Alice or Michael, he still was given unsuitable advice in areas he knew little about. His relationship with his stockbroker changed suddenly, and the recommendations were against Sheldon's stated goals. All three parties have good cases for suitability violations.

Personal Questions

Financial capacity is an element of suitability that a stock salesperson must also examine. He should learn how much you earn, but his inquiries should not be limited to your present income. If a broker is properly performing his job, he will ask his client what they have earned during the last few years and whether they believe they can maintain their income level over the next several years. In fact, a broker would best serve his client by reviewing the client's complete financial statement, even though most people don't feel comfortable parting with this information.

Having a working knowledge of a client's income is not enough information for a broker to determine the client's financial capacity. A reliable broker should ask, "What are your liabilities?" That is, how much is your mortgage? What does it cost to feed your children? How much insurance do you pay? What are your other debts? The answers to these kinds of questions can provide the basis for financial capacity. Most "new account forms" contain a section entitled "Client's Stated Net Worth Exclusive of the Family Residence." When the stock salesperson receives this information together with the income, liabilities, assets, and risk tolerance of a prospective customer, then—and only then—does he have the basic information to understand an investor's suitability requirements.

Misrepresentation

Misrepresentation is a violation that is just like it sounds—a stock salesperson misrepresents a product he is selling.

Misrepresentation falls into two categories: negligent misrepresentation and fraudulent misrepresentation. As with suitability violations, whether a broker intentionally deceives you or is unaware that his statements are false, the outcome remains the same: Money is lost, and it's not his. Were it not for the broker's statements and the client's reliance on those statements, the client would not have purchased the security recommended by the broker. In most cases, if you, the investor, knew the true facts of the recommended product, you never would have decided to purchase it in the first place.

Think back to Sheldon. His broker recommended a savings and loan stock that made Sheldon skittish but the stockbroker talked him into buying it anyway. Making a recommendation to purchase a savings and loan stock during a time in which the savings and loan industry is in deep trouble is questionable at best. Stockbrokers, we believe, are supposed to know things we don't—so we go ahead and listen.

This is the way a misrepresentation might occur:

The broker calls you up and says, "I've got a great buy right now. This stock is really depressed, and it's going to have a big move up. The name of the stock is Eldorado Savings. In spite of the savings and loan problems, it's got a great balance sheet. The stock is down to $25. It's got to go up. Headlines? No, the current savings and loan problems have been hyped by the media, and there's really nothing wrong with buying a savings and loan stock right now. There's very little risk in the transaction, and you're going to make a quick profit as soon as the stock pops back up to $35 a share."

This stock salesperson knows he is telling half-truths. He also knows that the recent quarterly report shows that pending lawsuits and the liabilities of the savings and loan exceed its equity (net worth). So, even if the broker feels for technical reasons the stock is due for a bounce, he has a duty to tell the customer about the disastrous balance sheet, the fragile condition of the savings and loan industry, and the grave risks in purchasing this kind of stock. Then, if the client wants to take the chance, the stockbroker has represented the risks adequately, holding nothing back.

But what if the broker didn't know all this? What if he hadn't done his homework to learn that the balance sheet of the Eldorado Savings and Loan was in serious shape? What if he had just relied upon word of mouth and his own instincts when recommending the purchase of the stock? Then the stock salesperson wouldn't have been committing fraudulent misrepresentation but, rather, negligent misrepresentation. He has failed to live up to a reasonable and prudent standard of research before recommending such a purchase.

Incidentally, a broker can commit a fraudulent or negligent act even if he provides you with most of the information you need before making an investment decision but he fails—or purposely omits—a key piece of information, which would have prevented you from following his recommendation.

If he'd said, "Oh, by the way, half of the Eldorado officers have just been indicted," would you have taken his advice?

Churning

Recently I watched a television interview in which an elderly lady was talking about her brokerage account. The reporter asked her if she was aware that her account had been churned, to which she replied, "No, I wasn't."

"Do you know what churning is?" the reporter asked delicately.

"Well," she paused, "isn't that like buttermilk?"

Churning is one of the most offensive acts that a stock salesperson can commit, and it has very little to do with buttermilk, aside from the bitter taste it leaves in your mouth. Churning occurs when a broker has either de facto or discretionary control of your account and makes a series of trades unreasonably excessive in frequency or dollar value per trade, with the intent to produce commissions for himself, not profits for you.

Liz: Churn and Burn

Churning is what happened to Liz. She received an inheritance from her father's estate, a whopping $250,000. Unsophisticated in financial matters, having never invested in the stock or bond markets, Liz went to see a stockbroker recommended by a friend. Liz bluntly admitted her lack of expertise but clearly stated that she wanted to invest conservatively with no more than $50,000 in the stock market at any time. The stock salesperson agreed with her. So Liz transferred all the assets over to the broker, who immediately began to purchase high-risk, low-priced, over-the-counter securities and limited partnerships of questionable value providing little or no income.

When Liz began receiving confirm slips in the mail, she would call the stockbroker to ask him what he was doing. "Don't worry," he said, "all these purchases comply with your wishes, I promise."

Liz had no criteria for judging the quality of a stock. She didn't know that a low-priced, over-the-counter stock might be substantially more dangerous than a New York Stock Exchange stock. Since her "counsel" was the one making the purchases, he was not going to educate her. So she continued to rely on the advice, counsel, and representations of this "I promise" stockbroker.

Within only a couple of months, reams of confirms started to pour into her office. Every time she would contact the broker, he would assure her that he was complying with her wishes. Finally, doing a little addition, she realized there was more than $50,000 invested in the stock market. She called her stockbroker and firmly pointed out that he was not fulfilling her wishes.

"But we'll make a lot more money by having the money invested this way," he said. "You're not going to lose any money."

At the end of the year, when Liz's income taxes were prepared by her accountant, she received a shocking phone call. The accountant told her she had lost a lot of money and the broker was doing a huge amount of trading. The quantity of stock purchased in the 11 months since she opened her account was approximately $700,000.

Liz was at her wit's end. What did that mean? Watching the national television show, "Smart Money," Liz saw an interview I was doing with the show's hosts, Ken and Daria Dolan, and called in. I was discussing arbitration and investors' rights to recover monies that were wrongfully taken from them. Ultimately, she sent me her statements, and I discovered that even the accountant was wrong. The turnover in her account—that is, how much stock had been purchased in that 11 months—was not $700,000, but $1,450,000! Based upon the confirmation slips, many of which did not show commission, I calculated the commissions to be over $100,000.

The stockbroker had taken her $250,000 and bought and sold and bought and sold—churning, churning, churning—almost $1,500,000 in stocks in a year. Why? For practice? To work up his trading muscles? No, for the commissions made on every single sale, every single churn—over $100,000 worth. Yet Liz had told him not to invest more than $50,000 in conservative stocks.

How could he do so much trading? As the frequency of trades increases or the dollar value of trades grows, a broker may engage in buying and selling securities on a short-term basis. This could be a "day trade," in which he buys and sells the product in one day. It could be a weekly or monthly trade if the dollar amount of the transaction is high enough. The stock salesperson is not making trades in the best interest of the customer to generate profits. Rather, he's making trades in his own best interest to generate commissions.

In fact, it's interesting to note that in churning cases, even if the account doesn't lose a single penny—or even if it makes money—the broker is still liable for damages resulting from the churning. I have seen cases in which the account has made a few dollars, while the stock salesperson has lined his pockets with $200,000 in commissions. The broker and the brokerage firm were required to repay the client all of the commissions earned.

De facto control invites this sort of manipulation. Greedy brokers see such trust as carte blanche to use money entrusted to them as they please, perhaps rationalizing their actions as long as they don't lose your money. But it's illegal. Unfortunately, the SEC and the NASD do little to push these individuals out of the business. If a broker is caught with his hand in the cookie jar, all he usually has to do is give back the cookies. Nothing else happens. A broker might lose a churning case before an arbitration panel, but frequently he can go straight back to work, "burning his bridges" with each churn, yet always seeming to get new clients.

Unauthorized Trades

Elizabeth and Jay had been investing in the stock market for years. They'd been able to build up a sizable nest egg—$100,000—which they managed themselves through the use of a retail stockbroker at a major brokerage company. They called their own shots, did all their own research, and always gave their broker explicit instructions when they knew they would not be in touch.

For six months they'd been planning a Panama Canal cruise. They knew they would be away for three weeks so they decided to leave instructions with their broker should something unexpected happen with their account while they were gone. Jay called his broker, Jenny, and specifically instructed her to purchase 1,000 shares of a particular company's stock if the stock dropped to $10 a share. He made it very clear that she was not to perform any other purchases or sales without contacting them.

Two weeks passed. Elizabeth and Jay were having the time of their lives cruising through the Canal. You can probably guess what happened. The company's stocks traded down to $10 a share. Jenny bought 500 shares for Jay and Elizabeth. In fact, by the end of the day, she was able to fill the rest of the order at $9.75 a share.

Then something unexpected happened. Jenny noticed that the stock continued to drop and drop. When she came to work Monday morning, Jenny noticed that the stock was down to $6.50 a share. Excitedly, Jenny tried to call Elizabeth and Jay on the cruise ship but couldn't reach them. So Jenny decided to purchase 4,000 shares of the company's stock at the $6.50 price. By the end of the week, the stock was back up to $9, and Jenny was feeling proud that she was able to make an additional $10,000 for her clients.

But what happened next, nobody could have predicted. Over the weekend, the company announced that it planned to cut back its work force and might not be able to pay its quarterly dividend. On Monday, the stock began trading at $6 and continued down from there. Elizabeth and Jay arrived home and called Jenny to see if she had purchased the 1,000 shares at $10 for them. Horrified, they found out that not only had Jenny bought the 1,000 shares but also another 4,000, increasing their loss by $9,000.

Unauthorized trading is just that: Your stock salesperson executes a transaction that you have not authorized. The purchases Jenny made were clearly unauthorized and are clearly a violation of the law. Now she and the firm can be held accountable for Elizabeth's and Jerry's losses.

I have seen people wiped out by unauthorized transactions. Unauthorized trades seem to go hand in hand with other fraudulent practices. Whatever the circumstance, it is your duty to immediately notify your broker that these trades were not authorized, and you do not accept them.

Even if you have never written before, it is not too late to begin. When something goes wrong in your account, you should put it in writing and bring it to the broker's and branch manager's attention immediately.

Failure to Obey

Ann, a lawyer in the Public Defender's office for 15 years, had built up $75,000 through prudent investments. Preparing for an upcoming trial, she realized she'd be so engrossed in the trial that she had better make some provisions for her portfolio. She decided that should American Express go below $30 a share, she should sell her stock to protect from possible loss. She also had a nice profit in Chrysler stock and didn't want to see that stock go down below $15 a share. So she called her broker and gave him instructions to sell both if either went below those stated prices.

Halfway through the trial, she got a break for the Fourth of July. After sleeping late, she browsed through the newspaper and discovered that both Chrysler and American Express had sold down below her instructed level. Before the trial resumed, Ann quickly called her broker to see why she hadn't received confirmation slips on the sales of the two stocks.

The broker's response: "I forgot." The stock salesperson had forgotten to place the stop-loss orders for the two stocks. He just forgot. Now, American Express was at $25 and Chrysler, $11. Ann has a large loss. And the broker and the firm are in trouble.

Or are they? Brokerage firms usually defend failure to obey claims by denying that they ever received a stop-loss or limit order from the customer. They also throw the responsibility back to the customer: Surely the client should have known to expect a written confirmation of the stop-loss order and should have contacted the brokerage company when he didn't see any in the mail. When the brokerage firm utilizes this defense, the customer's credibility and pattern of other trading activity in the account can substantiate the customer's claim. Unless, of course, once again, it was all put in writing.

P.S. Write that Letter

The stock salesperson has failed to obey your direct orders. Maybe he forgot, maybe he decided you were wrong and he was going to save you from yourself. Is it your word against his? Not if you've put it in writing. When you give a broker a direct order, it is best to follow it up with a simple letter to the effect that "this will confirm our conversation in which I told you to . . ." In this way, you are protected by having a written request with which the stock salesperson must comply and one that will prove what your request was. It's that clear.

Broker Guarantees

Brokers often make guarantees to their clients. In some cases, the brokers actually put the guarantees in writing. In other cases, the limited partnerships advertise guarantees of principal and income. In either event, as explained in Chapter 5, there is no such animal as a true brokerage firm guarantee. Well, the brokerage company's standard defense is that it doesn't guarantee any of your investments. Even if a broker puts a guarantee in writing, the brokerage company will say, "He had no authority to make that guarantee." Yet stock salespeople make guarantees every day.

Failure to Supervise

All of the activities just set forth would not have occurred if there had been adequate supervision by the branch manager, compliance department, or other personnel at the brokerage firm.

It's their job, after all, to supervise their stock salespeople. It is the responsibility of the branch office manager to monitor all trades, all tickets, and all account activity occurring at his particular branch. With computer-generated "activity runs" and other commissioned printout schedules picked up by the compliance department, firms are supposed to supervise and catch illegal activities before they become a problem to the firm and to the customer. But their systems don't always work.

Remember, the churning in Don's and Ellen's account that we discussed in Chapter 5? Well, that's exactly what happened to Liz. In a year of churning, Don's and Ellen's stock salesperson had bought and sold $2,000,000 worth of stock with the $250,000 they'd entrusted to him. When they found out, they went straight to the branch manager, who admitted he was unaware of the activity generated by his stockbroker and would talk to him.

But how could $2,000,000 worth of trades take place in the same account and escape the branch manager's attention? He either looked the other way or he chose not to notice. The branch manager's failure to supervise his broker allowed the broker to blatantly juggle Don's and Ellen's money to his own ends. The branch manager has the duty to approve all new accounts, to review all orders, and to make sure that suitability requirements are not violated. Surely, if he'd been doing his job, he would have noticed that Don and Ellen were not high rollers, willing to trade a couple of million dollars a year off their $250,000. One look at their suitability forms with its stated conservative goals would have told him that.

The compliance departments at brokerage companies are also charged with supervision, as you might recall from your peek behind the scenes in Chapter 2. They should have caught all that trading and the excessive commissions in Don's and Ellen's account. The problem is so pervasive that major brokerage companies have written manuals for the branch managers, operations managers, and compliance staff to follow. The manuals set forth rules, procedures, and regulations that brokerage firm employees are expected to follow or act in accordance with. Stock salespeople are required to observe these firm rules as well as those of the NASD and the New York Stock Exchange.

So, when employees in these "safety net" areas "fail to supervise" and allow unlawful acts to slip through the net, the brokerage firms can be held responsible for the broker's improper conduct.

That goes for any mistake made anywhere along the line. As you recall, the compliance departments as well as the back office personnel of the various branch locations are understaffed, overworked, and underpaid. As a result, many problems slip through the proverbial cracks and end up on lawyers' desks. The back office might unintentionally remove a zero or move a decimal place here and there in your account. The firms are held accountable, and should be, for the activities of the stock salespeople and other firm personnel.

A Bag of Tricks

Some violations are best called what they are—tricks, sleight of hand, devices to maneuver and defraud—much like the hidden commission ploys discussed earlier. Here are several of the most practiced and most flagrant ones that are actionable:

Short-Term Trading of Mutual Funds

Both the New York Stock Exchange and NASD frown upon short-term trading of mutual funds. In fact, there is language contained within the NASD rules that prohibits stock salespeople from trading mutual funds on a short-term basis. This rule is found in the NASD Rules of Fair Practice, Article III, Section 2 (mentioned earlier). The Policy of the Board of Governors section entitled "Fair Practice With Customers" warns:

> Some practices that have resulted in disciplinary action and that clearly violate this responsibility for fair dealing are set forth below, as a guide to members. . . .
> Trading in Mutual Fund Shares
> . . . 3. Trading in mutual fund shares, particularly on a short-term basis. It is clear that normally these securities are not proper trading vehicles and such activity on its face may raise the question of rule violation.

This is because the product, by its very nature, is considered a long-term investment for the customer, and the only one who profits from short-term trading is the stock salesperson, because he can generate enormous commissions buying and selling mutual funds.

Front Running

Although brokerage firms frown upon it, front running does occur. Here's how front running works. A stock salesperson makes a solicitation for the purchase of a stock or option. At the same time or before he places the order to buy it for his client, he buys it for himself. If it is a "thin market"—a market that is lightly traded or has very little volume—and the stock salesperson makes a purchase for several clients, including himself, it's not uncommon for the security or option to go up in value. Then it's up to the broker to decide who gets the best price. In other words, if the stock salesperson buys a $20 stock for six different clients, including himself, and the stock goes from $20 to $21 per share, who's going to pay $20 per share and who's going to pay $21 per share?

It's illegal for the stock salesperson to put that stock in his own account at $20 a share and then place it in his client's account at a higher price. But what a temptation.

Front running can also apply to the sale of a security. For example, a broker has ten clients, including himself, that he wants to move out of a particular stock, and he sells the stock starting at $20 a share. By the time he's done, the stock has gone down to $18.75. Once again, the stock salesperson has to decide what price per share each client receives. If the broker places the sale into his account at $20 a share, and the other clients get the $18.75 a share, how is anyone going to know?

Offloading a Loser

A cousin to front running, but far worse morally and legally, is the practice of placing bad trades in a particular client's account. If a stock salesperson trades for his own account or for his favorite clients, it is possible, due to the nature of the system, for him to make several purchases of the same stock. For instance, the broker places 15 people into Intel starting at $110 a share, and by the end of the day, the stock ends at $112.50 a share. The stock salesperson can decide who gets to buy Intel at $110 and who buys it at $112. Now, to complicate matters, what if the stock salesperson wanted to purchase 1,000 shares of Intel at $110 per share, with the hopes of getting out of the stock at $113 a share, to make a $3,000 profit by the end of the day? And what if suddenly, in the middle of all this buying, a negative announcement about Intel is made and Intel plummets to $104 per share? If that broker didn't want to take a $6,000 hit (loss), and he was simultaneously purchasing the stock for a number of his other customers, guess where that stock loss could end up? That's right, in somebody else's account. Obviously the same can be said of selling stock.

How does anyone stop this? The ultimate responsibility for catching these illegal activities rests with the supervisory personnel of the compliance department. Most of the major firms have, as mentioned earlier, safety nets attempting to catch the unscrupulous stock salesperson who is performing these kinds of activities. But nonetheless, these acts fall through the cracks. As the size of the firm shrinks, the compliance personnel and departments also become smaller, and the ability of the compliance personnel, if there are any, to catch unscrupulous brokers becomes more and more limited.

Trading Away

This practice is so serious that the stock salesperson caught trading away is usually susceptible to disciplinary charges and possible suspension or revocation of his license. When a broker is trading away, he enters into a deal with a person not associated with the brokerage firm and sells that person's deal or product to one of his clients, who is *also* a client of the firm. This bit of moonlighting is self-serving at best and fraudulent at worst. I am handling a case in which the stock salesperson not only committed $600,000 in churning violations but had trade-aways of $700,000, receiving $70,000 personally for each outside deal. A broker who trades away knows he is violating both firm policy and rules of the New York Stock Exchange and NASD. Always be sure that any product you are buying is one that is being sold through the stock salesperson's firm and not an outside deal offered by the broker and some other party.

Your First Steps to Take

Sour Grapes

I need to be very clear about one point: Just because you have lost money doesn't mean you always have the right to take your stockbroker to arbitration to recover it. You have a reason to be upset, but you may just be experiencing sour grapes if your stockbroker did everything right. *If* you've been advised of the risk, *if* the transaction meets your suitability requirements, and *if* the broker's recommendation was reasonably based, you probably don't have a case. You made the decision, and you lost your money.

Sometimes, though, it's hard to accept that you're the culpable one. It is difficult to say goodbye to one's money and all too easy to blame someone else.

Susan, a stockbroker, worked for a regional brokerage firm. The firm came out with a recommendation to buy stock in a national toy manufacturing company. Part of the recommendation was based upon excitement over a video game the toy company was about to release. The firm's research department thought it would be a big hit. Believing that the video game would possibly cause the stock to double or triple in value, Susan went through her client list, pulled out ten clients she believed could afford to take the risk, and called them. With each client, she was careful to explain the great amount of risk in this type of investment. If the sales didn't materialize, she told them, other traders might take a dim view of the stock and sell it down, and that meant a possible loss, as in all investments in the stock market.

Bill, who had been a client of Susan's for six months, liked the idea and gave her permission to go ahead and buy 1,000 shares at $8 a share. Two weeks later, the video game came out and the stock shot up to $12. Susan told Bill the good news and advised him to take a profit; instead, Bill told her to buy another 1,000 shares at $12. Susan was quick to caution him about the risk involved in buying a stock that had just jumped 50% in value. Bill, though, was unconcerned, firmly believing he had a winner. So Susan bought the stock for him.

For the next month, the video games sold briskly, and the stock jumped another three points, to $15 a share. Then it slowed down and dropped back to $12.

"Why did the stock go down?" Bill asked Susan. She didn't know but told him that it was normal for a stock to give up a few points after such an enormous rise. At Bill's request, she probed further. After talking with her research department and searching for any news items released by the company, she found nothing to report.

A week went by. The stock dropped to $10, and suddenly, it was suspended from trading, pending a news announcement: The toy company announced that although sales were brisk, they were having difficulty meeting their production demands, and to make things worse, they would have to cease production at one of their facilities due to computer problems.

When the stock opened for trading after that bit of news, it sold down to $6 a share. Bill exploded, accusing Susan of incompetence and failure to properly advise him—a glaringly untrue fact. Accusation or not, Susan still felt an obligation to continue advising him. The smart thing for Bill to do, she said, would be to sell out now, at a loss, because the stock might go even lower if the company could not fix the production problems. Again, Bill ignored her advice. Three weeks later, the stock was at $3. Bill finally told Susan to sell.

Bill filed an action against Susan, accusing her of causing him to lose $14,000. But Susan did everything she was supposed to do. She advised him of the risks, advised him against buying additional shares, and then advised him to sell when the stock went down. In reality, Bill was blaming Susan for the vagaries of the stock market and for his own greed, not for her performance.

Sour grapes clients can't accept the idea that no one's to blame for a loss of their money . . . no one but themselves. They have lost money and someone's got to pay. In Bill's case, it will not be Susan, because everything was well-documented, just as I have recommended all through these pages.

Sour grapes clients like Bill have overtaxed the system. If you have a case, then by all means, investigate possible legal action. But investing in the stock market, remember, is never riskless. As long as you are completely aware of the risk, the recommendation is reasonably based, and the product is suitable for you, the stockbroker has probably done nothing wrong.

Your first step is to take a good look at your situation. Has there been a rule of law violated? Losing money is hard on anyone, but be sure you have a case before you pursue it.

Here are two more factors that an arbitration panel will take into consideration about you and your case.

Sophistication of the Customer

Were you able to understand the risk?

If you had prior trading experience, education, or business expertise that made you fully capable of comprehending the risk in an investment that lost money, an arbitration panel may not be persuaded that you should be awarded damages. One can't hide behind a mask of ignorance, the panel might say.

One important note, though: Sophistication in one area of business does not necessarily mean that a client would understand or comprehend the risk involved in a particular investment. Recent cases have established the proposition that even accountants and businesspeople who are sophisticated in their own specializations may be able to recover monies lost at a brokerage firm.

Similarity of Activity

When you file a claim against a brokerage company, your past can come back to haunt you. Your activities at other brokerage companies become, suddenly, an important and relevant issue.

If you have performed similar transactions at other brokerage firms, your claim for unsuitability will probably come to a screeching halt once that fact is introduced into evidence. It's not much more than sour grapes for a client to complain about improper recommendations by a stockbroker at one firm when that client engaged in the same or similar transactions at another firm.

Duty to Mitigate

You've decided you have a case.

Then there's an all-important question you need to answer: When you first noticed a problem in your account, what did you do—besides hit the roof? If the answer is sit and hope things would get better, you may have a hard time recovering your money. Your actions at that moment may weigh heavily during an arbitration hearing down the line.

In most cases, you'll become aware of a problem in your account before you are left with nothing. Once you notice there is something wrong, as mentioned in Chapter 5, you should fire off a letter to your broker instructing him to cease and desist from engaging in any further transactions in your account. Then fire off another letter informing the branch manager of the problem. You can make all the fiery telephone calls you like, but you must put this into writing.

Perhaps the most important step to take, however, is the liquidation of anything in your account that is subjecting you to a loss. Once you discover that your broker has committed an act which has caused a loss, you can't sit back and hope that things will improve or, even worse, not care under the mistaken belief that your broker is responsible for *all* losses in your account. Oh, no. You must *mitigate the damages* by liquidating your position immediately. Why? Because if you fail to mitigate—that is, you fail to *cut your losses*—an arbitration panel might deduct the money that could have been saved if you had liquidated immediately upon discovering the problem in your account.

Let me give you an example. Let us suppose you went away on a vacation and upon returning opened your mail to discover that your broker had purchased 1,000 shares of ZZ Best Carpet Company at $10 a share. He did this in your absence because he genuinely thought the stock was going to double in a couple of weeks. After all, it was one of the hottest stocks on Wall Street and everybody thought the company was really going to climb sky-high. You didn't authorize your broker to buy that thousand shares, and you're not very happy about the $10,000 that was debited against your account. However, you are delighted to see that the stock is at $12 a share. After all, who would turn down a $2,000 profit made during a one-week vacation?

Let us further suppose that you don't say a single word to your broker, even though you know that he had no right to buy the stock. Now let us suppose that one week later rumors start circulating that ZZ Best Carpet Company just might be in trouble. You open the morning paper to discover that your $12 stock is now $9 a share, but instead of calling your broker and complaining about the purchase, you sit back and wait to see what develops. Much to your dismay, a few days later the stock falls to $3 a share when it is announced that ZZ Best Carpet Company has taken *everybody* to the cleaners.

Do you think the brokerage company should be responsible for your losses? Many of you will say yes. But you didn't mitigate your damages. When you discovered your broker had performed an illegal activity, you should have called him and no matter what the stock was selling for, had him immediately liquidate the stock. That would have put a stop to his illegal activity and put a stop to his control over your account. When you learned of his illegal activity and understood it, you relieved the broker of his responsibility and his control over your account. You would then have the responsibility of managing that particular trade.

Because you did not inform your broker of your desire to liquidate at $12 a share, or certainly at $9 when you had a $1 loss, the brokerage company will defend the case by saying that you had every opportunity to liquidate your position before you had a loss, or certainly at $9 a share when you had a one point loss. This applies to any kind of trade in any kind of account. If you discover that your account has been churned and you continue to allow your broker to churn and burn with the hope that he is going to make back the money he has lost, you very well may be cutting off your chance of recovering any money.

I realize that it seems unfair to be forced to take a loss from a transaction that was not of your own doing, but it is essential that you mitigate to prevent further losses from occurring. Because if you don't mitigate, an arbitration panel might shift the responsibility from the broker to you.

Write Another Letter

After you have "mitigated your damages" and fired off those letters, you're not quite finished writing. Now a cooler head must prevail. You should sit down and outline what, in particular, you feel the stock salesperson did to cause your loss. Every fact you write down must be correct and accurate. State whatever rule of law the stock salesperson broke, and state the actions (or inactions) he took that directly caused your loss.

Don't forget, if you were aware of the risk or were fully informed prior to making that investment decision, you may not be able to recover anything. But if your stock salesperson misrepresented a fact, omitted a fact, churned your account, failed to obey, or committed any of the violations described earlier, you should outline all the events that occurred from the time of the sale to the time of the loss, and then reduce them to a letter that you should send to the branch office manager.

You might find it useful to contact an attorney and make sure that the letter is properly worded so that nothing in the letter exposes you to further problems. Within 30 days, the brokerage firm should respond, no doubt setting forth why it believes you are responsible for the losses.

That is the time you decide whether you will try to recover your money and whether you will do it on your own or with the help of competent legal counsel—the topic of Chapter 11.

CHAPTER 11

When All Else Fails: How to Get Your Money Back

The Arbitration System

You've lost money and you discover that your broker, through incompetence or outright fraud, is responsible. What do you do? Do you just kiss your money good-bye and kick yourself, or can you recover your money? If you find yourself a victim, you won't be going to court—you will be going to arbitration.

So what is arbitration?

Since the landmark United States Supreme Court case of *Shearson–American Express, Inc. v. McMahon,* arbitration has become the most frequently used method of resolving securities disputes between investors and brokerage companies. Prior to the Supreme Court holding in the *Shearson-McMahon* case, investors had a right to file an action against their brokerage company through the court system. However, all of that changed when the Supreme Court ruled in *McMahon* that investors who had signed predispute arbitration clauses in their brokerage account agreements could be compelled to resolve their disputes by way of arbitration and not be allowed to proceed through a court action.

Today, as a condition of allowing an investor (customer) to open an account with a brokerage firm, virtually all brokerage companies require an investor to sign an agreement that contains a predispute arbitration clause. This clause, which is usually contained within the new account form, option agreement, or margin agreement, requires that any dispute between the customer (investor) and the brokerage company be resolved through arbitration rather than litigation. Most brokerage firms even have clauses that specify which industry forum may be used when invoking the arbitration process.

The Arbitration Explosion

In 1872, the New York Stock Exchange became the first securities exchange to provide an alternative to litigation by means of the arbitration process. Then, in 1925, Congress passed the Federal Arbitration Act, which made arbitration a legitimate alternative to litigation. The purpose of the act was to provide aggrieved parties a quicker, more economical resolution of their claims than was available in the court system.

Commercial arbitration has been used with great success for decades as an alternative method to resolve disputes not related to the securities industry. More recently, state courts have been ordering parties to arbitration as an alternative method to relieve congestion in the overburdened court system. Labor relation claims between an employee and an employer, contract disputes between a motion picture studio and an employee, and construction defect claims between a customer and a contractor have seen a dramatic increase in the use of arbitration as a means of resolving these disputes.

But nothing can match the explosion seen in the filing of arbitration claims related to securities matters in recent years. The United States General Accounting Office (GAO) published a report to congressional requestors in May of 1992 entitled *Securities Arbitration, How Investors Fare.* This report, over two years in the making, evaluated issues relating to the arbitration process sponsored by the securities industry self-regulatory organizations (SROs). The NASD is the largest SRO governing securities in the United States. Many of you undoubtedly recognize the NASD as the regulator of the over-the-counter market known as the NASDAQ system. The

NASD is also the largest forum in which arbitration proceedings are commenced.

The GAO report found that during the last decade, the number of arbitration cases filed with the SROs had increased approximately 540%, from 830 in 1980 to 5,332 in 1990. Also, between 1980 and 1990 the annual share volume in securities at the NASD increased about 400%, from 6.9 billion shares to 33.4 billion shares (see page 18, second paragraph, of the report). The report further states that in 1990, the NASD and the New York Stock Exchange together processed 94% of the disputes filed for arbitration at the securities industry forums. The NASD received almost four times the case load as did the New York Stock Exchange.

Well, what do all these numbers mean anyway? What they mean is that if you have a problem with your broker, you are no longer going to court, you are going to be involved in this arbitration process. Except in rare circumstances, it is a panel of arbitrators who will decide whether you should be allowed to recover your losses from the brokerage company. Let's take a journey through the arbitration process and find out how the arbitration system works and what people make up this panel of arbitrators who will be deciding your case.

The facts are taken from a real-life case history. The names have been changed to respect the privacy of all parties to the controversy. Before we embark on this journey, you might be asking yourself, "Well, it's great to hear about one case, but what chance do I really have of getting any money back?" Well, I'm glad you asked that question. Before I answer it, however, I want to talk just a moment about statistics.

Juggling Numbers: The Truth About Statistics

I have heard it said that you can do almost anything with statistics. The case we are about to delve into was interesting from a statistical point of view because the brokerage company tried to show, by numbers-juggling, that my client had made $5,000 during the history of her account, when in fact our numbers showed that she had lost about $65,000. During my closing argument, I stood up in front of the three arbitrators and said, "You know, statistics fascinate me, but they also frighten me; and in this particular case, they downright scare me to death. We should conclude this case as soon as possible because if the brokerage company is allowed to juggle its numbers any further, we're going to end up owing the brokerage company money before this hearing is over."

I was referring to our calculations, which established a $65,000 loss while the brokerage company's pencil pushers attempted to prove that my client had made $5,000. Now what does this mean in relation to arbitration awards? It means that statistics are nothing more than numbers and that each case should be decided on its own merits. No two cases are exactly the same, just as no two people are identical. Scott, an attorney who represents brokerage companies, once remarked to me that he believed 50% of the cases brought by aggrieved investors were nonmeritorious. That's right. In 50% of the cases filed against brokerage companies, the investors didn't have a case; they were just suing their stockbroker because they lost money, not because the stockbroker had done something wrong. These sour grapes investors didn't have too much difficulty finding an attorney either.

Sour Grapes and Sour Lawyers

Unfortunately, there are many attorneys who have hung out their shingles during the past decade only to find a crowded arena in which cases are fewer and fewer, and the bills higher and higher. What this means is that many lawyers unqualified to handle securities cases are taking them because they need the money. These less than scrupulous lawyers are accepting cases that should be rejected. This is unfair to investors because it gives them false hope and this is unfair to brokerage firms because it sticks them with unnecessary and expensive legal fees. This is the bottom line: The statistics take into consideration all of the cases filed—the sour grapes cases, as well as the sour attorneys who represent clients who might have legitimate claims.

Is Arbitration Fair?

Now that you have been duly informed by my statistical caveat, let's take a look at the results of the GAO study on the fairness of arbitration. First of all, it is comforting to note that the study did not find any difference between arbitrations commenced under SROs and those filed under independent organizations like the American Arbitration Association (AAA). This is important because many attorneys had felt that the results were significantly better under the AAA than they were under SROs.

The GAO found that arbitrators decided in favor of investors in nearly 60% of the cases in which investors filed claims against broker-dealers. Investors receiving awards got an overall average of 64% and 52% of the amount claimed, respectively, at the NASD and New York Stock Exchange. The analysis did not include punitive damages claimed or awarded. In some instances, investors received more than the total amount they claimed. This was because arbitrators awarded the investor attorneys fees, interest, and other costs that investors requested in their claims by name, but not by dollar amount. Surprisingly, arbitrators awarded investors the total amount claimed or more in 30% of the cases. Also interesting was the fact that securities investors whose cases were decided after a hearing were 1.4 times more likely to receive an award than investors whose cases were decided only on a review of written evidence.

Later in this chapter we will discuss why you might need to have an attorney sitting beside you when you present your case at the arbitration hearing. Before we get there, I thought you might like to note that attorney representation, according to the GAO report, did not affect whether an investor received an award—however, it did affect the size of the award when made. According to the GAO report, investors who were represented by attorneys were 1.6 times more likely to receive an award in excess of 60% of their claim. One more statistic before we meet Mary—claims under $20,000 were 3.7 times more likely than larger claims to result in awards greater than 60% of the amount claimed. I guess you could say arbitrators felt less constrained to give away money when it was under $20,000.

Mary: A Case Study

Now I would like to introduce you to Mary, a lady who used the services of a securities litigation expert—me—and, although I'm turning to the last page of our story before we get there, she met with a very positive result. The arbitration panel awarded Mary $65,000—her out-of-pocket loss plus the interest she would have received had she left her money in a bank.

Mary had lived the life that many women dream of but few fulfill. Quitting school in the eleventh grade, Mary began an active professional dance career that included Broadway hits such as *A Chorus Line*, several tours of Vietnam with Bob Hope, and numerous appearances on television shows such as "The Tonight Show." However, the image and allure of professional dance also has its dark side. Mary succumbed, as do many dancers, to multiple and recurring injuries that became so severe she was forced to terminate her career prematurely. What made matters worse for Mary was the fact that she had a learning disability that severely reduced her ability to read. In fact, Mary found it difficult to go on auditions because she wasn't able to read the scripts for casting calls. The only way she could prepare for a part was to receive the script in advance and then painstakingly, word by word, slowly put the sentences together so that she could understand what she was reading.

Her learning disability had far more impact on her ability to understand or comprehend simple arithmetic. In fact, she felt so uncomfortable trying to decipher her bank statements that she didn't even bother to balance her checkbook. During her years as a successful dancer, Mary's talents were managed by her agent, Don. Mary and Don developed a close personal relationship, as do many agents and entertainment personalities. He guided her through the major decisions of her career: negotiating contracts, deciding which parts to take and which to turn down, and generally advising her. Don knew a great deal about Mary's character and personal tastes.

Before the torn ligaments and ripped cartilage ended Mary's career, she had switched to another theatrical agency, thus terminating her relationship with Don. Following her dancing career, Mary fell in love with and married Richard. After approximately five years, the marriage ended in divorce. The glitter and glamour of Broadway seemed farther and farther in the distant past. Because Mary was unable to work after her marriage and knew that she could not secure any jobs in the entertainment field, it was of the utmost importance that she conservatively manage her savings and the money she received from her divorce settlement.

Mary's learning disability coupled with her limited education made it difficult for her to find employment. The learning handicap affected her ability to work in service-oriented jobs such as a sec-retary or a bookkeeper, and Mary had no formal training other than dance. Mary had received $300,000 from her divorce settle-ment and deposited the money into CDs and a mutual fund.

One night, while dining with a friend at a famous Hollywood restaurant, Mary bumped into her former agent, Don. For several hours Don and Mary reminisced about her glory years and how fun it had been to work with Bob Fosse, Bob Hope, and other notables. Don asked Mary what she was doing now, and she told him about her recent divorce and the funds that she was going to need to live on for the rest of her life. He asked Mary where she intended to invest her money. Mary said, "My mom and dad always told me to keep my money in a bank account, so all my savings, together with the divorce payments, have been kept in CDs at dif-ferent banks. That way I know I will always be protected, and I can sleep at night. The one thing I never want to do is to become a bag lady. You know I see those women on the streets of Los Angeles, and it terrifies me. I've even had dreams about pushing a shopping cart around with all my worldly possessions inside the cart. I just don't want it to happen to me."

The Hustle

Don looked at Mary with a puzzled stare and then said, "Well, you know, I work for Shearson Lehman Brothers as a financial con-sultant, and I manage a lot of money for famous people in Hol-lywood. I've got to tell you that your money just isn't safe in a bank. You know, Bank of America is having lots of problems right now, and if your bank should fold, it could take up to one year to get your money out of the bank. To make matters worse, your money is losing value every day that it's in a bank. The reason for this is that inflation is eating away at your dollars every minute, and if you don't make enough money on your money, your dollar is going to be worth less when you get it out of the bank. I think what you should do is come meet with me at my office, and let me set up a savings plan for you that will be guaranteed. You won't stand the risk of losing any of your money, and inflation won't eat away and ravage your savings." Mary thought that sounded like a good idea, and instead of going into the office to meet with Don, she invited him to have dinner at her apartment the next week.

A few nights later, Don arrived with flowers in one hand and a bottle of wine in the other. When they sat down to dinner, Mary's mother joined them, and, for the first part of the evening, they talked about old times. But when it came to money matters, Don was quite emphatic. "Your money just isn't safe in a bank. We all know about your learning disability and how much trouble it is for you to be able to balance your checkbook. I think the best thing for you to do is to turn the money management over to me. You go enjoy your life; let me worry about how to invest your money. After all, you know I would never do anything to harm you. Wherever I invest your money, it will always be safe, conservative, and risk-free." Mary's mother emphasized how worried her daughter was about becoming a bag lady. Her mother lived in a federal housing project and knew the importance of making every penny count. Mom felt good about Don because he and Mary had worked together before, and she knew that Don would watch out for her daughter.

Later in the week, Mary and her mom went to see Don. During the ride in the elevator to the 20th floor of his Century City office, Mary felt a bit of trepidation about embarking on this new journey. Her mom comforted her with reassuring words like: "You know, Don will always look out for you, don't worry about anything. It will be all right." Stepping out of the elevator into the well-appointed lobby of Shearson Lehman Brothers, the two ladies were asked to have a seat while the receptionist called Don to announce their arrival. A few moments later, Don appeared and escorted them back to his new office.

The Sting

As Don spoke to them, you could see how animated and excited he was about his recent promotion. "Don't let me forget to show you the award I just got as one of the top brokers in this office." The tone quickly changed when they reached Don's office. "Well, let's get down to business. I've given this a lot of serious thought, and I've come up with the best game plan given your unwillingness to risk any money, your desire for safety, and my desire to see your money grow to protect you against the ravages of inflation."

Mary looked at Don and said, "I'll follow your advice, whatever you say, as long as I can sleep at night and not have to worry about watching my investments."

"Don't worry about watching your investments," Don said. "That's my responsibility. You just worry about having a good time and see if you can get a script or two early enough so that you're able to go out on an interview. I'll watch everything from here, and if anything needs to be done, I'll give you a call."

Don went on: "Here's what we're going to do. First, we are going to liquidate all of your CDs. I'll put your money into a limited partnership and bonds. The bonds will give you a good return for your investment, and the limited partnership will give you the growth needed to protect you against inflation. That way your portfolio will be safely invested for growth and income."

That sounded great to Mary. Looking at her mother for reassurance, she took her mother's hand and squeezed it gently.

"See, darling," her mother said, "I told you there was nothing to worry about; Don will take care of everything."

At the conclusion of their meeting, Mary signed the necessary documents to open the account and said good-bye to Don, who got up from his desk to escort her out. Don didn't forget to point out the plaque next to his name as they walked back through the hallway to the reception room.

Unsuitable Investments

Well, all would be fine indeed if the story ended here. But this was just the beginning, not the end, and things went downhill once Don got his hands on Mary's money. Don's initial investments were Macy's junk bonds, a tax-free mutual fund, and an illiquid high-risk limited partnership. The truth was that the Macy's junk bonds were an extremely high-risk investment suitable only for those willing to take the enormous risk commensurate with bonds yielding such a high rate of return. To make matters worse, the limited partnership was a start-up company with no previous track record investing in the cable industry, a highly competitive market and a newly developing industry looking years into the future before generating any real income. And finally, let us not forget the tax-free mutual fund from which Don earned a 5% commission. Given Mary's income, there was no reason to put her into tax-free investments because she could not derive the benefit of tax-free income unless she was in a much higher tax bracket. In fact, she was losing money from investing in a tax-free mutual fund because she could not avail herself of the tax benefits and she was earning a much lower yield than available from taxable investments.

Further complicating the picture was the ludicrous strategy of putting Mary's assets on margin. That's right. Don borrowed money against Mary's portfolio to make the purchases of the tax-free mutual fund and junk bonds. He did this with the idea, so he claimed at the arbitration hearing, of increasing her overall return. The real reason he borrowed against her portfolio was to make purchases that generated commissions for himself that he otherwise would not have been able to make without the use of the margin. In other words, he borrowed against her assets strictly for the purpose of buying more so that he could make more money.

For the first three months, everything seemed fine. Everything that is but Mary's ability to read, much less comprehend, her monthly statements. Remember that Mary had difficulty deciphering her monthly bank statement. Well, Mary couldn't even get past the first line of her monthly brokerage statement. So what did she do? She did the obvious and correct thing. She called Don to find out how to read her statement. It was difficult for Don to walk Mary through her brokerage statements. She made no less than three trips to the brokerage company and sat down in his office to try to understand what all the mumbo jumbo meant. Finally, after the third session, Don gave up.

"Listen, Mary," he said, once again playing the old mentor and friend, "you're just not going to be able to understand these statements. Frankly, most clients have a hard time understanding them, so don't feel bad about it. You just call me whenever you want, and I'll pull up your account on the ol' computer and tell you exactly how you're doing."

Mary felt reassured and left the office knowing that she could call Don at any time to find out what was going on in her account. Once or twice a week, and sometimes as little as once or twice a month, Mary would call Don to find out how her account was doing. He would always paint a rosy picture about the limited partnership acquiring more and more cable companies, the bonds earning more and more income, and the mutual funds making her all of that tax-exempt income.

Mary Discovers Her Problem

After four years, Mary thought that everything was going along just fine. During those years, Don had switched Mary in and out of several products—all in her best interest—to keep her income high and her long-term growth at its fullest potential. In reality, he had moved her from one junk bond to another, and from one mutual fund to another, generating unnecessary commissions clearly in violation of exchange rules and policies. His supervisor, the branch manager, had duly approved all of his trades, including the original investment in the junk bond. Now understand, I am not talking about a junk bond mutual fund, which is made up of hundreds of other bonds. I am talking about taking Mary's life savings and placing 62% of all of her money into one junk bond—and what junk bond was that? Well, if you didn't think that Macy's was bad enough (it later went into bankruptcy), Don jumped right out of the frying pan and into the blazing furnace of TWA junk bonds. Wall Street was quite concerned about the earnings reports of airlines, but TWA had been at the forefront of worries and eventually went into bankruptcy.

Four years after she had opened her account, Mary met Charles, a literary agent and business manager. Deciding to live together before their intended marriage, Mary asked her broker to change the address on her statements and have them sent to her fiancè's address. The first month at her new abode, Mary was going through the morning mail when she noticed her monthly Shearson statement. Opening up the envelope, she turned to Charles and asked him if he wouldn't mind taking a look at her statement to assure her that everything was in order.

As Charles sorted through the description of the items in her account, his forehead developed a frown, which turned into a puzzled, worried look.

"You know, Mary, I think I ought to have Paul take a look at these statements. As my investment advisor, Paul manages all my assets and makes all decisions regarding my investments. I don't think what this broker has done is right for you. I think you're exposed to a lot of undue risks, and I certainly don't like the cable company limited partnership you own."

That afternoon Mary and Charles went over to see Paul, who also happened to live in the same townhouse complex. After he examined the statements, Paul became very concerned. He asked Mary to show him some earlier statements so that he could get a handle on what had gone on in her account. Fortunately, she had kept most of her previous statements, and, after a couple of days, Paul was ready to meet again with Mary and Charles.

"I've got some bad news to tell you," he began. "I don't like what I see going on in your account, and, in fact, we've got to do something about it right away. In the first place, I think you've lost a lot of money from the improper trading that has gone on in your account. But you've got something that's much worse. You have a deteriorating position in TWA junk bonds, and you own a limited partnership whose value I have been unable to ascertain. I have called up several friends of mine who are going to get back to me with a quote, but as you might not know, limited partnerships are very difficult to liquidate. If you can sell them, it's usually at substantially less than what you paid for them, even though your statement shows them at full face value."

Mary began to cry. The more she cried, the more hysterical she became until finally even Charles' comforting could not calm her down. Luckily for Mary, Paul knew what to do. He immediately called the broker to arrange for a meeting to discuss what had gone on in Mary's account and what could be done to rectify the substantial losses that had occurred. He somewhat calmed Mary's fears, but in the back of her mind the image of the bag lady had once again reappeared. She kept trying to keep the bag lady out of her thoughts, but each night as she fell asleep, the image of herself wandering from street to street pushing a shopping cart brought her to tears.

The Wall Street Defense

Early the next week, Mary, Charles, and Paul went to see Don, the broker. Don denied any wrongdoing and emphatically stated that he had done everything with Mary's best interest at heart. Paul pointed out that Mary had lost close to $80,000 in her account, and with an overall investment of approximately $240,000, this represented one-third of everything Mary had in the world. Don pointed out that while it was true Mary had lost approximately $80,000, she had nonetheless received income of $85,000; so, in fact, her account had made a $5,000 profit over the four-year period. It's interesting to note that Don's perspective of the accounts' performance is precisely the defense the brokerage companies use when playing their statistical numbers game.

If you recall my caveat about statistical maneuvering and numbers juggling, you will remember that statistics can be shown to do just about anything you want them to. In Mary's situation, although it is true that she received $85,000 in income over a four-year period, the brokerage company and Don failed to consider the time value of money. What would have happened had Mary left her money in a perfectly safe CD? What would that money be worth today? If Mary had bought one-year CDs during the last four years, she would conservatively have earned at least a 7% return. That would average out to just over $65,000 of interest with *no* loss of principal. In other words, if Mary had never met Don, her $240,000 would have been intact and she would have earned another $65,000 on top of that. So her savings would have grown to $305,000. But through Don's splendid investments, Mary's savings grew from $240,000 to $245,000 in a period of four years.

Don just would not listen to reason. Paul kept hammering at the time value of money and tried to explain to Don the irrational strategy of borrowing against the portfolio and thereafter investing in tax-free mutual funds and an illiquid limited partnership. Yet even with the reality of Mary's losses hanging in the air, Don just would not get the point. Finally, Charles could no longer contain himself. He and Don began to shout at one another over the desk until it was painfully obvious that Don didn't intend to do anything to restore Mary's losses. On the way out of the office, Paul suggested contacting the branch manager to see if he could work something out.

Later in the week, Paul did speak with the branch manager, who said that he would look into the matter and get back to him. As is the case in just about all brokerage company disputes, the branch manager gave the well-known and deeply overused brokerage company defense, which goes something like this:

Well, you know, I'm really sorry about what happened. The broker did try to do the best job he could for his client; but as we all know, none of us can accurately predict the future, and, after all, it was only an opinion. I guess what I'm trying to say is that we at Shearson Lehman Brothers are not guarantors of our clients' money. We all try to do the best job we possibly can to see to it that our clients' money is properly and prudently invested. Unfortunately, sometimes investments just don't seem to work out the right way. And I guess this is one of those times. While I feel deep regret about the losses that Mary suffered, there's just nothing I can do about it. My hands are tied. If I could do something about it, I really would. But the market is a risky place, and Don did explain all the risks involved in Mary's investments to her. If she really wanted to have safe investments, she should have kept her money in a CD . . . blah, blah, and further blah.

That, ladies and gentlemen, is exactly what you are going to encounter when something goes wrong in your account and you write that first letter to the branch manager. But don't let it dissuade you from continuing on and making Wall Street pay you back.

Branch managers, compliance officers, and Wall Street attorneys are all trained to tell investors that there is nothing they can do when a client suffers a loss. It's all part of the game. Wall Street does not want to have the image of a soft touch. They want to make it as difficult as possible for you, the investor, to recover money, no matter how improper the broker's actions.

Let me make one point perfectly clear right now: I am not saying that in every case a brokerage company will not offer one single dime. However, even in the most egregious of complaints, a brokerage company will usually propose a settlement that is less than your out-of-pocket loss. It might offer to return a portion of the money you lost if a broker performed illegal acts subjecting the broker to criminal or severe civil penalties, but the key word is "portion." Unless a brokerage company is exposed to damages in excess of the out-of-pocket loss such as attorneys' fees, costs, and punitive damages, only then will it enter into a discussion concerning payment in full.

Cutting Your Losses: The Duty to Mitigate

Paul was unflustered by the branch manager's negative approach. He immediately liquidated the limited partnership and all unsuitable assets in Mary's account. Paul elected to hold on to the TWA bonds because he felt that if there was a settlement between the creditors and TWA, Mary would probably get more than the bonds were selling for at that time. This brings up an important point mentioned in Chapter 10. If something goes wrong in your account (that is, if a broker performs an act that may subject him or his firm to liability), you may be duty-bound under the law to act immediately to prevent any further losses from occurring. This duty about which I am speaking, you might recall, is the duty to mitigate damages or (in nonlegal terms) the duty to cut losses. Remember you just can't sit back and allow that broker or that position to continue to your detriment. So Paul did the right thing by liquidating Mary's account. He mitigated her losses and set up the right sequence of events for her to recover her money.

The Solution

What should Paul do now? He certainly wasn't in a position to commence an arbitration proceeding, having never done this before. But who does he turn to? How does he find an attorney? Which attorney is really an expert? All of these are difficult questions to answer. Searching for a competent attorney, one that is familiar with all the nuances of the arbitration system, is not a simple matter. You can't just look them up in the phone book. Well, one day Paul was watching "Smart Money," hosted by Ken and Daria Dolan. Their television show is an informative, enjoyable walk down Wall Street that is interesting and can teach you how to invest, how to protect yourself, and where to get help when you need it.

Paul was watching Ken and Daria while they were interviewing me. I was talking about broker abuse and the remedies available to investors for the recovery of their money from a brokerage company. Paul contacted the show, and eventually we met to discuss Mary's case.

When we sat down together and went over the statements, Paul made it abundantly clear what had happened. As a seasoned trial attorney and a former prosecutor, I knew no matter how good Mary's case looked on paper, the brokerage company would try to portray her as a sophisticated investor who fully understood all the risks which were adequately explained to her. Therefore I knew that my next job was to interview Mary to determine her degree of sophistication, what she knew or didn't know about her account, and what kind of witness she would make—that is, was she believable, would the arbitrators like her, and was her story believable.

The key element of any brokerage company dispute is the credibility of the witnesses. If a client is credible and believable, it will go a long way toward winning their case. Obviously I cannot evaluate the credibility of the broker because I have not met him. I must rely upon my client's description of the broker and any information I may obtain about his previous history or background.

Shortly after my meeting with Paul, I interviewed Mary. I found her to be a friendly and likeable woman, lacking any degree of sophistication in financial matters and particularly handicapped in her ability to read brokerage account statements. I felt that her story was believable, and that *she* was believable. Having evaluated her case from a documentary standpoint and feeling comfortable about her ability to testify, I informed Paul and Mary that I would be pleased to represent her.

We have already learned that you should never throw away anything you receive from a brokerage company. Although Mary had kept most of the brokerage documents, there were several internal documents that I wanted to see before I filed her claim. Mary filled out a request for information form, which I forwarded to the brokerage company. After receiving the requested documents, I was ready to prepare her claim.

Claim Preparation

There is a substantial difference between arbitration and court proceedings, which can be seen right from the beginning with the drafting of the claim. As you might already know, when someone wants to commence litigation in a court setting, a complaint is filed. This is a legal document prepared under strict rules of the court, which require the correct paper size, color, margins, and other arbitrary rules, which if not met will prevent your complaint from being accepted for filing. The rules of pleading not only vary from state to state but can even vary from county to county and court to court. Thus it becomes a very onerous, complex, and expensive job to file a proper complaint in a proper forum.

Arbitration, on the other hand, is far simpler. There are no specific standards for filing a claim, and, in fact, many lawyers file a claim as they would a complaint in a court proceeding. This I believe is a mistake. Arbitration has many advantages over a court proceeding, and one of them is the lack of complexity. One should write a claim as though it were a simple story, setting forth in chronological order what happened, what the broker said or didn't say, and what he did or didn't do that caused the loss that is the subject of the claim.

Arbitrators are not judges. The panel that sits in judgment over your case does not want to read a bunch of legal mumbo jumbo and documents drafted under complex rules of pleading that take forever to get to the bottom line. They want a clear, easily understood, concise accounting of what happened. I have also seen attorneys go to the other extreme and write a one- or two-page claim without any details about what occurred.

It is my belief that the best drafting of a claim lies some place in the middle ground. Don't make it so short that the arbitrators cannot get a feel for what happened nor so long that it puts them to sleep. The middle ground offers the arbitrators the unique opportunity to hear your case without the rules of evidence and pleading that must be followed in a court proceeding. More importantly, it gives you the opportunity to have that first strike against the broker—unobstructed and unbounded by the complex rules of the court.

This, I believe, gives you a distinct advantage over the respondent brokerage companies. My job is to write the best possible claim that can be written, even if that means six, seven, or eight rewrites. I do this because the claim represents my office's work product and it is my first encounter with the individuals who are going to sit in judgment over my client. I want that first encounter with the arbitrators to present my client's case in the most favorable light possible while painting as negative a picture of the brokerage company's actions as is reasonable, given the facts of the case.

This leaves an impression on the arbitration panel even before I commence my opening statement. Furthermore, it leaves a lasting impression on the attorney working for the prestigious Wall Street law firm that is going to represent the brokerage company. If that attorney is aware that he is up against a competent, knowledgeable attorney who will do everything possible within the ethical bounds of the practice of law to win a case for his client, that attorney is going to be far more likely to entertain the notion of negotiating a settlement on a case that he clearly cannot win.

I include in my claims all of the legal grounds upon which I base a case. I would not expect you, in the preparation of your claim, to use any legalese or state any specific legal grounds upon which to base a claim. This is because an attorney is accountable for the preparation of a claim, and if he fails to include a specific legal principle while he has included other ones, the arbitrators may be persuaded to exclude the offering of evidence concerning a legal principle that he failed to plead. So to make life simple for yourself when preparing your claim, just stick to the facts; tell your story and don't get bogged down in a legal quagmire. If your case is complex or your losses are substantial, you're probably going to use an attorney anyway, and then you can let him worry about including the proper causes of action in your particular case.

After completing a claim, I always send it to my clients for approval, so off this claim went to Mary and Paul to be sure that all the facts, dates, and statements were correct. I also sent Mary three uniform submission agreements, which are the formal documents that the SROs require the claimant (investor) and the respondents (brokerage company/broker) to sign. The uniform submission agreement is the formal request for arbitration. Unless the information is properly filled out on the uniform submission agreement, the SRO will not accept the case for filing.

In Mary's particular case I chose the NASD to be the SRO of choice. As we have learned at the beginning of this chapter, whether you file a claim with an SRO or an independent organization like the AAA, the probability of success in your case will be substantially the same. There is one SRO, however, that under most circumstances I would not file a case with. That is the New York Stock Exchange. The reason for this is that, based upon the procedures available, the enforcement of the discovery rules, and the apparent "old boy network," the New York Stock Exchange does not seem to offer as fair and impartial a setting as other SROs. Members of the New York Stock Exchange might differ with my opinion, but members of the panels that make up the arbitrators for the New York Stock Exchange seem to be older, more conservative, and less likely to give you your money back. I would choose either the NASD or the AAA.

I file most of my cases with the NASD because I know many of the people who work there, and it seems that in this hectic world if you know someone by a first name, things tend to run a little more smoothly. Once the claim, together with the uniform submission agreement, is received back at the New York headquarters of the NASD, the claim will then have been "filed" and the next act that occurs is for the SRO to serve the claim upon the various respondents. After the respondents have been served, they have

20 business days in which to file a response or an answer to your claim.

The Enemy's Counterattack

Answers vary, as do claims, from person to person. I have seen answers as short as two pages, but I have also seen answers that have been quite long. Every brokerage company has its own method of preparing an answer, and each attorney who works for either the brokerage company or an outside law firm has his own method of preparing and filing an answer. While we are on the subject of brokerage company attorneys, let me give you an inside tip about how the defense of these cases evolves.

When a brokerage company receives a claim, it will make a decision regarding which set of attorneys will handle the case. After the claim is assigned to a particular division within the legal department, it is then assigned to a particular attorney. For political and other reasons, the brokerage company might opt to have the claim sent to outside counsel. This is a term referring to attorneys who work for firms that are not employed directly by the brokerage company. In other words, these are outside law firms that might represent several brokerage companies and perform legal services in areas other than just securities litigation. In most cases, the division of the law firm that receives your claim will have had extensive experience in defending securities claims and will undoubtedly place a competent, experienced trial attorney in charge of defending your claim.

Space does not permit an explanation of why a particular case might be sent to outside counsel or be retained at the brokerage company, but one point of observation is quite relevant. Without casting a stone at the defense industry (and I don't mean the military defense industry), it has become apparent to me during my years of practice that when a case is sent to an outside law firm, in most instances it becomes more difficult to settle that case until it gets fairly close to the arbitration hearing date. You might ask yourself why. The answer becomes painfully obvious once you realize that defense firms (law firms that handle securities defense work) are paid on an hourly basis for the work they perform in defending the brokerage company from a lawsuit. Now if you're operating a defense firm as a business, the bottom line is very important, and it isn't really in your best interest to settle a case as soon as the claim is delivered to you. In fact, it might be in your best interest to fight that claim right to the doorstep of the arbitration proceeding. Why? Because the more hours you bill, the more money you make. Now there it is again, that old conflict of interest rearing its ugly head in the practice of law. I am not painting with one brush stroke the picture that all defense firms are the same, because clearly they are not. I have experienced ethical, professional relationships with many attorneys on the other side of the table (the broker-dealer side), and together we have discussed the strong points and shortcomings of our particular cases. With that in mind, I have settled many cases well before the arbitration date. On the other hand, there are defense firms I have fought against whose marching orders, whether from the brokerage company or from management at the law firm, have been to not settle the case and instead see it through to arbitration. Mary's suit was just such a case.

Early in the proceedings, the case was sent to outside counsel and assigned to a professional, well-dressed, highly polished attorney. Jim was a very able attorney—conscientious, thorough, and thoroughly convinced that we had no valid claim in this case. Jim and I held many discussions about the possibility of settling Mary's case, but every time it came down to dollars and cents, it was always Jim's position that Mary had made $5,000 in her account and therefore we had no claim to talk about and no damages for the brokerage company to pay.

I don't know how much money the brokerage company spent on defending the case, but I can tell you that I would have settled Mary's case for less money than the brokerage company paid for its defense. That's right. I would have settled her case, if the brokerage company was willing to pay Mary the same amount of money it was willing to pay the attorneys, experts, and other people used in defending the matter. In this particular case, I don't believe the defense firm, that is the outside counsel, was doing anything other than what they were ordered to do by the brokerage company.

It is my belief that several political factors entered into the picture. For one, Dan Dorfman, a well-known columnist with *USA Today*, had published a cover story in the business section about another New York case I was handling against Shearson. As one might imagine, this did not set well with Shearson Lehman Brothers, and I suspect, and again this is only an opinion, that they wanted to teach me a lesson in Mary's case. That, coupled with their position that Mary had in fact made $5,000 in her account, led them to the conclusion to proceed through arbitration.

What all of this means is that there is a lot more to the arbitration process than meets the eye—politics, geography, dollar losses, the types of activity, the name of the defense firm, who in the brokerage company is responsible for overseeing the case, and the company's financial condition at that time of year. All of these elements of the puzzle have to be put together to determine what a brokerage company is willing to pay and what a case is worth. It is the attorney's responsibility and obligation to consider all of these elements when taking a case through the arbitration process. That is one of the reasons why, if you need the help of an attorney, you should be very careful in selecting an expert who is qualified to work in this specialized area of the law.

Back to Mary's Case

When I received Jim's answer to Mary's claim, I was not surprised by the broker's statements. Don claimed to have explained thoroughly all the risks inherent in each of the products he had recommended for Mary, and that Mary had fully understood those risks and was willing to assume them. The answer continued, stating that Mary had consistently requested the highest possible yield and she was dissatisfied with the return she was getting on her CDs, so it was for this reason that she began investing with Don.

I routinely send a copy of the respondent's answer to my client to have the client review it. I have the client write out in detail each of the misstatements, errors, or incorrect conclusions in the respondent's answer. I am usually greeted with a phone call from an indignant client who could not possibly understand how the brokerage company can print such vicious lies. The degree of frustration and anger varies only with the number of mistruths and inaccurate statements contained within the answer. On the other hand, I am quite sure that there are many cases in which a broker might feel the same way when he gets a copy of a client's claim based on a sour grapes case.

In Mary's case, I was alarmed by the manner in which the broker dealt with her claim. Basically, he stated that Paul, Mary, her mother, and her boyfriend, Charles, were all liars; that the only one in the whole world who was telling the truth was Don; and that Mary was, although not sophisticated, fully capable of reading her statements and understanding the nature of her investments.

Discovery: Just the Facts, Ma'am

The answer having been received, it was time to go on to the next step—the discovery process. Discovery in court cases is dramatically different from discovery in arbitration proceedings. Let's take a closer look.

Discovery is a procedure in which each side makes demands of the other side to produce documents and other evidence that will help them place a value on the case and prepare the case for trial or arbitration. Discovery under the court process is formalized and allows the lawyer to have tools that are not available in the arbitration process. One of the best weapons a lawyer has in his arsenal is the use of depositions. As you might already know, a deposition is a process whereby the person to be deposed (the witness, party, defendant, or plaintiff) is asked questions under oath (under penalty of perjury) while a stenographer records the testimony. The record is later transcribed and made into a booklet. The purpose of a deposition is to gather information and facts about a case in order to prepare for trial. Some of this information might not be allowed into evidence at trial, but it's still pursuable under the discovery rules.

Two other tools not available for arbitration are interrogatories, a type of question-and-answer document, and request for admission, a list of questions such as "Do you admit that you did . . . ?"

Because none of these are allowed in arbitration, it saves the claimant a great deal of time and money. Were this case to proceed in a normal litigation mode, the client could spend several thousand dollars just in taking one deposition. The sad state of circumstances in law today is that the courtroom is now used as a hearing room for motions to produce, sanctions, more motions to produce, motions to compel, and other delaying tactics that can rob you of both money and time.

Because arbitration is designed for quick, relatively inexpensive litigation, the rules of discovery are severely limited. You don't get bogged down in a quagmire of hearings, motions, and rulings by a judge necessitating an attorney to go to court 15 or 20 times only to get that which should have been produced the first time.

Each SRO has its unique rules regarding the production of discovery. The NASD has certain guidelines concerning which documents should routinely be produced by each side and what period should transpire before those documents are produced. When a discovery request is served upon a party in NASD proceedings, the party has thirty calendar days in which to respond to that discovery request. If a client does not have his statements, his attorney will ask the brokerage company for a copy of any of the missing statements, together with all account forms signed by the client and several important internal documents.

The brokerage company is also entitled to discovery, and it will generally ask for copies of your statements. You might ask yourself, "Why in the world would the brokerage company want a copy of a statement when it already has the original?" Well, that's a good question. Generally, the brokerage company wants to take a look at your statements to see if you made any written notations that might reflect your understanding of the account, the suitability of the products you purchased, or your ability to comprehend or compute what was going on in your account. As an example, let's say you have a claim in which margin interest is at issue—that is, whether or not it was suitable for you to have maintained a margin account. The brokerage company may wish to show that you knew you had a margin account, and furthermore that you were able to understand how much margin interest you were paying. How? By obtaining a copy of your account statements and showing that you had computed the margin interest on your statements or had circled the interest charge each month. Therefore, you were fully informed and aware of how much margin interest you were being charged and what it was costing you to maintain this margin account.

The brokerage company might also ask for your income tax returns. Whether they are relevant or not depends upon your particular case and the areas of law upon which your case is based. As a general rule, I object to providing income tax statements except in those cases in which I feel the statements will not harm or impinge upon the client's right to privacy. In some cases it's better to turn over the income tax statements to show just how unsuitable the investments were.

Setting the Case for Hearing

Upon the completion of the discovery stage—that is, when both sides have all of the documents needed to prepare for arbitration— the case is ready to proceed to the next step, the setting of the case for a hearing. Generally speaking, depending on the location, arbitration hearings will be held from nine months to one year from the date a claim is filed. In Mary's case, the arbitration hearing was set ten-and-one-half months from the date her original claim was filed.

Arbitrators: Who Are These Guys?

In most cases, you will be assigned three panelists to serve as arbitrators on your case. They are chosen from a panel of arbitrators on file with the NASD. Two of the arbitrators will be selected from candidates serving outside of the securities industry. That is, they may be members of a law firm that specializes in securities law, trustees at a bank, or accountants—in other words, not affiliated with the securities industry. The third member of the panel will be a securities industry arbitrator, a person directly associated with the securities industry. Such a person might be a branch manager, compliance officer, attorney working in a securities defense firm, economist at a brokerage company, etc.

The NASD will then provide you with a sheet listing the job description of each of the three panelists, their former employment history, and their brokerage account history. This will provide you with the opportunity to see whether there is a conflict of interest between any of the panel members and you, other parties to the arbitration hearing, or the brokerage company. If one of the panel members has a former or present relationship that might interfere with his fair and impartial ruling on the case, he will be relieved for cause. Otherwise, you are entitled to only one preemptory challenge—that is, a challenge to eliminate an arbitrator for no reason whatsoever. You might ask why you would want to eliminate an arbitrator? Well, I'm going to let you in on a little secret: You have the right to ask the NASD to provide you with the awards background of each arbitrator who is going to serve on your panel. What does that mean, "awards background?" It literally means each award that the arbitrator has rendered in the past when he served as a panelist in an arbitration proceeding. Obviously, if you represent a brokerage firm and have an arbitrator before you who has made numerous awards against brokerage companies, you might wish to eliminate that person from the arbitration panel simply because you feel he might be biased in favor of claimants. On the other hand, you as a claimant might find an arbitrator who has dismissed his last nine cases and, therefore, feel you might not receive a fair and impartial hearing from that particular arbitrator.

Now I don't want you to jump to the conclusion that you can always judge an arbitrator by his award history. Each case should be decided on its own merits, and although an arbitrator might appear to be partial, it is possible that he could have heard six sour grapes cases in a row and had no other choice but to dismiss them. Recently, I presented a claim in New York at the NASD national headquarters where three seasoned arbitrators sat in judgment over my case. Several of the panelists had not made substantial awards for quite some time; yet I was very well satisfied with the result when they returned a $250,000 plus award in a case in which the out-of-pocket loss involved a great deal of imputed interest—just like Mary's case. (Imputed interest is the money you would have earned from an appropriate investment rather than from the inappropriate investment made with the brokerage company.) So, as the old saying goes, don't judge a book by its cover.

The Arbitration Hearing

A Peek Inside

Now we are just about ready for the arbitration hearing. Before walking into the hearing room, though, you must be sure that your case is properly prepared and you are ready to withstand the cross-examination of opposing counsel. What follows is a close look at these two subjects as well as a peek inside a hearing room.

Stage Preparation: Getting Everything Ready

You've gone through the challenge process and the arbitration panel is selected. Now it's time to complete your final preparation for the hearing. Make sure you have all your documents ready and placed in chronological order; that is, the order they will be introduced at the hearing. Be sure that your testimony has been prepared, and that doesn't mean rehearsed or memorized. It means that you must thoroughly understand your case, what you are going to testify about, and what questions might be asked of you during cross-examination. You should always tell the truth and nothing but the truth in concise, relevant language. However, it is not what you say but how you say it that can affect the outcome of your case. That is where the use of an attorney—a seasoned trial attorney— can make the difference between winning and losing a case.

Many people use the old phrases "to tell the truth" or "to be honest with you" or "to be frank with you" in general conversation. However, if an arbitrator hears you use such phrases, his natural inclination will be to say, "Oh, gee, hasn't this person been telling me the truth throughout his testimony? Hasn't he been frank or honest with me up to this point in time? Is this the only time that this person can be depended upon?" This is just one small example of a larger picture of trial preparation that is critical to the successful outcome of your case. You should also spend time preparing your testimony and readying yourself for any hard-fired, cross-examination questions you might be asked.

Movies and television paint a glorious picture of a robust trial attorney pleading his case before a jury, which listens to his every word and anticipates, with great expectation, each new fact that the attorney brings forth from his witnesses. Many famous scenes from motion pictures focus on the cross-examination of an opponent's witness. The damning evidence resulting from these modern-day Clarence Darrows catching an opponent's witness in a lie produces great material for the cinema. However, any seasoned trial advocate is keenly aware that the secret to success lies not in courtroom antics but in trial preparation. Preparation, preparation, and more preparation are the three keys to success. There is no shortcut to this fundamental concept. If you think that you can go to an arbitration hearing on a wing and a prayer, it will be far better for you to save your time and your money and go on a holiday instead.

Now you might be asking yourself, "What does he mean by preparation?" Well, we've already discussed possessing a thorough understanding of what you want the arbitrators to hear. What facts are you going to present? How will you prove those facts? Are you going to do it through your own testimony, or do you have other witnesses who will testify to the facts of your case? Of course, you will be introducing important documents that verify, independent of your own testimony, those facts that you are trying to prove. In addition to what to say and how to say it, you must focus on how to answer cross-examination questions put to you by the defense attorney. If you are aware of every question that might be asked of you, then you will have come a long way toward surviving this key element of your forthcoming arbitration hearing.

What comes next? Well, by now you have arranged all of the documents that you intend to introduce in a concise order, and you are thoroughly familiar with them. You have provided yourself with a written sheet outlining your testimony and the key elements that are fundamental to your case. Don't forget you must make a copy of every document that you intend to introduce for each of the three arbitrators, opposing counsel, and the NASD staff attorney who may or may not be present during your hearing.

By the way, this isn't all work. You get to have some fun also. How? By cross-examining the broker. When the broker is finished with his direct examination (when his attorney is through asking him questions), you have the opportunity to ask questions of the broker. Unless you have previous experience in this specialized area of the law, meeting with an attorney to provide you with a list of questions to ask your broker may be the difference between winning and losing your case. You should outline all of the questions you intend to ask the broker and use them as a checklist when you interrogate him about his previous testimony.

Most likely you will be the claimant—that is, the person seeking recovery from the brokerage company. You will be allowed to go first in the presentation of your case and in making opening remarks to the arbitrators. Many attorneys prefer to write out their opening remarks and it might not be a bad idea for you to do the same—especially considering you probably haven't done this sort of thing before. Keep your opening remarks concise, not spending more than five minutes from beginning to end, and don't say anything that you cannot prove in your case. Defense attorneys love a lawyer who makes an opening statement that contains facts that he cannot prove.

While we are on the subject of opening statements, let us not forget that once both parties to the hearing have rested—that is, have completed presenting their cases—each side will be given the opportunity to make closing remarks or summation. Some trial experts believe that the summation is the single most important aspect of a trial. How many of us remember Gregory Peck in *To*

Kill a Mockingbird, or Spencer Tracy in *Inherit the Wind*, or any one
of a number of other great movies in which the attorney's argument
persuaded the jury to rule in his favor?

Closing argument or summation is important because it is your
last opportunity to speak to the arbitrators before they make a
decision in your case. If your argument is persuasive enough, it
might even convince a reluctant arbitrator to rule in your favor.
Be sure to summarize, as briefly as possible, the facts you have
proved, the deficiencies of your opponent's case, and why you believe the arbitrators should rule in your favor. Don't be afraid to
tell the arbitrators how much money you want and what your damages are, which, of course, you have already presented during your
case.

The Hearing

Well now, here we go. All of our documents are ready to be introduced, we've prepared our opening statement, and we have outlined our closing argument. What should we expect?

Arbitration hearings, when held outside the NASD headquarters in New York City, will usually take place in a hotel convention
room. There will probably be one large conference table in the
middle of the room or two conference tables making up a T. The
arbitrators will sit at the top of the T. The defense team, consisting
of the attorneys representing the brokerage company, the broker,
and the branch manager, typically sit on one side of the conference
table while you will be seated across from them on the other side
of the table. The entire arbitration hearing, including oral testimony
and all motions, is tape-recorded, thus producing a permanent record. Motions may address rather complex legal principles such as
case law regarding the propriety of your claims, arbitration rules,
and other procedural matters. This area of the law is far too complex to address in our overview of arbitration. However, as I have
pointed out previously, a securities arbitration attorney will know
what to expect and how to respond to any motions that might be
filed by the defense attorney.

Walking into the hearing room, you will be greeted by three arbitrators, with the chairperson seated in the middle of the panelists. Prior to the commencement of the proceeding, the chairperson will introduce himself and the other two arbitrators and read from the NASD *Rules of Procedure,* explaining how the arbitration will be conducted. After he concludes his opening remarks, the chairperson will then ask if the panel is acceptable and if you have any preliminary motions. After the panel is accepted and the motions have been made, the chairperson will ask any witness who may testify to be sworn.

It is now your turn to begin with your opening statement, and thereafter the defense attorney will present an opening statement. Be sure to have a pencil and paper handy so that you are ready to take down any facts that the defense intends to prove, paying particular attention to those facts that you feel are misstatements or outright lies. After the defense attorney concludes his opening remarks, it is time for the show to begin.

You'll probably want to testify first and then call any witnesses who are going to testify on your behalf. After you have introduced all of your evidence, documentary and otherwise, the chairperson will ask if you "rest," which means you have no further evidence to introduce. Now it's time for the defense attorney to put on his case. Don't forget that just as the defense attorney had the opportunity to cross-examine you at the conclusion of your testimony and each of your witnesses at the conclusion of theirs, you have the same opportunity to cross-examine the defense attorney's witnesses. After the defense attorney "rests," you may then introduce rebuttal evidence—that is, evidence to rebut or disprove any new evidence the defense attorney raised that you had not already raised. You may do this by further testimony of yourself or other witnesses.

After you have put on rebuttal evidence, the defense attorney may put rebuttal evidence to your rebuttal evidence. When both sides have "rested," it is now your turn to present your summation followed by the defense attorney's chance to make his closing argument. Upon the conclusion of the defense attorney's closing argument, you will be given the opportunity to rebut the defense attorney's closing argument. Legal experts differ on whether you should be the first party to commence closing argument. Some attorneys believe that you gain a slight advantage by proceeding last because the defense attorney isn't given the opportunity to refute your argument. But keep your remarks very short. You don't want to put the arbitrators to sleep.

Once you have finished your closing remarks, the chairperson will thank each of you for your presentation, read a short concluding statement, and officially end the arbitration hearing. Both sides will then be asked to leave the room, and, depending upon time constraints, the arbitrators may discuss the case and reach a conclusion right then and there. If time does not allow, the arbitrators will convene sometime in the future to decide the outcome of your matter. Each of the three arbitrators must sign the award and send it back to the NASD, which will then prepare the award and send it to you via the mail. You should receive the results of the arbitration in four to six weeks from the conclusion of the hearing. There is not much to do during that period except to be a "Monday morning quarterback," which I strongly advise you not to do. You will undoubtedly have felt great when your testimony was concluded, and you will have reached a low point when the defense attorney cross-examined you. Don't beat yourself to death thinking of what you could have done or should have done. Now that it's all over, you just have to sit back and wait.

The End of the Story: Mary's Hearing

To get a taste of what it's really like at a hearing, let's go inside the hearing room with Mary. Mary's case was heard at the Beverly Hilton Hotel during the week immediately preceding Easter. When I met Mary in the lobby of the hotel on Tuesday morning, the day of our first session, she looked very nervous and had circles under her eyes.

Her voice quivered as she said, "I've had a lot of trouble sleeping the last three nights and my stomach is really upset. Do you think this will be over by tomorrow?"

We had originally thought the case would require two days, but I always add an extra half-session because things just never seem to go as planned—you know, Murphy's Law.

In as calm a voice as I could muster, I tried to reassure Mary: "Everyone seems to get butterflies before their first session, especially if they are going to be the lead-off witness. You're comfortable performing in front of audiences and cameras so just imagine that you're about to go on stage, in front of a live audience that can't wait to hear what you have to say. And remember, Shearson already has your money. The worst that can happen is that you don't win. Keep a positive outlook—you have nothing to lose and everything to gain." Mary sighed deeply and together we entered the conference room.

Two of the arbitrators were seated reading the morning newspaper. By sheer coincidence, an article had appeared in a recent *Barron's* concerning a case I had just tried at the NASD headquarters in downtown Manhattan. The case had been well-publicized because of the nature of the wrong and because it had been against a mutual fund company instead of a brokerage firm—a highly unusual situation. The arbitrator sitting at the center of the table identified himself as the chairperson and asked me, "Are you in any way related to the John Allen mentioned in this article? It's quite a coincidence to have two John Allens specializing in securities arbitration on both coasts. This seems like an interesting case."

"Yes," I said, "I am intimately acquainted with that John Allen; he and I are one in the same person."

The arbitrator looked a little bewildered. He wanted to know how a Southern California attorney ended up with a case in downtown Manhattan. I told him that I actually represented more clients on the East Coast than I did on the West Coast and that securities arbitration was my primary specialty.

While we engaged in further conversation regarding the mutual fund case and its unusual circumstances, the third member of the arbitration panel walked into the room and introduced himself as the industry arbitrator. The chairman then asked all the parties to leave the room so the panelists could prepare for the hearing. As I walked outside I met Jim, a tall, handsome man in his early thirties, who worked for the securities defense firm representing Shearson. This defense firm represented most of the major brokerage companies west of Chicago.

Over the past few months, Jim and I held several discussions concerning Mary's case, but we found it impossible to reach a compromise because we each valued the case so differently. Even during the arbitration hearing, Shearson remained firm in its conviction that Mary had made $5,000 and therefore she was not entitled to any monetary award.

Jim and I were still talking when the door opened and the industry arbitrator asked everyone to come into the room. Mary sat down to my right and Paul to my left. Jim sat next to Paul, while Don, the broker, pulled up a chair next to Jim. While we were unpacking our briefcases and lining up our hearing exhibits, Dean, the branch manager, strolled in. He was wearing an elegant Italian designer suit, as if to say, Business is really great, and this arbitration is a real inconvenience; I should be at the branch office making sure my staff is productive instead of wasting my valuable time at this hearing. Dean pulled out a chair at the left end of the conference table, next to Don.

After his opening comments, the chairman asked if we were all ready to proceed. The witnesses were sworn and I commenced my opening statement.

Keeping my remarks brief, I suggested to the panel how preposterous it was for Shearson to assert that Mary had made $5,000 in her account because had she left her money in a bank, she would have earned $65,000; that's $65,000 more than her caring, honest, and trusted friend Don had made for her. Looking right at Don, I then said, "And let us not forget that this confidant earned $30,000 from his grossly negligent handling of Mary's account. How did Don accomplish the production of such large commissions? By purchasing products whose commissions were three to four times what he could have earned in prudent, suitable investments. Just think, had Mary never met Don, she would have been $30,000 ahead from the commission cost alone. What a high price to pay for friendship."

Upon the conclusion of my opening statement, Jim stood up and painted Don as a kind, caring man who would never do anything to harm Mary. However, Mary's chief concern had always been income and Don was merely complying with Mary's desire for high income, regardless of the risk involved. After Jim was finished with his opening statement, the chairman asked me to proceed with my case, and I called Mary as my first witness.

To make Mary feel comfortable, I began by asking questions about her childhood, her learning disorder, and why she had left high school without graduating. As her life story began to unfold, she became a little more comfortable, but the quiver in her voice had not yet disappeared. While we went through the chronology of important events in her life, she started to talk about her dance career. Once she began discussing Broadway musicals, feature films, and television appearances on "Johnny Carson," she was quite at ease describing who she had worked with and the numerous injuries that eventually had resulted in "bronzing her shoes," as she put it. As she was going through her story, my eyes were switching back and forth between the arbitrators, trying to get a sense of whether or not they were paying attention to her testimony. All three arbitrators were paying close attention to every word that she was uttering. Nothing worries me more than an arbitrator who either sleeps through the proceedings or stares off into space with a blank look, wishing he was anyplace else but in the hearing room.

Once I sensed that Mary was comfortable and relaxed, I sped past the background information and dove right into the issues of the case. Mary, like most people, did not enjoy having her private life exposed to a room full of men. To make matters worse, Mary's ignorance of financial matters, while highly positive to her case, was less than flattering to her ego.

An interesting event occurred regarding this very subject. I was questioning Mary about her inability to understand her monthly statements. When asked about the equity portion of her Shearson statement, Mary's answer seemed to indicate (or at least I thought it indicated) that she knew what equity meant and that she could locate it on the statement. Well, I knew that Mary didn't know about equity any more than she knew how to speak Russian. The problem was that she just didn't want to appear stupid in front of the arbitrators so she was trying to present herself in the best possible light. This might be fine to do in front of your peers but in an arbitration hearing, your lack of sophistication or understanding of financial matters only helps to strengthen your case, not weaken it. That left me with a problem. How do I impeach my own witness? How do I ask her questions that can show the arbitrators that she really doesn't know what is going on without humiliating her?

Reaching for one of the exhibits, I handed Mary a copy of a monthly Shearson statement.

"Now Mary," I said, "I want you to take a close look at this Shearson statement for the month of February and tell me what your account was worth."

Mary looked over the statement and began to read off numbers without knowing what they were. But no matter how hard she tried, there were so many different numbers with so many names attached that she just couldn't figure out the account balance. I asked her to find the long market value of her account and recite the number to the arbitrators. Mary could not find the long market value. When I pointed it out to her, she misread the number. Finally, when I knew that I had made my point, I took the statement away from her and went on to another area of examination.

When I had concluded my direct testimony, the chairperson asked if we would like a short recess before Jim began his cross-examination of Mary. Acknowledging that we would, I thanked the chairperson and accompanied Mary out to the hallway where we discussed the impact of her direct testimony.

"I was very pleased with your testimony. The only word of advice I have for you is to make a little more eye contact with the arbitrators and don't look down as much."

Mary commented that she was looking down because she was nervous and that the butterflies in her stomach were still flying around. She wasn't sure whether she could go on any longer without eating. In addition to being unable to sleep, Mary had eaten only one meal a day for the last week and had lost seven pounds.

It was time to go back into the hearing room. I cautioned Mary to answer only questions addressed to her and not to volunteer any information that was not asked of her. Jim began his cross-examination, obviously trying to show Mary to be more knowledgeable than she really was.

The truth does have a way of emerging, and no matter what Jim tried to do, he couldn't put Mary into the boxes marked "Sophisticated" or "Knowledgeable" or "Intelligent." In fact, the more he tried, the worse it looked for Shearson. The attorney's role in interposing objections during the cross-examination of his client is radically different in arbitration than in a court trial, but I'll have to leave that subject to a chapter in another book. Let's just say that few, if any, objections should be interposed during an arbitration hearing. In this particular case, I didn't object even once. I just sat back and let Jim go at Mary for as long as he wanted, knowing that it would only help our case and damage his.

At the conclusion of Jim's cross-examination, the chairperson asked if anyone had any further questions of Mary. Both the industry arbitrator and the third panelist indicated they did. The industry arbitrator proceeded first: "Mary, did you perceive you were incurring any further risk by investing with Shearson than if you had left your money in a bank?"

For the next five or ten minutes, both the industry arbitrator and the third panel member posed various questions to Mary in order to get a better picture of what had gone on in her account. The asking of questions by members of the panel shows that the panel members have a keen interest in the case and really do want to get to the truth. I was happy with the questions they asked and the responses that Mary gave. So remember that it isn't just the attorneys who may ask you questions; it could be any member of the panel. Let's hope they will ask the right questions.

After the arbitrators were finished asking questions of Mary, we adjourned for lunch. Realizing that she would not have to answer any more questions, Mary was finally able to enjoy a meal. During lunch we discussed the order in which we would call our witnesses. I decided to have her mother testify next, followed by Paul, her new money manager, and to close with our strongest witness, Dr. Richard Wallace. Dr. Wallace was going to testify as an expert witness—an essential element of our case.

Now, you might already be asking yourself, Why would it be necessary to call an expert to testify at an arbitration hearing? Well, the world continues to become more and more complex, and the world of arbitration is no exception. Panel members are required to make decisions based upon complicated industry rules, and complex strategies and products not easily understood by those people unacquainted with the securities industry. Besides providing guidance in the use and/or abuse of those products and rules, experts can also testify to the custom and practice of the securities industry. Expert testimony aids the arbitrators in making an informed decision about whether those customs and practices were violated.

In Mary's case, Dr. Wallace's testimony was necessary to provide an expert opinion regarding suitability, supervision, damages, and rule violations. I feel compelled, however, to provide you with one important caveat about the use of expert witnesses. If you use the services of a lawyer unfamiliar with the arbitration process, guess what might happen? You could end up paying for the education of that lawyer through expert witness fees. That's right. I have seen attorneys hire experts to enlighten the attorney regarding the arbitration process and related rules and procedures at a significant cost to their client. So, get the jump on that attorney by consulting directly with the expert or making sure that your attorney is an expert as well.

As we were finishing our lunch, Dr. Wallace joined us and we began to discuss the key points of his forthcoming testimony. Because he was to follow two other witnesses, we felt it was unlikely that he would testify in the afternoon session. On the way back to the conference room, I could see from Mary's expression that she was finally starting to unwind. I told her to sit back and enjoy the rest of the show, especially the cross-examination of Don.

The second session went rather well and, as we had predicted, left our final witness for the morning session of the next day. At the beginning of the third session, Dr. Wallace clearly showed the branch manager's failure to supervise Don and the unsuitable nature of the investments in Mary's account. In addition to testifying about the actual loss Mary had suffered, Dr. Wallace also discussed why Don's actions were motivated more by greed than by a genuine concern for Mary's welfare.

I felt reasonably sure that the arbitration panel had understood Dr. Wallace's testimony and that he had provided the expertise necessary to overcome the defense's position that Mary had enjoyed a profit in her account. But his role in this real-life drama was not yet concluded; the toughest part, responding to cross-examination questions, lay ahead.

Jim was not afraid to mix it up with Dr. Wallace, and Jim tried everything he could to discredit him. Aware that the true test of an expert witness lies not in direct- but in cross-examination, Jim was going to make certain that Dr. Wallace "knew his stuff." However, even before Jim had completed his questioning of Dr. Wallace, the panel had grown tired of Jim's antics and was ready to move on to another witness. Since I had no further evidence to present, I rested and it was now the brokerage company's turn to present its defense.

The morning session was now over, and it was time for the lunch break. Instead of eating, Dr. Wallace and I took advantage of the extra time to review my cross-examination questions to make sure that everything was in order—I didn't want to leave anything to chance. Returning to the conference room a few minutes early, I found Mary anxiously waiting to speak with me. "I really am afraid that I might start to cry when Don testifies," she said. "I don't know how to control myself if he lies the way he did in the answer." I told Mary that Don's testimony would be consistent with his answer, which meant that he was not going to tell the truth during the hearing.

That people lie is an unfortunate circumstance of life, but as I said earlier, the truth does have a way of emerging, and one can give it a little nudge through an effective cross-examination. I told Mary she would feel vindicated by the time I had finished questioning Don. It is usually a very satisfying experience for a client to watch a dishonest broker impeached for not telling the truth. Getting caught in a lie is the surest way to lose an arbitration hearing.

The fourth session began with Don taking the witness stand. He proceeded to spin one yarn after another. By the time Don was finished with his direct testimony, Mary was so upset that I had to ask for a ten-minute recess to allow her to regain her composure. When we returned to the room, I began my attack.

Attack may seem like a strong word, but in certain circumstances it is quite necessary to confront a dishonest witness so that his true character can be discerned, and this was such a case. To achieve an effective cross-examination, I had to give the panel members the opportunity to hear Don discredit himself, which he more than amply did.

At the conclusion of my cross-examination, it was obvious that Don's one and only concern was the production of exorbitant commissions—without any consideration for the welfare of his client. It became painfully obvious that Don's never-ending quest for greater commissions continually exposed Mary to greater and greater degrees of risk.

Don was followed by Dean, the branch manager. At the conclusion of Dean's testimony, Jim called his final witness, George Parris, the brokerage firm's expert witness. His job was to prove that Mary's account had actually made $5,000. George also tried to establish the suitability of the products purchased in Mary's account. During George's testimony, I kept a watchful eye on each arbitrator to see if they were buying the expert's story. I couldn't tell from their expressions whether or not they believed his dialogue.

Jim completed his direct-examination and it was my turn to engage in the last cross-examination of the hearing. By the time I had finished with the brokerage firm's expert, it was obvious that he was a "hired gun" called to say anything necessary to win, despite the facts of the case or the truthfulness of his testimony.

The chairman asked if either party had any more evidence to present. After acknowledging our negative responses, he requested that we commence our closing arguments. Jim went first, trying to persuade the panel that Mary was a sophisticated investor who hadn't lost any money. As Jim was speaking, I felt like a horse at the starting gate—I couldn't wait to get my turn. Jim finished his statement in less than 20 minutes, and now the last opportunity to speak to the arbitrators was mine.

I kept my remarks brief; my entire closing argument was less than 15 minutes. Space does not permit a recounting of my closing remarks, but I do recall reminding the panel that Mary had confided in Don because of her long friendship with him. I finished by saying, "Safe and frequented is the path of deceit under the name of friendship," and then one last time asked the panel for an award in favor of Mary.

The hearing was over, and there was nothing left to do but wait for the result, which as you already know was an award of $65,000.

For most people, an arbitration hearing is physically fatiguing as well as emotionally draining. The thought of cross-examination has kept more than a few of my clients up at night. Having your financial history exposed, even in the privacy of this nonpublic forum, is a great burden for many people to bear. It is only after they have finished testifying and the defense attorney has concluded the cross-examination that clients generally feel a little more at ease.

The best advice I can offer is to get plenty of rest, be sure you are physically and emotionally prepared for the proceeding, and don't let your opponents wear you down. Remember that consulting with a securities litigation attorney may improve the likelihood of winning your case. After all, if you lose your case, all the regrets in the world won't help you get your money back. As long as you tell the truth and are honest with your responses, you can expect to get a fair and impartial hearing.

Your Own Happy Ending

You've waited weeks for your arbitrators' decision. Then, one day while you are going through the morning mail, you notice a letter from the NASD. After a mild anxiety attack, you open the envelope to find that you, just like Mary, have won your case, and the arbitrators have rendered an award in your favor. You have been vindicated and the brokerage company has been found to be responsible for your losses. Feel great? You bet you do. It was all worth the effort, wasn't it? What next? Well, in all but a few cases, you should receive a check from the brokerage company within 30 days from the date of the award.

One note about the right to appeal. There is no right to appeal an arbitration award—it is binding and final. However, there is a special proceeding, called a "Motion to Vacate," in which a losing party can request a court of law to set aside an arbitration award. The grounds for bringing this motion are so limited and the burden of setting aside an award is so great that it is rarely undertaken. In virtually every case both sides accept the arbitration results, close their files, and go on with their lives.

A Final Word . . .

Having read this book, you now command the power to take control of your own financial affairs. But I must impart one more warning: Your education in financial self-defense is not over. In fact, it has only just begun.

Why? Because the rules of the game are always changing. Shifts in government policy bring about new laws, and the ebb and flow of economic cycles inevitably lead to new investment fads. Wall Street firms are forever conjuring up novel products to fatten their bottom lines and then inventing clever buzzwords to help sell them. The folks who make their living through outright fraud work day and night dreaming up still more ingenious deceptions with which to cage their pigeons. It goes on ceaselessly.

Your best defense is to keep informed. Read intelligent business publications to stay abreast of the changes taking place in the investment world. Study other books about the markets in which you have an interest. Learn more about how investments work, whom they benefit, and why. Keep this book handy for reference. It will deepen your understanding of the stories you read on the business pages of your daily newspaper.

What is most important, always be a skeptic and never assume that investment professionals are placing your financial interests ahead of their own. The investment world presents many dangers, but the knowledge you have gained has sharply improved your chance of enjoying a financially secure future.

Glossary

AAA   American Arbitration Association.

Account Activity   That portion of a brokerage account statement that indicates what occurred in an account during the reporting period, i.e., purchases, sales, dividends, interest charges, disbursements, etc.

Arbitration   The process by which the parties to a dispute submit their differences to the judgment of an impartial person or group selected by mutual consent or statutory provision.

Back-End Mutual Fund   A mutual fund that charges no commission when bought if the buyer holds the fund for a certain period, but charges a declining balance of commission if the fund is liquidated early.

Bear   One who believes that market prices will fall. A bear market is a declining market. A bear spread in futures or securities is one that should yield a profit if the market falls. See also **Bull.**

Beta   A volatility measure of the tendency of a security to move with the market. A beta of less than 1 means that the security moves less than the entire market; a beta of greater than 1 means that the security moves more than the entire market.

Blue-Chip Stock   A common stock issued by a major company with a reputation for stability, financial strength, and good dividend return.

Bond   A long-term certificate evidencing ownership of a debt due to be paid by a government or corporation to an individual holder and usually bearing a fixed rate of interest. Interest on American issues normally paid semiannually. Face (par) value usually $1,000, but may be more or less.

Broker One that acts as an agent for others in negotiating purchases or sales, usually for a fee or commission.

Bull One who believes that market prices will rise. A bull market is a rising market. A bull spread in commodities or securities is one that should yield a profit if the market rises. See also **Bear.**

Call (1) The option to buy a security at a specified price on or before a specified date. (2) The redemption of a preferred stock or of a bond before its due date.

Call Writing The selling of a call option, granting to the buyer of that option the right to exercise the option to purchase the security on which the option is based, on or before the date the option expires.

Churning Excessive trading by one who controls a securities account belonging to someone else and who benefits from the trading usually by sharing in the commission revenue. Control may be formal (power-of-attorney) or de facto (actual control).

Closed-End Bond Fund A fund made up of bonds that offers a finite number of shares on its initial public offering and thereafter trades on the stock market.

Closing Total Net Worth Portfolio's total net worth at the end of the current month's reporting period as shown on the monthly statement.

Commodities A basic product, usually but not always agricultural, mineral, or financial, which is traded on a commodity exchange. See also **Futures.**

Common Stock Equity securities that represent an ownership interest in a corporation and usually have last claim on residual assets and earnings of a corporation. Common stock dividends usually are paid only after preferred stock dividends are paid. Usually having voting rights of one vote per share, common stockholders normally have the power to elect directors, authorize new stock issues, and approve or disapprove of major corporate changes.

Confirm The confirmation document sent to a customer containing details of a purchase or sale. It generally provides a description of a transaction, including such details as the date, purchase or sale price, commissions, and the amount owed by or to the customer.

Corporation An association of individuals created by law and having an existence apart from that of its members as well as distinct and inherent powers and liabilities.

Discretionary Account An account in which the customer gives the broker or someone else the authority, which may be complete or within specific limits, as to the purchase and sales of securities or commodities. Authority may not be verbal but must be given via a general or limited power of attorney. The latter is often called a trading authority.

Diversification The purchase of varying assets in order to minimize the risk associated with a portfolio.

Dividend A distribution to stockholders declared by a corporate Board of Directors. It may consist of cash, stock, or property.

Duty to Mitigate The obligation imposed on an injured party to exercise reasonable care in attempting to minimize the damages or avoid aggravating the injury.

Equity (1) The share of security value in a brokerage account belonging to a customer. In effect, the difference between total value and debit balance. (2) A portfolio's total net worth. (3) The net worth section of a corporate balance sheet.

Fundamental Analysis An analysis of industries and companies based on such factors as sales, assets, earnings, markets, and management.

Futures Contracts for the sale and delivery of commodities at some future time.

Guaranteed Bond   A bond on which the principal or income or both are guaranteed by another corporation or parent company in case of default by the issuing corporation.

Guaranteed Stock   A stock whose dividends are guaranteed by a company other than the issues. Usually preferred stock.

Hedge   Protecting a long position in one asset while being short in another in order to reduce overall risk. In commodities, one side of the hedge is in the cash market and the other in the futures market.

High-Yield Bonds   See **Junk Bonds.**

Individual Retirement Account (IRA)   A retirement program that may permit an investor to set aside a limited amount toward retirement each year and deduct some or all of the amount from taxable income.

Insider   An individual who has special information dealing with the financial status of a firm before that information is released to the public or to stockholders. Insiders may be officers, directors, large stockholders, attorneys, investment banking personnel, and others.

Investment Company   A company organized primarily to invest in the securities of other companies. Organized either as closed end or open end. Shares of closed-end investment companies are traded like any other stocks either on or off exchanges. Shares of open-end companies are bought or sold directly from the company or its sponsors. Open-end investment companies and mutual funds are synonymous.

Investment-Grade Bonds   Bonds rated Baa or higher by Moody's bond rating system, BBB or higher by Standard & Poor's system.

Junk Bonds   Bonds with ratings below "investment grade," i.e., below Baa by Moody's or below BBB by Standard & Poor's. May be new issues associated with leveraged buy-outs or restructuring or may result from the downgrading of outstanding issues. Also called high-yield issues because of the high yields needed to compensate holders for high risk.

Limited Partnership   A partnership in which limited partners are not personally liable for incurred debts of the partnership but may lose up to the entire amount of investment.

Liquid   Easily converted into cash.

Long   The position of one who has bought and holds a security. A long position does not always result from a purchase because the buyer could be converting a formerly established short position. A long position is held by one who expects an increase in the price of the securities or holds these securities for income.

Margin   (1) The funds required to be deposited by one purchasing securities. (2) The percentage of equity in an account owned by someone who has bought on credit.

Margin Account   Any brokerage account where securities can be bought with the aid of credit given by the buyer's broker.

Margin Call   A demand by a broker that a customer deposit additional funds either because additional securities have been bought or sold short (original, federal, or Regulation T call) or because there has been adverse market action (maintenance call). See also **Regulation T.**

Margin Interest   The interest paid on securities bought on credit.

Market Makers   See **Principal Transactions.**

Money Market   A financial market in which funds are borrowed or lent for short periods as distinguished from the capital market for long-term funds. See also **Money Market Instruments.**

Money Market Fund   A mutual fund that invests its assets in money market instruments.

Money Market Instruments   Short-term debt instruments such as Treasury Bills, bankers' acceptances, Certificates of Deposit, commercial paper, repurchase agreements, and certain Eurocurrency instruments.

Mutual Fund   See **Investment Company.**

National Association of Securities Dealers (NASD)   An industry association of brokers and dealers created under the Maloney Act of 1938. Regulates in a quasi-governmental manner over-the-counter dealers in corporate securities, investment banking, and mutual funds.

National Association of Securities Dealers Automated Quotation (NASDAQ)   A system for providing a network of competing brokers and dealers electronically with current price quotations to enable them to operate in effect as a stock market without a trading floor.

New Issue   A security about to be offered to the public.

New York Stock Exchange   The largest, most prestigious security exchange in the world, reorganized under its existing name in 1863.

Offloading a Loser   The illegal practice of placing bad trades in particular clients' accounts to rid the broker of them.

Opening Total Net Worth   The closing balance from your last month's statement shown on current monthly statement.

Open Order   An order to buy or sell securities that has not yet been executed. May be placed at market price or at a fixed price. Synonymous with *good-til-canceled order.*

Option   A privilege sold by one party to another that offers the buyer the right to buy (call) or sell (put) a security at an agreed-upon price during a specified period or on a specified date. May be listed (exchange options) or traded over the counter (conventional options).

Option Spreading   The simultaneous purchase and sale of options within the same class.

Order   Instructions to a broker to buy or sell securities.

OTC Trades See **Over the Counter.**

Overbought Reflecting an opinion about price levels. May refer to a security that has had a sharp rise, or to the market as a whole after a period of vigorous buying.

Oversold The reverse of overbought.

Over the Counter Trading among firms usually by telephone in which orders are not filled on floors of exchanges. Firms may act either as brokers or dealers. Sometimes called "off-board."

Preferred Stock Corporate stock that has a claim on earnings, dividends, and assets ahead of the common stock but behind debt. Sometimes regarded as quasi-debt because of the pressure, if not obligation, to pay dividends. Dividends frequently are cumulative.

Principal Transactions Those transactions in which you are purchasing securities directly from the brokerage firm or from the issuer of the securities. The brokerage company is not acting as your agent but is selling securities that it either purchased in the open market or has held in its own inventory. Also known as *market making.*

Prospectus A summary of the registration statement filed with the Securites and Exchange Commission for most new issues. The prospectus is partially a selling device and partially a means of making certain that buyers of new issues have had all essential information about the issue disclosed to them.

Put An option that gives the holder the right to sell the underlying security at a specified price for a certain, fixed period of time.

Real Estate Investment Trust (REIT) An investment company that invests in real estate rather than securities.

Regulation T A rule determining the amount of credit a customer may receive from a broker when trading securities. The percentage may vary as to the type of securities bought or sold short and may be raised or lowered by the Federal Reserve Board.

SEC See **Securities and Exchange Commission.**

Secondary Market   Any market in which securities can be readily bought and sold after their initial issuance. The national listed securities exchanges provide secondary markets.

Securities and Exchange Commission A U.S. government agency established in 1934 to regulate the issuance and trading of securities and securities markets, including options but not commodities, and personnel including investment advisors operating in the securities business.

Security   An investment contract containing the following elements: (1) a transaction in which money is invested; (2) the investment is in a common enterprise; and (3) there is an expectation of profit resulting from the efforts of others. Important examples of securities are stocks, bonds, and options. Commodity futures have been held not to be securites.

Short   The sale of a security that is settled by the delivery of borrowed securities rather than by delivery of securities owned by the seller. The seller may wish to retain his securities for such reasons as tax advantage or control. He may not own the securities at all.

Short Sale   A transaction made by a person who believes a stock will decline and places a sell order, though he does not own any of these shares.

SRO   Self-regulatory organization.

Standard & Poor's (S & P) 500-Composite-Stock Index   An index of stock prices composed of 385 industrial firms, 56 financial firms, 44 public utility firms, and 15 transportation firms.

Stock   The legal capital of a corporation divided into shares.

Stop-Loss Order   An order to sell stock at a particular price. A stop order becomes a market order when the stock sells at or beyond the specified price and thus may not necessarily be executed at that price.

Suitability   A determination of whether a strategy or trading philosophy is in accordance with an investor's financial means and investment objectives.

Technical Analysis Analysis of the market and stocks based on supply and demand. The technician studies price movements, volume, and trends and patterns that are revealed by charting these factors and attempts to assess the possible effect of current market action on future supply and demand for securities and individual issues.

Ticker Tape The instrument that prints prices and volumes of securities transactions in cities and towns throughout the U.S. and Canada within minutes of each trade on any listed exchange.

Total Return The amount of dividend or interest income plus the difference between the purchase price and the sale price of the security.

Trading The act of buying and selling securities or commodities.

Trading Away A practice by some securities salespeople of recommending the purchase by their customers of products not handled by their firm. May be considered unwise if not unethical.

Unauthorized Trading Trading that takes place in an account without permission of the customer or account holder.

Volatility A measure of the amount by which a security is expected to fluctuate in a given period of time.

Index

Account Activity, 88–89, 263
Active Market, 120
Activity, Past Transaction, 214
American Arbitration
    Association (AAA), 222,
    236, 263
American Depository Receipts
    (ADRs), 185
American Express, 206
American Stock Exchange, 120
Amusement
    as reason for stock market
    activity, 112
Anticipation, 49–50
Appreciation, 111
Arbitrage, 151
Arbitration, 79, 80, 119–20,
    125, 204, 218–44, 263
    American Arbitration
    Association (AAA), 222
    arbitrators, 242–44
    case study, 222–34
    claim preparation, 234–37,
    245–48
    closing remarks, 247–48,
    249–50, 258–59
    cross-examination, 246–47,
    249, 255, 257, 258
    discovery, 240–42
    end of, 259–60
    expert witness, 255–56, 258
    explosion in, 219–22

fairness of, 221–22
Federal Arbitration Act, 219
hearing, 242, 248–59
lawyers in, 221, 233
margin, 241–42
opening remarks, 247, 249,
    252–53
rebuttal, 249–50
response to claim, 237–39
statistics used in, 220–21
testimony in, 249, 253–55
"As Of" Trade, 89, 92–93
    See also Cancellation trade
AT&T, 178, 180
Attitude of Brokers, 44–45
Attorneys, 221
    and arbitration, 221
    class action, 77–80
    defense, 237–39
    searching for, 233

Back-End Loaded Mutual
    Fund, 76–77, 93, 263
Back Office Personnel, 39–40
Bad Recommendations, 197–99
Bait and Switch, 94–96
Bank of America, 224
Barometer, Risk, 137, 138–40
Bear, 263
    See also Bull
Beta, 140–41, 263
Blue-Chip Stock, 66, 113,
    144–45, 180, 198, 263

Bonds, 66, 87–88, 93, 177–79, 226, 228, 263–64
  commission on, 35
  guaranteed, 266
  investment grade, 266
  maturity, 178–79
  principal transaction, 190
  risk, 6
  Treasury, 137–38
  See also Junk bonds
Branch Office Manager, 38–39, 207–8, 231, 258
Bredan, Richard, 72
Broker, 7–19, 28, 264
  advice, 165–66
  arbitration proceeding with, 119–20, 257–58
  attitude of, 44–45
  Cold-Calling Clara, 12–13
  communication with, 134–35
  compensation for, 121
  contact with, 98–99, 102–4
  credibility of, 125
  discount broker, 102
  dishonesty of, 42–43, 93–100
  failure to obey customer, 206–7
  fraud by, 134
  Good News Gus, 10–12
  guarantees given by, 207
  guarantees, no investment, 99–100
  investment philosophy of, 121–22
  jargon of, 29–30
  lawsuit against, 119–20
  licensing of, 125
  logging conversations with, 124–25
  No Brain Bill, 14–15

  own investment, 43–44
  picking, 107–26
  Professor, The, 17–18
  quarterly reporting with, 122–23
  questions to ask, 117, 118–22
  registration of, 125
  relationship with, 117
  research reports of, 57–58
  selling incentives of, 35–36, 173–75
  Seminar Sam, 16–17
  tenure at firm, 118–19
  Trader Dick, 13–14
  training of, 9, 119
  unethical, 42–43, 131–32
  verifying reputation of, 125–26
  where does blame lie, 211–13
  working for whom?, 20–21
  See also Commissions
Brokerage Firms
  attitude of, 44–45
  back office personnel, 39–40
  bankruptcy insurance for, 126
  behind the scenes, 23–45
  branch office manager, 38–39, 207–8, 231, 258
  capital requirements, 126
  credibility of, 125
  dishonest salespeople of, 42–43
  knowing history of, 125–26
  professionalism, air of, 31–33
  profits, losing, 28–29
  purpose of, 5
  selling incentives of, 35–36, 173–74, 174–75

trading department of, 40–41
upper management of, 41–42
working for whom?, 21–22
Broker of the Day, 171
Bull, 264
  See also Bear

Calls, 145–46, 264
  See also Call writing; Options;
  Puts
Call Writing, 61–62, 113–14,
  264
  See also Calls; Options
Cancellation Trade, 89, 92–93
Capacity, Financial, 199–200
Capital Requirements, 126
Certificates of Deposit (CDs),
  6, 115, 141, 198, 224, 226,
  230, 239
Certified Board of Financial
  Planners, 125
Chrysler, 206
Churning, 43, 64, 91, 114,
  184, 185, 202–4, 207–8,
  264
Claim Preparation in
  Arbitration, 234–37
Class Action Attorneys, 77–80
Closed-End Bond Funds, 76,
  176–79, 264
Closing Total Net Worth, 264
Cold Calling, 12–13, 36–37,
  174
Commissions, 20–22, 113–14,
  173–74, 179, 183, 184,
  203–4, 227, 228, 252
  bonds, 35
  cost, 14
  hidden, 34–36

limited partnerships, 35–36
lumping, 34–35
and mutual funds, 76–77
not shown on confirmation
  slips, 93
shown on confirmation slips,
  92
switch idea, 34
trailing quarter, 15
Commodities, 145–46, 181–82
Commonsense Rules for
  Investing Alone, 128
Common Stock, 264–65
Communication, 134–35
Company Stock, 72
Compensation for Broker, 121
  See also Commissions
Compliance Department, 208
Condition, Financial, 114–15,
  116, 122–23
Confirm, 265
Confirmation Slips, 90–93, 203
Corporation, 265
Customer Sophistication, 214,
  233
Cutting Losses, 161–63

De Facto Control, 196–97,
  202, 204
Default Risk, 137
Discount Broker, 102
Discovery in Arbitration,
  240–42
Discretionary Account, 265
Diversification, 144–46,
  180–81, 199, 265
Dividends, 87, 265
Dividend Yield, 139
Documents and Statement of
  Account, 123–24

Dolan, Daria, 203, 233
Dolan, Ken, 203, 233
Dorfman, Dan, 239
Duty to Mitigate, 214–16, 232, 265

Economic Forecasting Group, 62
Efficient Market Hypothesis, 52–56
Emotion versus Reason, 143–44, 154–55
Equity, 85–86, 265
Errors and Omissions Insurance, 72, 101–2
Expert Witness for Arbitration, 255–56, 258

Failure to Obey, 43, 206–7
Federal Arbitration Act, 219
Federal Reserve Bank of St. Louis, 138
Financial Condition, 114–15
changes in, 116, 122–23
Financial Goals, 109–14, 127
appropiate investment for, 121
list of, 111–12
overlapping of, 112–14
See also Suitability
Financial Help, Seeking, 7, 109–16
Financial Planners, 70–73, 100–102
communication with, 134–35
errors and omissions insurance, 72, 101–2
verifying reputation of, 125, 134

Firm Jumping, 118–19
Foreign Stocks, 185–86
Fraud, 43, 134, 194
Fraudulent Sales, 79
Front Running, 209–10
Fundamental Analysis, 17, 60–61, 265
Futures, 145–46, 181–82, 265

General Accounting Office (GAO), 219–20, 221–22
General Electric, 180
General Motors, 180
Goals, Financial, 109–14, 121, 127, 198–99
Good News Gus, 10–12
Good-Till-Canceled Order
See Open order
Government Protection, 133–34
Grant, James, 188
Guarantee, No Investment, 99–100
Guaranteed Bond, 266
Guaranteed Stock, 266

Hedge, 181–82, 183, 184, 266
High-Yield Bonds
See Junk bonds
Hypothetical Returns, 96–97

Imputed Interest, 244
Income, 199–200
with Risk, 111
with Safety, 111
Individual Retirement Account (IRA), 266
Inflation, 6, 127, 198, 224–25, 226

Information, 240–42
  importance of, 46–64, 186
  insider, 44, 46, 51–52, 266
Insurance
  bankruptcy, 126
  errors and omissions, 72,
    101–2
  personal, 200
Interest Rate Risk, 137–38
Interest Rates, 178
International Board of
    Standards and Practices for
    Financial Planners, 101
Investment Advisors, 70–73
  philosophy of, 121–22
  picking, 107–26
  training of, 119
  verifying reputation of,
    125–26
Investment Company, 266
Investment Letter Writers,
    67–69
Investments
  appropriateness of, 121
  done alone, 127–49
  description of, 86–88
  long-term, 116–18
  philosophy of, 121–22
  protecting, 122
  psychology of making,
    143–44
  speculative, 98–99
  success of, 65–66
  unsuitable, 226–28
  See also Suitability
Investor Sophistication, 214,
    233

Jargon of Brokers, 29–30

Junk Bonds, 10–11, 187–90,
    226–27, 228, 229, 232,
    266–67
  mutual funds, 3–5
  packaging of, 189–90
  risk versus reward, 188–89
  victims, 3–5

Law, 194
Lawsuits, 77–80, 119–20
  See also Arbitration;
    Attorneys; Litigation
Lawyers
  See Attorneys
Letter Writers, Investment,
    67–69
Liabilities, Personal, 200
Licensing, 125
Limited Partnerships, 73–75,
    87–88, 93, 100, 113,
    171–76, 188, 197, 202,
    226–27 228, 229, 231,
    232, 267
Liquidation, 215, 232
Liquidity, 116–18, 120, 127,
    137, 143, 173, 197, 226,
    229, 231, 267
Litigation
  determining blame, 211–13
  and customer sophistication,
    214, 233
  duty to mitigate, 214–16,
    232, 265
  steps to take, 211–14
  and rules of suitability,
    194–200
  and past transaction activity,
    214
  written letter, 216–17
  See also Arbitration;
    Attorneys; Lawsuits

Log Keeping, 124–25
Long, 267
Lose and Win, 158–59
Losses, 141–44
  accepting, 160–61
  blame for, 211–13
  cutting, 161–63
  offloading a loser, 43,
    210–11, 268
  taking, 215, 216
Lumping Commissions, 34–35
Lynch, Peter, 9

Magellan Fund, 9
Mail, Reading, 84–89
Malpractice Insurance, 72,
  101–2
Margin, 196, 199, 227,
  241–42, 267
Margin Call, 196, 267
  See also Regulation T
Margin Interest, 267
Market, Bottom of the, 165
Market Makers
  See Principal transactions
Market Making, 269
Maturity of Bonds, 178–79
Merrill Lynch, Inc., 9
Milken, Michael, 187, 188
Misrepresentation, 43,
  200–201
Mistakes, Learning from,
  164–65
Mitigate, Duty to, 214–16, 232,
  265
Mitigate Losses, 232
Money Advisor
  picking, 107–26
Money Managers, 100–102

Money Market Fund, 267
  See also Money market
  instruments
Money Market Instruments,
  267–68
Monthly Statements, 84–89
Murphy's Law, 155–57
Mutual Funds, 66, 72, 224
  junk bonds, 3–5, 189–90
  managers, 75–77
  new, 76
  short-term trading of, 209
  tax-free, 226–27, 228, 231
  See also Investment company

National Association of
  Securities Dealers (NASD),
  9, 43, 63, 92, 101, 112,
  125, 194, 204, 208, 209,
  211, 219–20, 222, 236,
  241, 242, 243, 247, 248,
  249, 250, 251, 259, 268
National Association of
  Securities Dealers
  Automated Quotation, 120,
  219, 268
Negligence, 194
Net Worth, 200
New Funds, 76
New Issues, 97, 182, 268
News and the Stock Market,
  47–52
New York Stock Exchange,
  112, 120, 195, 202, 208,
  209, 211, 219, 219–20,
  222, 236, 268
  constitution of, 43
No Brain Bill, 14–15
North American Securities
  Administrators Association
  (NASAA), 125

Nothing, Investing, 146–47, 166–67

Offloading a Loser, 43, 210–11, 268
Open-end Investment Company
  See Investment company
Opening Total Net Worth, 268
Open Order, 268
Opinions, Second, 135
Options, 61–62, 113–14, 145–46, 182–85, 268
  See also Calls; Puts
Order, 268
OTC Trades
  See Over-the-counter
Overbought, 269
Oversold, 269
Over-the-Counter, 63, 92, 198, 202, 219, 269
Overtrading, 43, 164

Paper Trading, 155–57
Philosophy, Investment, 121–22
Plan for Trading, 153–57
Portfolio, Financial, 115, 180–81
Portfolio Value, 86–87
Preferred Stock, 269
Price and Value, 147–49
Principal, Safety of, 111
Principal Transactions, 92, 185, 269
  bond, 190
  division, 62–64
Product Suitability
  See Suitability

Professor, The, 17–18
Profile, Preparation of, 108
Profits, Run with, 166–67
Prospectus, 74, 269
Protecting Yourself, 102–6
  stay in touch, 102–4
  telephone log, 104–5
  written evidence, 105–6
Prudential Securities Incorporated, 29, 175–76
Psychology of Investing, 143–44
Puts, 269
  See also Calls; Options

Quarterly Reporting, 122–23
Questioning, 133

Real Estate Investment Trust (REIT), 269
Reason versus Emotion, 143–44, 154–55
Recreational Investors, 132–33, 145–46, 181–82
Registration, 125
Regulation T, 269
Research, 133
Research Reports, 56–58
Responsibility for Investment Activities, 129–35
Risk, 6, 115–16, 120, 177–78
  barometer, 137, 138–40
  beta, 140–41
  bonds, 187–90
  default, 137
  identifying, 135–41
  interest rate, 137–38
  liquidity, 137, 143
  speculative investments, 98–99

understanding, 214
versus reward, 136–38,
138–44, 188–89
See also Safety of principal;
Speculation
Risk Dollars, 96
Risk-Free Investments, 136–38
Risk Tolerance, 115–16, 127,
142, 180–81, 199, 226–27
Rules, Commonsense, 128–49
Rumors, 52

Safety of Principal, 111
SEC
See Securities and Exchange
Commission
Secondary Market, 270
for limited partnerships, 173
Securities and Exchange
Commission (SEC), 43, 72,
101, 134, 194, 204, 270
Securities Exchange Act, 194
Security, 270
Self-Evaluation Rules for
Trading, 159–60
Self-Regulatory Organizations,
219–20, 222, 236, 241,
270
Seminar, 16–17
Seminar Sam, 16–17
*Shearson-American Express, Inc.
v. McMahon*, 218
Shearson Lehman Brothers,
Inc., 9, 18–19, 29, 224,
225, 231, 239, 252
Short, 270
Short Sale, 270
Sophistication, Investor, 214,
233

Southern California Edison,
180
Speculation, 111, 150, 181–82,
184, 198
see also Risk
SR4 (The Hoot 'n Holler Box),
30–31
SRO
See Self-Regulatory
Organizations
Standard & Poor's (S&P) 500
Stock Index, 140, 270
Statement, Monthly, 123–24,
253–54
Statistics in Arbitration,
220–21
Stockbrokers
See Brokers
Stocks, 180–81, 270
blue-chip, 66, 113, 144–45,
180, 198, 263
common, 264–65
company, 72
foreign, 185–86
guaranteed, 266
preferred, 269
reasons for investing in,
129–33
risk, 6
Stop Loss Orders, 142, 206,
270
Strategy, Testing of, 155
Stress, 167–69
Suicide, Financial, 130–32
Suitability, 43, 142, 270
rules of, 194–200
Supervise, Failure to, 207–8
"A Sure Thing," 195–96
Switch Idea, 34

Technical Analysis, 17–18, 59,
    69–70, 271
Telemarketing
    See Cold calling
Telephone Log, 104–5
Teweles, Richard, 53
Thin Market, 209–10
Ticker Tape, 271
Time Value of Money, 230
Tips, 52
Total Net Worth, 85–86
Total Return, 271
Trader, 150–69
    accept losses, 160–61
    amateur versus professional,
        151–53
    before entering trade,
        157–58
    bottom of the market, 165
    broker advice, 165–66
    cutting losses, 161–62
    don't add to losers, 162–63
    learning from mistakes,
        164–65
    lose and still win, 158–59
    making a living, 150–51
    money management, 157–59
    Murphy's Law, 155–57
    avoid overtrading, 164
    planning, 153–57
    profits, 166–67
    reason versus emotion,
        154–55
    rules, 152, 153–69
    self-evaluation rules, 159–60
    strategy testing, 155
    stress, 167–69
    where am I wrong, 159–61
    win and still lose, 158–59
Trader Dick, 13–14

Trading, 271
Trading Away, 211, 271
Trading Department, 40–41
Training Brokers, 9, 119
Trans World Airlines (TWA),
    228, 229, 232
Treasury Bill, 136–38, 138–39
Treasury Bonds, 137–38
Treasury Notes, 137–38
Tricks of the Trade, 93–100,
    209–11
    bait and switch, 94–96
    no investment guarantee,
        99–100
    hypothetical returns, 96–97
    "I guarantee," 99–100
    increased broker contact,
        98–99
    "my mistake," 94
    new issues, 97
    reach out and touch, 98–99

Unauthorized trading, 43,
    204–5, 271
Unethical Broker, 131–33
United States General
    Accounting Office (GAO),
    219–20, 221–22
Unsuitable Investments,
    226–28
Upper Management, 41–42

Value and Price, 147–49
Vancouver Exchange, 186
Variables, Investment, 127–28
Volatility, 271

Win and Lose, 158–59
Written Evidence, 105–6
Written Letter, 206–7, 216–17